ultimate game design

design

→ building game worlds

ABOUT THE AUTHOR

Tom Meigs is a game producer and designer with a decade of experience in electronic gaming. He has worked on several award-winning titles for a wide array of game platforms, including: Nintendo Game Boy, Sega Game Gear, Sega Genesis, Super Nintendo, Sega Saturn, Sony PlayStation/PlayStation 2, PC, Macintosh, mobile phones, theme park kiosks, location-based entertainment, online, and even the short-lived Bandai Pippin. Some of the game titles he has worked on include: *Madden Football '95, Sports Illustrated Golf, Sea Quest DSV, Akira, Jungle Strike, Bassmaster's Classic, The Mask, Angel Devoid 2, Youngblood: Search and Destroy,* and several titles for Disney. Tom received an M.A. in philosophy from California State University, Long Beach.

ultimate game design

design

→ building game worlds

Tom Meigs

McGraw-Hill/Osborne

New York   Chicago   San Francisco   Lisbon   London   Madrid   Mexico City
Milan   New Delhi   San Juan   Seoul   Singapore   Sydney   Toronto

*The **McGraw·Hill** Companies*

Publisher
Brandon A. Nordin

Vice President & Associate Publisher
Scott Rogers

Editorial Director
Wendy Rinaldi

Project Editor
Monika Faltiss

Acquisitions Coordinator
Athena Honore

Technical Editor
Jon Orwant

Copy Editor
Bill McManus

Proofreader
Claire Splan

Indexer
Irv Hershman

Computer Designers
Tabitha M. Cagan
Tara Davis

Illustrators
Lyssa Wald
Kathleen Edwards

Series Design
Lyssa Wald
Peter Hancik

Cover Design
Tree Hines

McGraw-Hill/Osborne
2100 Powell Street, 10th Floor
Emeryville, California 94608
U.S.A.

To arrange bulk purchase discounts for sales promotions, premiums, or
fund-raisers, please contact **McGraw-Hill/**Osborne at the above address.
For information on translations or book distributors outside the U.S.A.,
please see the International Contact Information page immediately
following the index of this book.

Ultimate Game Design: Building Game Worlds

 234567890 FGR FGR 01987654

ISBN 0-07-222899-7

This book was composed with Corel VENTURA™ Publisher.

DEDICATION

This book is humbly dedicated to Vivian E. Meigs, MCW, and Larry Siegel. Each, in their own magnificent turn, made this content possible.

Contents At A Glance

Contents

Acknowledgments

MANY people helped me in a variety of ways to complete this book. First, I have to thank David Fugate, Wendy Rinaldi, Dr. Jon Orwant, Athena Honore, Monika Faltiss, Bill McManus, and everyone at McGraw-Hill/Osborne for supporting me at every step along the way.

Next, I'd like to extend special thanks to each of the chapter interview participants. These individuals represent a wide array of gaming expertise and influence, and their contributions amidst very busy schedules should be applauded. Thanks go to Andrew Holdun, John Kreng, Rick Sanchez, Nathan Hunt, Aaron Odland, Andrew Forslund, Melinda White, Mike Weiner, Dave Warhol, and Bill Roper for taking the time to offer unique and valuable insight from their own vast experience. I couldn't have asked for more generous spirits, or more informed interview subjects.

Special thanks go to Andrew Forslund for his large and timely contributions to the scripting sections, and to Andy Wang/Netamin for permission to use many images from *Ultimate Baseball Online*.

On a personal note, I'd like to thank Art, June, and Jeanette Meigs; Larry, Sandy, and Scott Kessenick; Kevin Wright, Gene Hoglan/SYL, the *Tommy Lasorda Baseball* team, the *Metroid* team, Professors Richard Holmes and Simon Schama, Gordon Sumner, Disney, Eitetsu Hayashi, MLB great Darrell Evans, Tomahawk, The Melvins, Michael and Julie Allen, Dave Moses, Adrian Belew, Roscoe's, Mykonos, Harbour House, everyone at Waterside Productions, The Gnomon School of Visual Effects, Alex Alvarez, Tao Tong, The Long Beach Ice Dogs organization, Patrik Augusta, Master Kreng, Dr.s: Paul Tang, Charles Hughes, George Spangler, Shane Andre, Doug Deaver, and Bill Hyde; Harold Budd, Trey Gunn, Marjorie Stettbacher, Brendan Perry/Quivvy, Jim Wright, Andy Summers, Elvis, and Baloo.

For their support, inspiration, and the shared learning of various kinds, I'd also like to thank the entire Black Pearl Software/THQ development team, the Electric Dreams development team, the Realtime Associates family, the Disney games group, the UBO/Netamin development team, everyone at Blizzard Entertainment, the Orange County, CA International Game Developers Association, UC Irvine extension, and Art Institute-LA.

Introduction

THIS book was written for anyone interested in learning about applied game design. It is skewed somewhat toward new game developers, but it has plenty to say about the design process itself that should be useful to game developers at all levels of familiarity with the process of building games.

The material is organized chronologically from the roots of the design process right on through to the final or "gold" development phase as a game comes to full fruition and is delivered into the hands of game players.

Each chapter, read in order, will guide you through a basic game development curve and introduce you to many fundamental design areas and challenges. However, you also can jump directly to specific chapters of particular interest to you, or start with the support information located in the associated appendixes, which can be a useful starting point for further exploration into several of the key chapter topics presented here.

My purpose in writing this book is to try to provide new developers and seasoned pros alike with some common ground in their own approaches to game design specifics. Much has been written about game design theory, but far less has been written about what might be called applied game design. Make no mistake: I still believe that game design theory is important. I think it can be safely assumed that theory tends to inform and inspire application. I simply wanted to try to move much closer to a discussion about applied game design for all interested parties, and I have some very practical reasons for doing so.

As you begin to understand the development conditions under which most games are made today, it should become very clear that there is a great need to consider applied game design. After all, there is always a demand for compelling game content in many genres, yet even for the most successful developers, it is regularly extremely difficult to deliver. This stands in direct opposition to the idea that commercial viability for game makers often depends on repeatable results in game design quality.

There are many reasons why the development of great gameplay frequently faces many obstacles—as we'll soon discuss. In order to succeed, game developers need to be able to build up fun and addictive play into their games quicker and more surely than ever before. Yet prototyping play mechanics and experimenting with many aspects surrounding gameplay still poses several layers of challenge for many game developers. It is still not very easy to prototype and experiment with game dynamics while keeping costs under control.

With this firmly in mind, one of the most important questions this book tries to address is: What might be required to make applied game design more feasible for game developers in general? I try to offer up several answers.

I think that looking into applied game design in the way I've tried to for the purposes of this book gives all budding game developers a chance to learn first hand about design challenges, while asking established developers to think about solutions that might help to ease some of the same challenges. I see this as a dialogue that might help make more interesting kinds of gameplay possible.

Of course, as we'll soon see in detail, it often comes down to the brute development specifics: tools, smooth tool-to-engine interface, adequate ability to prototype and experiment, beginning your development cycle with solid concepts that can be altered and adjusted on-the-fly for improvement and refinement toward the fun zone, and so forth.

Those game developers or middleware providers that succeed in supporting game content construction in the most powerful and dynamic ways, thereby enabling developers to build-in the best kinds of gameplay possible, will probably find themselves on the top of the game sales charts. It isn't a secret anymore that several of today's top-selling games are based on technologies like RenderWare that conceivably allow game makers more time to flesh out exciting content details and worry less about jumping over gargantuan technology hurdles. My point can be summed up here: if content is king, it's time to build the throne.

It's in this spirit that the book was created. It's time to ask tough questions and find solid answers in the area of applied game design. It's time to move away from having to learn an entirely new design tool every 20 minutes. I know that if you use the material assembled here as a starting point, you'll soon find many ways to quickly build or reinforce your understanding of the many forces that help to shape game design.

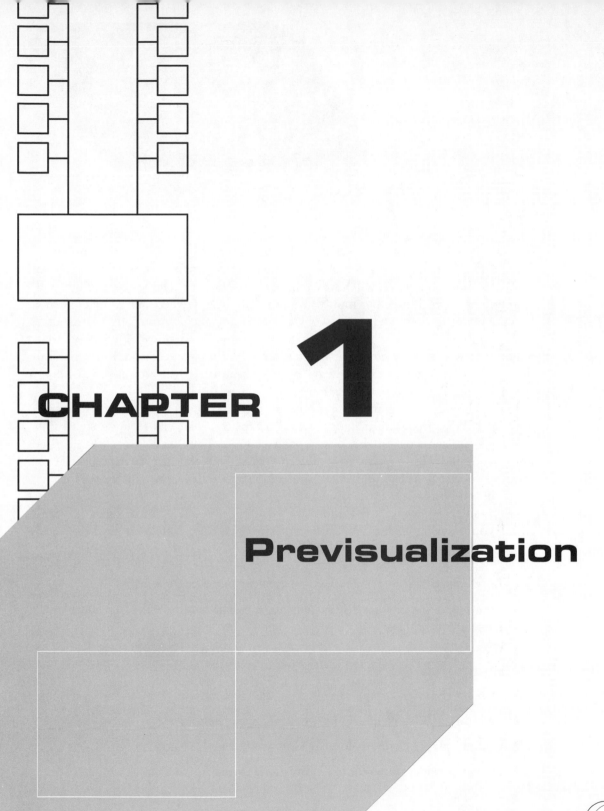

CHAPTER 1

Previsualization

THE game design process begins by synthesizing and harmonizing various gameplay ideas and concepts. The very early stages of game design are, by nature, heavily conceptual. Game concepts have to be pulled down to Earth and given shape and definition. These concepts, when working together to form a gaming experience, will have to share a small boat on a large ocean. They will be required to work together tightly and forcefully. Only when our game concepts row the boat together in harmony will we achieve any exciting motion. A game that seems "only to float" hasn't achieved this harmony. In some cases, concepts that might otherwise have worked out well are not given life in execution. Keep in mind that professional game design always occurs in parallel with a multitude of constraints, objectives, and considerations.

In this chapter, we will focus on the initial stage of game concept harmony, sometimes called the *previsualization process*. Perhaps the best way to understand this process is by discussing it in the context of an example. Thus, we'll look at the "cathedral" example. This specific example could be the game setting for a first- or third-person action title, but the previsualization process that we will discuss for this example can be applied to many game genres.

Each subsequent chapter will address in detail the process of "building up" or executing your own game ideas. We'll cover many topics that relate to giving shape and form to your own game concepts. In summary, we will consider the following:

> **Level construction** The process of creating game environments

> **Lighting, texturing, particle systems, effects, and audio** How we detail our game environments

> **Props, items, and behaviors** How we stage or set up our game environments

> **Camera considerations** How we handle camera issues

> **Scripting action events** How we create event behaviors

> **QA and player feedback loops** How we test and refine game titles

> **Design considerations for emerging game forms** New venues for games

INTRODUCING THE PREVISUALIZATION PROCESS

It helps to know where you're going before you get there, so that you can be prepared. Tropical jungle? Bring the bug spray. Exotic island? Bring the suntan lotion and spear-fishing gear. Similarly, when you are developing a game, title planning and attempting to predict trouble spots are critical to successful execution. Thus, most game titles, in the early days of production, go through a quick series of previsualization passes, the goal of which is to lock down a visual style—even if you're building the next frantic puzzle game based on alien octopus larvae marbles! What do alien octopus larvae marbles look like? Can somebody show me? Is there a museum? Is it open? Some development teams keep this process informal, while others take it very seriously. Whether you're building the next fighter, shooter, or environmental action game, you need a visual roadmap.

The real point of previsualization is to help take your game vision in an agreed-upon direction and to create a visual or stylistic reference point; a visual anchor, so to speak. Of course, deviations from this reference or anchor point can be made. The visual style can and will evolve over the development cycle. It might evolve slightly. It might change dramatically. Previsualization simply creates a useful starting point for everyone involved in the project.

Next, as we look at the previsualization process itself, we'll examine the following:

❭ Utilizing concept and reference drawings

❭ Implementing basic level architecture and environmental design. (A level is a self-contained section of the game experience with its own beginning and end. Most games feature many levels that must be completed in order to finish the game as a whole.)

❭ Doing concept work on paper and building topographic reference maps

❭ Making simple asset breakdowns from your design

STEP-BY-STEP PREVISUALIZATION

Since most game development cycles rarely allow for lengthy preproduction cycles, developers often face the challenge of delivering creative and technical design documentation rapidly. Any previsualization work that can be accomplished under tight time constraints will normally be done as the overall project details settle into place. Previsualization will happen during a small slice of time while a game title ramps up toward full production.

For many game developers, having the time to do aggressive previsualization is a luxury. Yet, those who scramble together the time to do some previsualization often save substantial amounts of time over the course of development. If a team is forced in midproduction to determine many of the visual formatting details that might have been resolved in a previsualization sequence, progress may be stalled and precious resources may be wasted.

In what follows, we'll walk through the process of completing a basic previsualization sequence, culminating in the construction of a "cursed cathedral" as our example.

Utilizing Environmental References and Sketches

Every game has an environmental setting—a physical location created to "host" gameplay. We're not just creating floor plans for a retirement village (that's a side project). We're hosting gameplay! Whether you're trying to simulate the atmosphere of a Western casino, a colorful and sugary cartoon world, or the burned-out remnants of a mining tunnel system on a distant star (or maybe all three at once—yikes!), the environment will in large part help define and dictate the mood. Mood forms a part of the player's emotional connection to the game. Gameplay mechanics and gameplay devices are what keep the player engaged, active, and excited, which supports a mood-driven or emotional experience. If you don't engage a player's emotions, the player will have a flat, nondynamic experience. Most of the games that we all love to play seem to blend mood and game mechanics seamlessly. You can't tell where one stops and the other begins. If you're not screaming at the monitor or television, whoever created that game might not get to make another game.

Simply put, the environment should support and complement gameplay—not detract from it. Environments, by their very visual style, can shift or alter the mood substantially. Warm and happy might describe the mood generated by a well-crafted Sugar World. Dark, anxious, and brooding might be the mood generated by your own private Apocalypse World. Thus, when trying to set the visual style for an environment, it's often very helpful to use plenty of reference material, such as photographs, drawings, illustrations, and pictures that help influence a visual or stylistic direction. This point may seem obvious, but it's sometimes forgotten in the fray of development. Reference material gives a team something concrete to talk about. Suggesting that a game should look like *Blade Runner* is useful at a conceptual level, and suggests a certain style, but really doesn't help lock down the messy details. What does a pay phone/telecom unit look like in the *Blade Runner* world? Inquiring minds want to know—especially when it's due on tomorrow's schedule.

The basic point is that providing adequate visual reference is always helpful to artists and designers and is usually very helpful to the development team when establishing a reference point. Many aspects of game development begin with useful and substantial reference points. Not all of them are visual. Some are conceptual. Some are concrete game devices that have worked to great effect in other games.

As an example of a drawing that could be used as reference material, consider Figure 1-1, which shows The Mole of Hadrian (from "Antichita Romane") by Giovanni Piranesi (1720-1778). Hopefully, you can see immediately how such a drawing could influence environmental construction, mood, texturing, and lighting. Not bad for one drawing. You wouldn't necessarily try to replicate the look and feel of the drawing—although you might be tempted. Better still, it would stand as a great reference point and starting point for developing the visual style for the parts or whole of a game—a springboard for visual ideas with a common starting point. This is the critical point in using environmental references and sketches to support your regularly rushed previsualization phase.

Architecture for Game Levels

Game worlds offer definite freedom in architecture. It is a "controlled" kind of freedom because as you are building up game environments, you must constantly weigh options and make trade-offs. For example, you might want certain physical features and complexities that would look wonderful to the player, but those same features

FIGURE 1-1

Piranesi's The Mole of Hadrian

may end up degrading the game's performance or running speed to a degree that is way too slow to be any fun to play. This won't do at all, because when the lights go off at night and Junior gets tucked into his racecar bed, it's all about the fun! Chugging frame rates are not fun. Remember that a *game level* is a self-contained section of the entire game experience, and each particular level will have its own unique performance challenges.

Frame rate refers to the speed at which a single frame can be redrawn to the screen following another frame; kind of like a flipbook animation. How fast can you make the pages flip? That's your frame rate. A "chugging" frame rate is a frame rate that is too slow to provide adequate game play performance or satisfaction. You want as much visual pop as possible, while maintaining fundamental performance. This is the crux and crisis point. Let the trade-offs begin! At its simplest, for modern 3-D games, the more stuff you put in the scene that uses polygons on drawing the scene, the more performance speed you stand to lose.

Also, what works in traditional architecture doesn't necessarily make for compelling game environments. Generally, interior levels—such as the inside of a castle—can be adapted from real architecture and "bent" into game shape. You want architecture that makes sense as a level layout, but you also want architecture that's fun (and fast) to navigate or move around in. So, it often helps to start with an existing reference point, like the floor plan of a castle, and then tweak and modify it into game shape. Or, you can start with something entirely new if you wish. Either way, you'll need solid reference material.

The nice part about working in the digital world is that you can combine bits and pieces of architecture from several different castles to build the ultimate castle interior. If you tried to build the real thing, it would fall apart like a sand castle in the surf, but it sure looks good. No matter what game genre you're building for, it always helps to start with a reference point and then adapt and refine it for gameplay. In fact, gameplay itself should determine level layout. Remember, environment supports play, but play is the deciding factor.

Basic Environmental Design

In a networked multiplayer environment, characteristic of many of the games made today, it makes sense to consider a couple of simple ideas about layout. After all, if you're going to have several players roaming a level or arena, you will want to consider carefully how they're going to navigate your map.

Entry and Exit

In general, bottlenecks and dead-ends don't work too well in a multiplayer environment. However, this is considered a "soft" rule because there are always exceptions. For example, someone may point out a case in which a bottleneck makes for a perfect gameplay foil. (A "hard" rule is one for which no exceptions exist, such as "Avoid frustrating your player!") When it comes to environmental design, the softer rules often give way to solid *testing feedback,* player comments about what works and what doesn't. We'll learn all about this process in Chapter 7. It's up to you and your team to figure out why something works or doesn't work. Testing feedback is the single most important measure of whether you've succeeded or failed at building a great venue for play.

If you create a *stock point* or *power-up point* (a space with a variety of power-ups like health or ammunition available together) in a dead-end area, the player may have to risk much to get at it because the corridors leading to the dead-end area may have high traffic—plenty of enemies stalking the player. This suggests that having multiple entry and exit points is a good thing. If certain areas have only one way in and one way out (see Figure 1-2), it becomes pretty obvious where a player might take their first step toward their own undoing. It's generally better to have multiple entry and exit points so that players can flee a situation easily, and so that their arrival/departure point is not so easily predicted (see Figure 1-3).

FIGURE 1-2

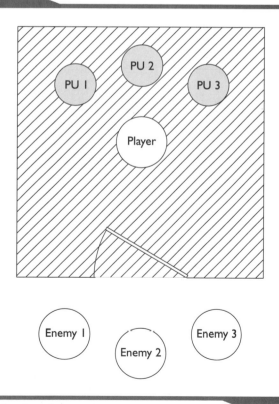

Player caught in a bottleneck

FIGURE 1-3

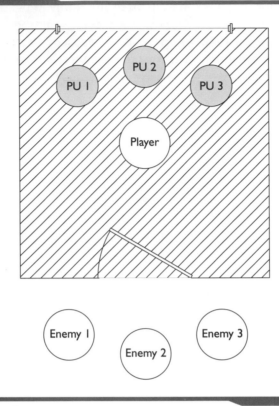

Player can flee north

FUNCTION

During the previsualization process, it is always useful to consider function, which in this context is something akin to "gameplay purpose." A well-crafted game environment has several simultaneous goals (for example, support actions and character abilities in an exciting way, perform at optimum speed on the given hardware, display logic in the environmental lay-out, and be navigable). At a minimum, you want your game environment to support in the right physical ways the kind of play dynamic you are trying to build or graft into the environment. This is a cross-genre principle. It makes little difference what kind of game we're talking about—from a state of the art first-person shooter (FPS) to a multiplayer party arena game—in all cases, you want to give forethought to the environment and its function (gameplay purpose) and direct your thoughts toward supporting gameplay. In the end, the environment that you're building will be built to host gameplay.

Building an environment to host gameplay is quite different from building an environment for visual impact alone. You want both—an environment that hosts gameplay well and is visually striking. The primary idea here is that for your levels (first- or third-person games), arenas (death match or player vs. player scenarios), maps (real-time strategy games or role-playing games), and playfields (action, twitch, or shooter-style games), you want an environment configured in the right ways to support your main objective: solid play. If you give little or no thought as to how best to construct an environment in support of gameplay (for whatever reason, whether it be a tight development schedule time or resource shortages), the results are often frustrating and do not support solid play.

So, as you consider function and layout, think about the play mechanics and play goals you're trying to build. How you begin to set positions or lay out your play space will depend on the kind of play mechanic you're trying to build. Of course, this varies according to which game genre you are working in.

Start by asking yourself a question: What is my game's heartbeat? The "heartbeat" refers to the primary or fundamental game mechanic that lies at the root of your game. It is your game's driving force. It is why players will want to play your game. Always try to keep your game's heartbeat in mind. No doubt, this heartbeat will suffer many palpitations and skipped beats along the beating path of game development, but your game's heartbeat should be kept in mind to help guide the thousands of decisions that will be posed to your development team along the way.

If you forget about a game's heartbeat, the game can grow into a surly five-headed beast almost overnight, and you'll be hacking and slashing at your game's Hydra heads for some time to come. This is a difficult situation. Many game development decisions along the development curve will be informed by keeping simple principles clear in your mind. It's always a challenge to learn how to do this under real-world resource constraints. As a team, you will have game direction ideas coming at you from 4002 sources—including those paying for your game development and those who own the character and world rights you are currently meddling with.

What is the heartbeat? Clear up the answer in your mind. Clear up the answer with your fellow team members. Act on it.

Although many game developers disagree on the deep details, many game heartbeats are deceptively simple to express and remain true across genres:

> Kill or be killed by other players or things (examples include *Quake III Arena*, *Asteroids*, and *Twisted Metal Black*)

> Let me grow my skills, abilities, powers, influence, or recognition in some way (*Everquest* and *Diablo II*)

> Let me control the simulation of a process (*Rollercoaster Tycoon* and *The Sims*)

> Take me on an adventure of type X, Y, and Z (*Grim Fandango* and *Myst*)

Is this level of reduction and simplicity even useful? Definitely. Your heartbeat might combine a couple of these statements, but be careful. Most successful games don't go too wide with their heartbeat statements. You should be able to reduce your game's heartbeat to one or two sentences at most. Don't try and be everything to everybody. How do simple statements like these have any power in an age of never-ending technological advance and gaming possibility? All I can say is, there is great power in reduction sometimes.

How do you use a heartbeat statement? After you have defined your heartbeat statement, you and your development team should evaluate the potential of each feature, function, mode, asset, or ability based on whether it adds to or subtracts from accomplishing your heartbeat statement. Game building is exploration. You may not know until you try it, but you can limit the pursuit of "peripheral ideas" by checking your idea for a feature or function against your game heartbeat. If it doesn't move you closer to presenting your heartbeat statement for the player, then don't bother with it. If it does, then weigh its true impact further and consider its feasibility.

Keep in mind that building a next-generation game is a team function. You will be working as a team member to help establish the heartbeat for your game. You will not be working in solitude sending down "heartbeat" declarations from your throne, after servants have set up an afternoon tea. In other words, part of the game design process itself is learning how to work as a team to reach a "buy-in" or group agreement for the game heartbeat. Each team member will bring their own particular game experience, orientation, and passions to lend support or rejection for game direction ideas. Normally, game producers and designers help to guide this process through many iterations and revisions toward establishing a clear game heartbeat—a game heartbeat vision that an entire team can share and charge toward.

With respect to function, start by asking yourself the following questions:

❭ Are you building a game where competitive racing gives players the ability to enhance and customize their vehicle over a series or race circuit?

❭ Are you building a game based on collection and combat with offense and defense?

❭ Are you building a game based on simulating a growth process?

Knowing the game heartbeat is fundamental and will help answer these questions. Establish the heartbeat first and build from there. The heartbeat will help inform the details. It will help determine the function. It will help show you how to build and evolve the right kind of environment in the right ways for your game.

Room Flow

Room flow is important because it gives shape to your game play function ideas. Many current games depend on room-to-room interiors as environments for play. For example, first- and third-person shooters are routinely set within building interior components. At the high concept level, rooms must connect in some fashion, such as through direct or implied hallways. An "implied" pathway (such as a well-worn dirt path would be an obvious example, a logical connection in level areas from front to back or top to bottom might be another less obvious example) is generally very helpful for the player in navigating your level, if a path isn't obvious. Different room types and room scales (such as the size of a room compared to the size of your character or vehicle) are connected through implied pathways. For example, you might be exploring a "prison cell" section of a level, which connects with a subterranean command center, which in turn connects with a tunnel system that connects with a vehicle hangar.

Room interiors vary in function, mood, scale, purpose, and many other particulars. So, then, how are the rooms put together into a cohesive level? Previsualization for room flow often requires a look at two critical areas: logic and symmetry.

When considering the logic of your room layouts during previsualization, you need to ask some basic questions: Is there a logical connection between rooms? How will basic room flow work as a transition from one playing space to another? What kinds of play and primary action elements do you expect these rooms to contain? Gameplay direction should always influence and shape environmental design choices. If you're going to be using long-range projectile weapons, you probably don't want short or cramped spaces. Room spaces can even be used to prompt certain responses from players; for example, the lay-out logic of a room space may suggest to players that it would be a good area to search, that it would be a potential high-conflict area, or that it would be a great cover and resupply area.

Physical symmetry is probably most important for team-based games like capture the flag (CTF) and others. When you're invading another team's area to capture something and bring it back home, the distance your team must cover should be the same as the distance the other team must cover; otherwise, you have an immediate imbalance. Yet, even for two player co-op or single play maps, those that offer some kind of physical symmetry are often less confusing, easier to navigate, and generally more enjoyable than those that feature no symmetry at all. Maps or levels with an unending series of connected rooms laid out in a serial chain, one after the other, quickly lose their sense of "place." It becomes hard to tell where you are as a player in relation to anything else in the level. On the other hand, levels that have a direct or implied symmetry in their layout provide the player with valuable visual reference points (for example, the tower is at the center ring). Symmetric levels seem to "feel" better and make traversal (running around) easier than levels that offer little or no direct symmetry at all.

In fact, you can see the symmetry when you start with an overhead map or topographic map as the basis for your level layout. It's part of what you're trying to work out on paper. When you're running around your favorite levels, stop and take a moment to consider symmetry. Are you even aware of it? It's actually best if you're not aware of it as a player. In that case, symmetry is working its magic. As a designer, though, you're looking for patterns like symmetry. You're looking for patterns that help drive the play.

Interior to Exterior

Interior to Exterior transitions are an important expression of function. Many popular titles use environmental features that segue between interior and exterior environments. Interior to exterior transition spaces should be planned for and, again, a logic check should be made to insure that these transitions make sense by viewing the larger picture of an overall level layout. Interiors that change rapidly to unrelated exteriors on a room-to-room basis usually don't keep a player believing that they are "within" a certain environmental setting for very long. If a player makes two close exits from an interior to two unrelated exterior scenes (for example, from a prison row exit to a jungle exterior through one door, and through another immediate door into a desert setting), it may look cool, but it doesn't support keeping a player's belief state suspended. We're always striving to provide a player with a "continuous" feeling or belief that they are where we've put them. A prison camp in the desert is a good example. If you want both jungle and desert simultaneously, you need to think about transition for the player.

Reinforcing Mood

Building mood supports and details your gameplay function ideas. The previsualization sequence should attempt to "ask and answer" questions about how a game will transfer mood to the player. Early concept drawings should deliver notes and sketches that help define the mood. How will audio and visuals come together to transfer mood? If you're building a fantasy fighter based on a cartoon world, how will you transfer mood? Location sets mood.

You want the mood to mirror the experience you're trying to transfer. Sports games or first-person shooters offer fast and frantic action, but the mood is reinforced by immersion via visual and auditory cues. Relatively small touches can transfer plenty of mood. For example, hearing an in-stadium broadcast announcer that sounds like a true in-stadium announcer, such as you would hear while playing in a football stadium, does much to transfer mood. Audio should never be neglected in game design, although historically it has been. Our understanding of mood is greatly enhanced or diminished by the presence or absence of audio cues. Audio is fundamental to creating and supporting mood. Audio is fundamental to designing a game world.

PAPER-BASED LEVEL BLOCKING

Every map, level, arena—in short, every game environment—should still begin on paper. There are a couple of reasons for this. First, it's just plain easier to edit, update, and try out ideas. Second, it can save large amounts of time and money spent on wasted resources. You can play around with spacing, room flow, and the logic of the level very easily. I've found that huge dry-erase whiteboards are very helpful. They are great for team brainstorming sessions, from which useful notes and ideas can be quickly gleaned. Paper-based level blocking is also great for discussing and making quick changes to level flow ideas, boundaries, prop placement ideas, and segue areas planned for your level.

Quick Topographic Maps

Yes, we live in a world of amazing editors and 3-D packages—each with its own subtle and frustrating nuances—but many "concepts" can be tested faster and easier on paper than by using any other medium. You can more easily identify flaws in logic, build out transition spaces, and test your ideas, and really get a more solid grasp on the global view for your level. Also, it's important to start thinking modularly, which means planning how to build up your level out of simple, adjoining, and reusable components. It's like building up a level with a toy construction kit out of several pieces joined together in a meaningful way.

Okay, you have your graph paper, now what? Generally, you want a nice topographic or overview-style map. Figure 1-4 is an example of what a section of your map might look like. I like to draw it out on paper or whiteboard, clean up the notes, and build a quick and clean version using the Microsoft Visio software application.

The small level section illustrated in Figure 1-4 might be a cathedral area for part of your level. The circles represent cathedral turrets or towers. The smaller circles are simply columns. You can use a legend that identifies what each element on your topographic map corresponds to, such as in this legend for Figure 1-4:

> **T**   Towers or turrets

> **C**   Columns

> **P**   Pews

> **O**   Pipe organ

> **OB**   Organ bench

> **A**   Altar

Now we have a basic positioning layout (not to scale, of course) and legend system. Keep in mind that a topographic sample like this is only a reference point, a way to start off on the often long road to a complete level. Now let's take an introductory look at how we begin to detail our level using textures, props, effects, and scripted events.

FIGURE 1-4

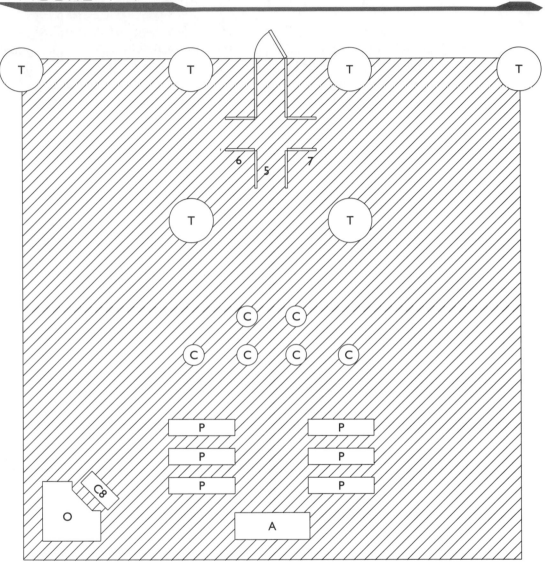

Topographic level map sample

Textures

Textures will be mapped or placed on our geometry constructions. Textures are sur-face material information—colors or patterns, contrast and hue, but they also indi-cate physical characteristics like bumpy, rusty, or stone-like, etc. Think of a texture as the wrapper on a paint can. It covers the surface of the cylindrical paint can with visual materials information.

We need to make a preliminary texture list for our cathedral example. A quick look at the textures we might want for this area include the following:

> Stained glass windows

> Stone floor 1 and stone floor 2

> Carpeted floor

> Turret steps

> Wall 1 and wall 2

> Turret wall 1 and turret wall 2

> Turret wall trim border

> Door 1 and door 2

> Altar covering

> Organ covering

> Organ bench

> Wooden pews

> Decorative columns

These should suffice as a first-pass listing. It's important to think of these textures in terms of how they support and define the visual look and feel you're trying to create or replicate. Make sure you have as much relevant reference material as you can gather. "It's bumpy" or "It's rusty" is not entirely helpful. In what way is it bumpy? What kind of rust? A visual reference is worth 1000 words. Be prepared to show your texture artist photographic or illustrative samples. This is why the previsualization phase, and the organization of this visual data, can be a helpful team time-saver.

Props

Props are 3-D models of objects that litter or populate a 3-D environment. Each of the physical objects you find around you in an environment are potential props in our created environments. Tables, chairs, phone booths, trashcans, and street lamps are all examples of props. We need to model these and include them in our environments. Again, this is where setting a visual style in a previsualization sequence is so important. We're not just making any street lamp; it has to be a street lamp that complements and supports the visual style we are working in or working for. A street lamp in the *Scooby Doo* universe is different from a street lamp in the *Blade Runner* universe, which is probably different from a street lamp in your universe.

So, what props might we want for our cathedral example? Some of the props are already indicated on our map:

- **O**   Requires a pipe organ
- **A**   Requires an altar
- **P**   Requires wooden pews

We also have props that are used to scatter around the environment to add some realism. Most cathedrals are not barren inside, so our first-pass listing of props might also include:

- Organ bench
- Candelabras
- Wall tapestries
- Frozen beast statues 1 and 2 (two versions)

Our frozen beasts in this case are props that serve to tell a short backstory point on our cathedral area. It has been frozen by a curse, and these poor unfortunate beasts have been immortalized as frozen statues—unless maybe you break up the curse later. Sound familiar?

Effects

Next, we want to consider some of the effects we'll require for our cathedral example. Yes, even the effects need to match up with the visual style that we are planning in our previsualization phase. An effect like "steam" in *The Simpsons* world looks different from "steam" in the world of *Minority Report*. How is it handled? Typically, a game engine like the *Unreal2* or *Doom III* engines (built up on core code modules like an input/output system, rendering and animation system, audio system, and game loop/game logic system) handles effects (like ice spray off a hockey skate) as sprite-based effects or as part of a built-in particle or dynamics system.

Although we're still in our first-pass previsualization phase, we already know that we'll need some effects to visually detail our environment, such as the following:

- Cold steam (rising from our frozen beasts)
- Magical glow (surrounding our altar)
- Candlelight fire (for our candelabras)

Effects add definite visual pop and excitement and help to tell us something about our frozen beasts' recent "confrontations." These kinds of visual details can be handled programmatically in a number of ways, but for previsualization purposes, we need to think about which effects we must create and how the game engine we're working with will handle them.

Scripted Events

We've made some solid previsualization progress! We have our topographic map, early texture and prop ideas, and effects breakdowns—and we're cross-checking them to our visual anchor point. This is why a flurry of conceptual drawing needs to take place very early in the production cycle.

Now we have to consider scripted events. *Scripted events* are actions or behaviors that we want to include in our environment to set up play possibilities, make story points, elicit behavior from nonplayer characters (NPCs—like the talking castle gargoyle), and build up action.

For our cathedral example, we might want enemies to come crashing through the roof once a player trips an action trigger on the floor. We might want the busting or shooting of an altar icon to prompt a mini-attack by cathedral minions. We might want a switch on the organ to reveal an area that is a hidden treasure trove. These are all script-based actions. We'll talk a lot more about scripting in future chapters (such as Chapter 6). The important point here is that we need to consider scripting events in the previsualization phase so that we can determine what additional art assets will be required to support script ideas. Do the scripted events create extra character models, props, or effects? Usually they do. To what degree will these scripted events require additional resources? How are these resources connected to the visual reference points established?

As previously stated, any previsualization work that you do up front can save time and help to avoid confusion among developers all along the development path.

CASE STUDY COMMENTS ON PREVISUALIZATION

In 1996, a development team I worked with was asked to complete an action/RTS (real-time strategy) title for the Sony PlayStation on a timeline of approximately 15 months. Production had to begin immediately on this licensed title, which was set in an elaborate futuristic world. Licensed games, like *Spongebob Squarepants* or *The Scorpion King II*, have to be built quickly because they often piggyback on a companion TV show or film that makes them known, popular, and attractive for purchase: "You saw it! Now play it!" (or so the thinking goes).

In our case, no aggressive previsualization sequence could "seemingly" be completed due to the already aggressive development schedule. Our team settled the design and production considerations as rapidly as possible, and proceeded to build the game. As game engine details and technical factors evolved, so did the design. This is common. We had the opportunity to use established characters and to create new ones. We were entirely responsible for environmental setting and execution. The world and characters needed a consistent look. It is immediately obvious when "look" planning fails. In our case, the look planning faltered. With the visual capabilities of consoles and the PC today, the lack of a consistent look is entirely unacceptable.

Because we were prevented from completing even a condensed previsualization phase, many details, despite our best efforts, were left hanging to be considered midstream in the heat of development. This did indeed create a stall factor, which burns valuable resources. When layers of approval phases are introduced, sometimes this stall is close to inescapable. However, as game developers, you are always looking to minimize this kind of development impact. One way to minimize the stall factor is to use your best efforts to build a previsualization sequence into every development schedule.

INTERVIEW WITH ANDREW HOLDUN

Andrew Holdun is an extremely versatile and talented artist with a track record of making hit games for developers like LucasArts, Disney, and THQ. His work can be seen in Jedi Knights *for the PC and* Shadows of the Empire *for the Nintendo 64. He received a B.A. in Architecture from Pratt Institute.*

TM: Is getting ready for the game industry the same as preparing for a bullfight?

AH: I read a lot of Ernest Hemingway ... and drank a lot of tequila. Before you knew it, I had a cape and a hat with these stupid furry balls on it, and I was running for my life from a ton of mean steam-snortin' mammals.

TM: Nice. How is previsualization usually done? Is it important?

AH: I think that previsualization is becoming more and more important in all aspects of the computer graphics area—from movies and TV to web and game development. In fact, I think that it has trickled down from movies and TV commercials as a descendent of storyboarding.

While storyboarding has been accepted for a long time in those areas, it's taken a while for that to seep into games. As games have become more cinematic and more complicated, there has developed a need to use devices like storyboarding to express what is happening—for both the creators and producers of the content.

While I was at LucasArts, the majority of the artwork was conceptualizing what was going to go on in the game ... the character's look ... the appearance of the environment. A lot of the timing was in the script of the game and worked out as a trial-by-error function. Not really previsualized or even storyboarded that much. To be fair, I believe that there was not even a lot or any previz going on at movie studios at the time.

Then with digital tools, people started to cut apart storyboards and have them become digital visualizations of the action in the movie or commercial or game. As movie studios like Industrial Light and Magic [ILM] started using previz more, they went from cut-up storyboards (animatics) to rough 3-D visualizations of the movie/commercial/video. The benefits are numerous.

Before committing large resources to the project, one can save a substantial amount of time and money and also try out numerous avenues of story, and look before committing resources. With the increase in production costs, this has become almost a standard in production rather than the rarity it was just a few years ago.

This has all trickled down to games. As the costs, complexities, and cinematic quality of games has increased, so has the acceptance of previz. In fact, it's almost become a necessity with tighter production cycles. Previz is usually done by going from script to storyboard and then converting that storyboard to a 3-D re-creation. Characters can be rough geometric shapes as can be the environment. The important thing is to create an understandable feel for what the project will be.

If you can make a rough previz exciting, then the rest (adding textures, higher quality models, environments, lighting, audio) will just be the icing on the cake.

TM: What's the best way to build up visual reference for environmental work?

AH: Photographs from the Web as well as from such great sources as National Geographic are all my favorites. Also, it's good to just troll the library and bookstores for interesting material, such as the book Dead Tech: A Guide to the Archaeology of Tomorrow [Manfred Hamm, et. al].

The other key resource is a digital camera that you carry with you at all times. You never know when you'll see a grain silo or a rust-covered industrial tank that will just excite your imagination. One should also always have a sketch book and pen handy…so you can draw what you see and play with variations on a theme.

TM: What kinds of art skills relate to building successful 3-D environments?

AH: I started out as an architect, and so that has been a very good training ground for seeing the environment around me in a more complete fashion. I think any training such as drawing, sculpture, and photography are bedrock skills that give one the foundation for the creation of 3-D environments.

Also, just educating oneself visually by seeing movies of all types, but especially visually compelling films like sci-fi and fantasy, and just religiously going to museums and theatrical presentations are all important to help you create a 3-D visual vocabulary that you will use knowingly and sometimes unknowingly in your work.

TM: How does traditional architecture relate to "digital" architecture?

AH: There is a great similarity, but traditional architecture is held back by the realities of client and gravity. Digital architecture is unfettered by these things. A certain reality has to be present or else the game can fall apart.

Gravity is an important thing to have working when you are developing a driving game, for instance…but you can stretch a lot farther with digital and develop environments that just wouldn't be practical in the real world.

TM: How have you used your background in architecture for 3-D game work?

AH: I have used it to create city plans. Mos Eisley in Shadows of the Empire comes to mind. And using the conventions of computer-aided design [CAD] that are pretty commonplace in architecture … layers for different objects.

I've also used my architectural knowledge about how the shape of a space (a tunnel verses a room with a high ceiling) can influence one unconsciously.

TM: How do you approach building architecture for game levels or arenas?

AH: First, I try to get a grasp of what the designer is going for in the game … what is the feel? Then it becomes more like film set design. First, rough out the environments based on the script and the concept drawings, and then provide some rough lighting and texturing and try to play in the area as soon as possible to see if it "works."

Are the areas too big, too small, too boring, or too confusing? Then it's just a question of feedback, refinement, and more feedback and refinement. Until, hopefully, a great environment is produced.

TM: Do "real" floor plans translate into exciting game geometry? Do you consider them a point of reference?

AH: They can, but I think that most often while one can start with a realistic house or town, one is going to want to tweak it. Exaggerate it for effect. Except if your game requires verisimilitude such as a baseball field or a car racing game.

TM: When it comes to basic environmental design, what would you say about room entry and exit, room flow (room to room), and transitioning from interior to exterior spaces? This happens plenty in most games.

AH: Well I think that the flow of spaces has to be somewhat grounded in reality. In the study of architecture, flow is an important aspect of designing any space and is equally important in the game world.

That being said, sometimes one needs to tweak the reality to get a more fulfilling game experience … I am thinking of Half-Life, for instance, where the spaces are almost caricatures of actual physical spaces.

TM: Do you build or plan on paper before geometry construction begins?

AH: Definitely. Yes! I sketch a floor plan and some elevations and then do some rough axon metrics (3-D views) of the space. I go back and forth … plan, elevations, and 3-D and back to plan again until I get something polished.

TM: What is the learning process like for 3-D environmental work? How does one begin?

AH: A lot of it is trial and error. I travel to unusual spaces or environments. I draw a lot and photograph as much as possible and then do research for the particular project at hand. Then it comes down to modeling the environment and experiencing it first hand to see if it works. Trial and error, and hopefully each time it gets a little easier because each time I am adding to my knowledge of what makes environments work.

TM: Should game geometry be built with more modularity?

AH: It depends on the nature of the beast. A lot of shooters can get by on modularity, where it's almost more the pursuit that's important.

But if your game required, say, rooms in a mansion, there would be a downside to having it all modular, as the aspect of uniqueness in the spaces contributes to the feel of the game and forces one to confront each room as a different puzzle to solve. So it really depends on the type of game you are making I think.

TM: What would modularity mean for game production speed? Could designers build environments faster that way?

AH: I think that is definitely a good thing to consider. When doing Mos Eisley we did it in a modular fashion because of the twin requirements of storage capacity, which was low, and the need for visual complexity, which was high.

By varying the appearance of the same object by using scale and texture, we were able to create the appearance of complexity while only drawing on the resources required for a few models. Thus, modularity was the way to go. And it is faster to build a level this way, since you are using a kit of parts approach to the design. It all becomes drag and drop … like Legos … complexity from simplicity.

TM: For game environments, what do you use as a source of visual inspiration?

AH: I hunt the Web for a general theme, and I also am religious about checking out bookstores—especially those with a large amount of art and architecture books and magazines. You never know when something will just slap you in the iris.

TM: What tips do you have for someone interested in learning more about building 3-D environments?

AH: I think just traveling to see cool spaces first hand, and then drawing and photographing these spaces, helps tremendously. And then, just hit the computer and have fun … that is what it should all be about.

TM: What do you enjoy most about working in 3-D? About building game (or other) environments?

AH: Well, I think there is the aspect of being God without any of the downside. I get to create real or imagined characters and environments and then watch as other people interact with them so that they become something greater than what they were originally.

I love to create in a medium that is still flexing its wings, and I love that by creating things on the computer I am able to experience the world around me in a more profound way. It has changed how I look at the world, and how I react to the world around me in a tremendous fashion.

TM: With large-scale MMOG-style games like Everquest out there, how will developers continue to deliver large environmental experiences? What will be some of the challenges?

AH: Well, I think to a certain extent there will be a modular component to this like we said, and I see more algorithmic practices developing where an environment becomes more complex by the more time you spend in it.

Level of detail on a massive scale. Terrain generation will become more important as will display of organic shapes likes plants and trees, etc. With computers getting more and more powerful, it should be no problem.

TM: With all of your experience across mediums, what three tips would you provide to someone interested in 3-D environmental work?

AH: 1. Draw like a banshee. 2. Photograph environments and shapes in the real world that interest you. 3. Research art, architecture, and sculpture all the time.

TM: Thanks for taking the time to talk! Offer up any tips, suggestions, warnings, or reprisals you would like!

AH: I think traveling, drawing, and reading are constants. It is possible to get burned out because of the constant trade-offs between what you want to create and what you can create based on technical constraints. Get away from the computer and experience the world so that what you do in 3-D is expressive of the world, and not just a rehashing of some computer game's look … and have fun … have a vision and have fun with it!

TM: Seriously, how does bullfighting relate to working in games?

AH: In the course of your career, you will see a lot of bullcrap … it's important not to take your eye off the bull, but you also have to watch your step.

TM: Reminds me of Rodney Dangerfield in the movie Back to School—"Look out for number one. And don't step in any number two." Try and look out for more than number one, try and look out for your team, your ideas, and your vision. Stay committed to your path. Andrew, thanks so much for the wise words!

MEGA TIPS

1. As resources allow, always complete a previsualization sequence and exercise for every project.

2. Organize and assemble abundant reference material to support the previsualization process.

3. Commit to saving development time later by doing work up front to establish all major visual reference points, a style bible (which is a formal document sometimes provided by licensors and sometimes requiring its own invention), and an understanding of how visuals will be used in support of gameplay. This process will evolve, but having locked reference points is meaningful and valuable.

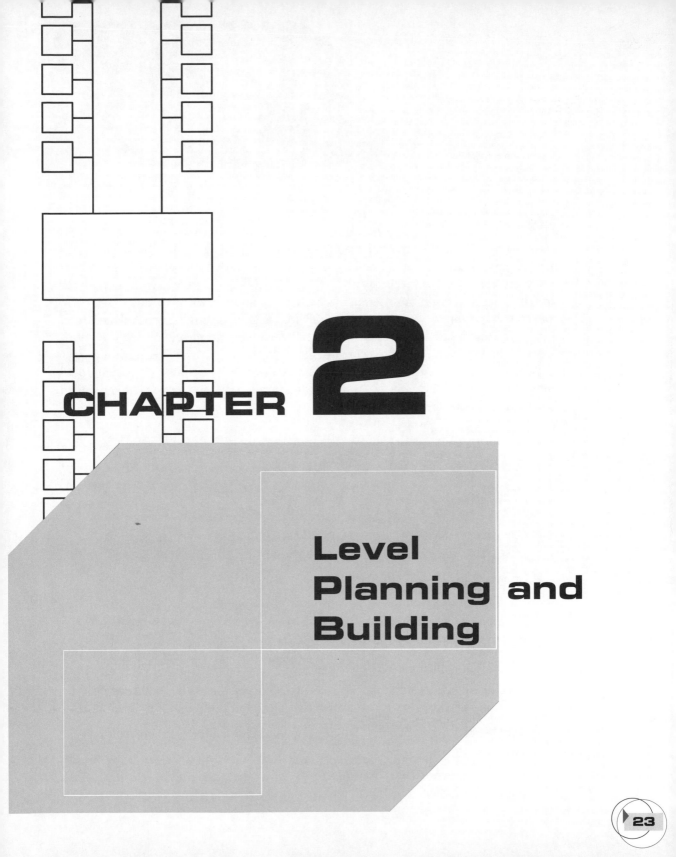

CHAPTER 2

Level Planning and Building

AFTER

you've completed your previsualization phase, it's time to gather up all of that information into a clean and ready-to-use design document. If you're interested in finding out how to build a complete design document, you can find a growing number of design document templates at www.gamedev.net. The specific type of information you'll include in your design document is dependent on your game's genre details and platform specifics. Platform specifics shape your design. Your platform hardware will determine in detail the largest aspects of your design. A basic shooter for a PDA or cell phone will have a vastly different design orientation than a third-person action title for the PlayStation 2.

When I'm writing the "Level or Mission Description" sections of a design document (for example, the game content specifications), I like to try to include detailed information about the following:

❭ **Location**   What is the action setting? A graveyard? A tunnel system?

❭ **Time of day**   Is it fixed time or dynamic? Does time change visibly during play?

❭ **Weather conditions**   Rain? Lightning storm? Hail? Wind gusts? Does weather change over time?

❭ **Story setup**   What main story points set up the player for the level or mission?

❭ **Story continuity**   What main story points need to be reinforced in the mission or level?

❭ **Mission or level summary**   Provide a complete general "walk-through" description of the mission or level.

❭ **Topographic map**   Provide a bird's-eye view of your level or mission.

❭ **Specific objectives or goals**   What will the player be asked to accomplish in the game setting?

❭ **Subobjectives or subgoals**   What peripheral challenges are required of the player, if any?

❭ **Terrain features**   Describe and specify. How do terrain features connect with one another?

❱ **Props**   What props are present? Are they static or can they take damage? How to behave?

❱ **Hazards**   Define all hazards. Open graves? Collapsing trees? Electric fences?

❱ **Puzzles**   What puzzle efforts will be required of the player, if any?

❱ **Enemies**   Which enemies will populate this level? How do their abilities mesh with the environment?

❱ **Nonplayer character (NPC) involvement**   What NPCs are present? What is their function and purpose?

❱ **Power-ups and collectibles**   Which power-ups and collectibles are present? What is their function and purpose?

❱ **Effects considerations**   What kinds of visual effects will be present? Disease clouds? Altar glows?

❱ **Sound and music**   How will sounds, ambiance, and music be used to support play?

❱ **Script lists**   What scripts will be required for the level or mission?

❱ **Artificial intelligence (AI) considerations**   What tricky "behaviors" will the player encounter in single-player mode?

❱ **Network or multiplay aspects**   What must the design account for to support network or multiplayer modes?

❱ **Team guidelines**   Establish grid size and workflow procedures.

❱ **Gameplay notes**   Collect notes and ideas from team brainstorm sessions.

This list seems like quite a bit of information to settle, and it is. In the end, success depends on having a roadmap that helps you know where you're going with a game.

Once you've tested and refined your level ideas on paper and have done your design document work, you are ready to begin the level planning and layout process.

The planning phase will help you lock down design and technical details, while the stubbing or layout phase will help you to bring out the rough and basic form for your level or mission. This chapter examines a number of workflow considerations for taking your ideas from concept toward execution.

With adequate planning, the idea is to begin to translate your topographic map and reference drawings into basic mesh or geometry form. This allows you to begin to test, at an early stage, most of your level's basic properties, like scaling, sizing, and jumping requirements for an action title.

Again, as discussed in Chapter 1, it's important to have a starting point and to have tested your ideas on paper. Don't begin by building blind geometry. Utilize reference drawings or reference points for all they're worth. Utilize your design document—it helps immensely to know where you're going. It seems simple, but it's a challenge for many game developers.

Building a game requires consistent forward momentum. If you don't know where you're going, you probably aren't going anywhere. For most level builders, it's far easier to start from sketches than to try to build up a level by holding it all in their mind and "free-forming" it. Now, let's take a look at what we should keep in mind as we begin to build levels.

PLANNING YOUR LEVEL WORK

These days, the game world stakes are pretty high, and the bar of measure is seemingly raised every day. Game worlds have to be built quickly and efficiently, and they have to deliver maximum impact. With the advent of massively multiplayer online games (MMOGs), entire new "world sections" or regions and updates must be created and delivered to the player to continue, support, and enhance their gaming experience. You'll learn much more about these kinds of games in Chapter 8.

In the recent past, many games were constructed using tile-based systems. Tiles are basically square 2-D "postage stamps" that link up or connect with each other along one, two, three, or all four of their edges. The pieces fit together like a jigsaw puzzle. By connecting many of these pieces in the intended way, you can build a game level. Oddly enough, even though most titles are done in 3-D today, some of the same construction principles apply. You might even say that, from a design standpoint, there is a small renaissance of old ideas applied to new technology. If you think about it, 3-D environments often can be reduced to an assembly of various simple components to form more complex ones.

The time that you commit up front to planning out your level and environmental work will generally save you time at many points along the way in executing it. Diving in to build "something" is usually both costly and inefficient.

Game development teams have several decisions to make in choosing software tools for level building. Here are some of the choices:

> Build custom level tool functionality into a 3-D package like Maya (www.aliaswavefront.com) or 3ds Max (www.discreet.com) using their own script systems (Maya Embedded Language [MEL] or MAXScript, respectively). You can build small- or large-scope level assembly and editing parameters right into Max or Maya.

> Use a game development package solution like RenderWare (www.renderware.com) and its Studio toolset.

> Use the tools that accompany a licensed engine technology like the Unreal, Quake, LithTech (www.lithtech.com), Serious Sam (www.croteam.com), or NDL/NetImmerse (www.netimmerse.com) systems.

> Write your own stand-alone editor to build content for your proprietary engine.

With the time demands placed on developers to provide new and exciting content, many developers are searching for game construction systems that rely on prefabrication, modularity, and maximum reuseability. There are also several scaling and world grid issues to consider, and a wide array of mistakes to try and avoid. Let's take a look at each of these concepts in detail.

Prefabricated Geometry and Modularity

Prefabricated geometry is simply geometry built to be used and reused in certain ways. A spiral staircase that you can use in a scene to transition from floor to floor is an example of a piece of prefabricated geometry. Its use is obvious—it's a stairway. You might see five to ten of these used in different locations throughout a level. A player might not even recognize it as the same piece used later, once it is retextured and scaled in size.

Piping system components and door moldings are two examples of prefabricated geometry that can be reused throughout a game environment. These days, for speed and efficiency, we have to think about building up environments out of components. Maybe the door molding can be flipped or mirrored in a scene to become something else. These prefabricated units become something akin to the 2-D tiles mentioned earlier. They become pieces in our toy construction set aimed at building up game environments.

Why modularity? Because we need "digital Legos." Game environments have to be built quickly and efficiently while offering maximum visual impact and maximum gameplay support. Development teams are under great pressure to create stunning worlds in short order. Although it seems obvious, only recently have game developers started to build tools that maximize efficiency with a "snap-together" Lego-like functionality. These tools now are essential to deliver large-scale environments.

Although some people may think that modular design is a recipe for repetition, that is not necessarily true. You can be very creative through crafty use of your construction pieces. All of your favorite 2-D titles were built with modular tile sets. 3-D offers new game vistas, but must share some of the same mindset.

Modular world design is a solid solution to several problems. If we didn't think modularly, and all environmental features and all prop features were entirely custom or unique, we would

> Suffer many machine performance issues.

> Constantly be building geometry and texturing, extending schedules, and burning valuable resources along the way.

> Not be able to build, refine, and test critical game play as efficiently.

> Not be able to make fairly large changes rapidly.

> Possibly never complete the game successfully.

In our planning stage, we need to think in terms of modularity and reuse. Commercial development schedules really don't allow for anything else. How can we get the most from the least? It's a design engineering issue, really. It always has been. Games are built with limited manpower and resources. Development teams regularly face the challenge of figuring out how to get the most complexity out of minimal resources.

From our topographic maps and basic asset breakdowns, demonstrated in Chapter 1's cathedral example, we now know some of the key environment components that define this part of a level section. This is how we start to go from concept to execution.

Scale and Grid Sizing Considerations

Scale, when thinking modularly, is usually dependent on game genre. Ask yourself and your team these questions: What are you trying to accomplish game-wise? What about genre-wise? You'll know the answers to these questions because you'll have done the planning. Yet, how you focus your *modularity scale* (how big or small you section up your pieces of geometry) depends on answers to these kinds of questions. Are maps built from entire village sections of terrain? Is a single hallway and room interior built up from many smaller individual pieces? These are examples of large modular scale and small modular scale, respectively.

If you're building a space-vehicle racing game through futuristic cityscapes, you can probably have larger-scale prefabricated pieces, like entire blocks of buildings in different combinations. On the other hand, if you are taking a player through intimate interior physical spaces, like abandoned mining tunnels, you need detailed components or building pieces that can be assembled to form complexity and detail from apparent simplicity.

This approach, in concept, works fine for first- and third-person action titles. It works for racing and sports titles, with track or arena layout, as well as for role-playing game (RPG) and real-time strategy (RTS) titles, depending on map detailing and population. It will even work for simulation-oriented games like *Zoo Tycoon* and *Rollercoaster Tycoon*. All of these can feature maps or levels made from geometry construction sets. This approach also can work with some elements of flight simulator design, like laying out airports and hangars. The "in flight" experience is handled somewhat differently by the game engine requiring the creation of custom scrolling and camera moves.

Grid systems are very important in game development. Programmers use grids to determine location and to handle other programmatic issues. Grids establish world scale, too. If a character is 128 units tall, then a fence that is 32 units tall may not have

FIGURE 2-1

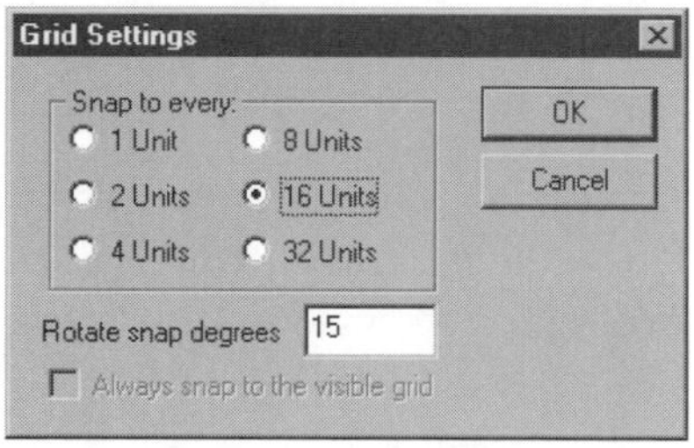

Global grid settings

the intended effect—Stonehenge being crushed by a dwarf. Figure 2-1 demonstrates the settings for a world or global grid scale. This setting means that every piece of geometry snaps to every 16 units on the grid. Figure 2-2 shows an example of the top view for your grid in an editor.

Also, keep in mind that character actions and interactions are grid-related. Characters can usually jump a certain number of units. They can reach a certain number of units. They can grab onto a ladder at a certain number of units from the ground. They can step up a certain number of units. The grid is always game-aware, so we have to

FIGURE 2-2

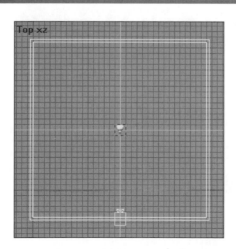

Top view of grid

build our environmental support for gameplay with constant reference to the grid system we have chosen. Developers should agree and lock down grid information early on. Otherwise, massive amounts of level reworking, which no one can afford, may be the result. It's important to remember that your design document should detail every action/object interaction.

Your action/object interactions will become part of your grid system guidelines. Most importantly, perhaps, the prefabricated pieces that form our level construction sets must be built according to the accepted grid system.

Avoiding Common Level Mistakes

Many types of maps and levels are built these days, including:

) Single player (player versus computer)

) Co-operative (two or more players in collaboration)

) Deathmatch (player versus player)

) Variations on capture the flag (player versus player or team versus team)

Each of these level types has several design nuances, many of which are still being explored. Before we begin to build out a level, let's take a quick look at some common mistakes that are made when building levels. These are generalizations only, and may not be a mistake in every case.

) **Hasty dead ends** Dead ends that suddenly and/or inconceivably "halt" the flow of the level.

) **Awkward room flow** Room-to-room transition that just doesn't work. Don't make your whole level a series of hospital rooms next to each other with a hallway down the center. Going endlessly in and out of cramped spaces is no fun. Plan your space-to-space transition carefully. Be mindful of it. Make sure that you provide variety for your player. Help guide the player through small to large spaces, small to medium spaces, medium to large spaces, and so forth. Offer up many kinds of space transition in your levels.

) **Using every enemy or power-up at once** Just because you *can* use everything at once doesn't mean that you should. Generally, you want to pace the use of your enemies. Use enemies dramatically. Allow for anticipation to build. It's not exciting if your player sees every enemy available up front. Having as many enemies as possible onscreen at once is not the point. Using enemies to build fear in a player, for instance, and create interesting play scenarios is closer to the point.

❯ **Overuse of switch systems**   Don't use too many switches. Nobody wants to switch doors open every other hallway. Also, don't make switch puzzles too tricky and trap your player. I'll just stop playing your level.

❯ **No surprises**   Where is my chance to discover something? Don't make everything too obvious. I'd like to find hidden areas and untold secrets. I want to explore this world you've put me in. Give me some humor elements. Let me in on a level secret not known to others.

❯ **No payoff point**   After I work hard at defeating your enemies and traps, what do I get? I want a satisfying reward. Give me mini-visual payoffs, too. When I work my way into new areas, I want a visual payoff point, at a minimum. Seed the level with visual payoff points. Identify areas where you seek to visually dazzle the player as a reward for progress.

❯ **Get me stuck**   You're not "giving it away" or "helping me" if I can successfully navigate your level. Test me with your enemy pacing, simple solution finding, and enemy challenges. Don't test my sense of direction. I don't have one. Use props and texture markers ("I remember this blue floor!") to help tell me where I am in your level. Build a simple location finder into your interface. Do both and I'll finish your game. Do neither and forget it.

❯ **No purpose or too much purpose**   Try not to leave me feeling disconnected from what I'm here to do in your game world. Help me to know what I'm after, but don't make it stale. On the other hand, once I know, don't bother me about it! Don't have an NPC or narrator keep popping up to remind me that I haven't found what I'm looking for yet.

❯ **Guide my every move**   Use NPCs wisely. Don't tell me what to do, when to do it, and how to do it from moment to moment. Try not to force me to do things. This is not the experience I'm seeking in buying your game. Teach me, but don't force me.

LEVEL STUBBING WALK-THROUGH

With prefab, modularity, asset breakdowns (our list of required environmental features, props, textures, and scripted events—like the cathedral example), and grid issues resolved, we can begin to build up our levels. Keep in mind that game developers use many different software tools to accomplish level construction and world building. For purposes of demonstration, this section shows you one of the most popular ways. In this phase, we start to translate our topographic maps into early level geometry or level meshes. In this context, *geometry* and *mesh* simply refer to the wireframe polygonal model of environmental features, like room definitions or spaces, arches, stairs, and so forth. Figure 2-3 shows a basic wireframe view.

FIGURE 2-3

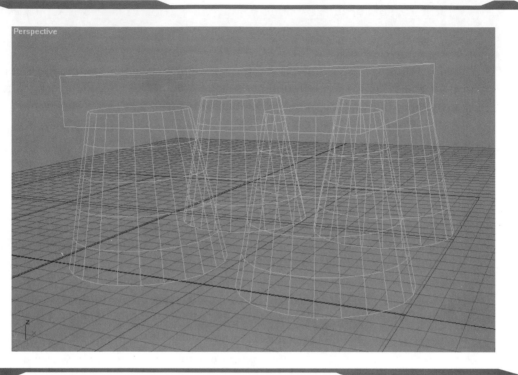

Perspective

Wireframe view

An important practical point needs to be made here. As previously stated, game developers have many choices in software tools when it comes to building up world geometry for their games. They can use commercial 3-D packages like Maya or 3ds max along with the script systems built into these packages for customization. They can use stand-alone level tools written specifically to generate assets compatible with their own game engine. They often use both in several combinations.

Figure 2-4 shows a sample Maya scene constructed using some of the game developer training materials available from Alias/Wavefront, the creators of Maya (www.aliaswavefront.com).

Some developers choose to use Maya for art and level work, whereas others choose to use 3ds max. There are some development studios that use a mixture of the two packages. In the final analysis, you use whatever works best in delivering the results you need (quickly). Maybe your programming team is more comfortable writing tools based around MAXScript. In this case, your team might use 3ds max. These days, both packages are extremely flexible, extensible, and powerful.

FIGURE 2-4

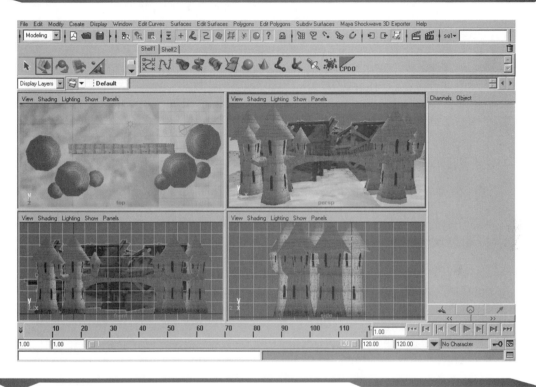

Maya scene

Next, we will consider the process of building up your initial level geometry, also called "stubbing out" your level. This process usually follows a fairly common five-step routine. You can adapt this to meet your own content needs.

Step One: Working from Your Topographic Sketches

The first step in stubbing out your level is to make sure you have a nice topographic sketch of your map, which describes the general shape and physical features for your level. It can include indications for general prop layout, rough enemy placement, encountered obstacles and hazards, and power-ups. Most importantly for modularity at this stage, it should describe environmental features to the best degree possible, such as the following:

> Terrain features (hills, valleys, outcroppings, rivers, pools, and so on)

> Terrain elevation information (stair placements, ramps, slopes, inclines, and so on)

❯ Description of the intended gameplay purpose (for example, fighting your way up the hill to capture a strategic enemy stronghold)

Figure 2-5 shows a sample of the kind of topographic sketch you might start working from. Keep in mind that these are only reference or starting points. We start at the macro level and work our way down toward level specifics.

The more work that you do up front to assemble conceptual drawings and collect quick reference material, the clearer the task of building environmental geometry becomes. This shouldn't come as much of a surprise, but in the heat of developing games on condensed schedules, it can easily fall by the wayside. Normally, there is scant time to do a robust amount of preproduction. It happens in parallel with game development. This is why it's usually so important to be able to create quick and easily evolved conceptual drawings to build from, and to plan to build in modularity with asset use.

Step Two: Create Contour Lines

You might choose to scan into an image file the paper map you've created for use as a template. Load the image into the 3ds max or Maya background image plane (a common starting point for several types of modeling, including environmental and character work). From there, you can trace the contour outlines of your image to create spline paths or shape outlines of your level's major features. Once you have the contour lines, then adjust all of your elevation information by raising and lowering the curves to end up with 3-D contour lines.

FIGURE 2-5

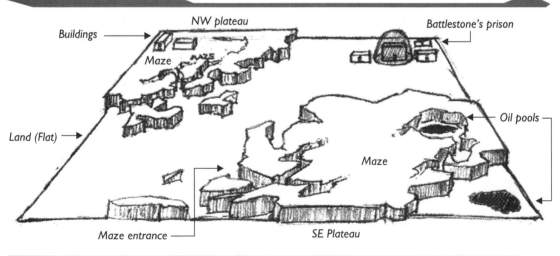

Topographic map example 1

Figure 2-6 shows the creation of contour lines, and their final position with basic "elevation" information included. You can see that they are now 3-D lines, if you look at them from each of your views (Top, Side, Front, Perspective) on the screen.

Step Three: Build a Mesh from Your Contour Lines

If you were using an image file in your image plane background to draw your contour lines, hide that now and create some basic geometry from the splines you've created and adjusted. We just want to create a basic mesh that can be used to run a player around on in order to check out level basics, like sizing and scaling issues and so forth.

Figure 2-7 shows a "loft" operation, a basic modeling move, to create a polygon mesh from the contour lines. You can see that we now have a basic wireframe model of our environment starting to take shape.

Step Four: Utilize File Referencing to Build Up and Populate Your Level

Now you can begin to create prototype files, commonly called "file referencing," which will associate certain heavily reused pieces of geometry with a button, and al-

FIGURE 2-6

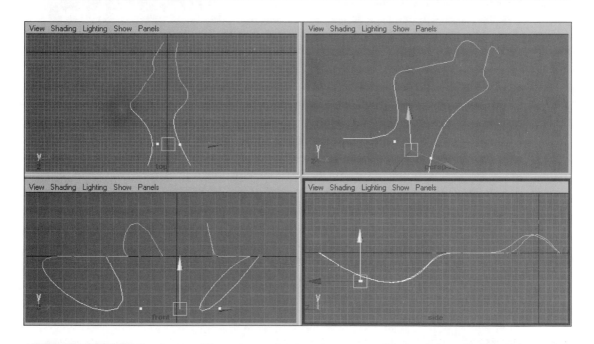

Create contour lines

FIGURE 2-7

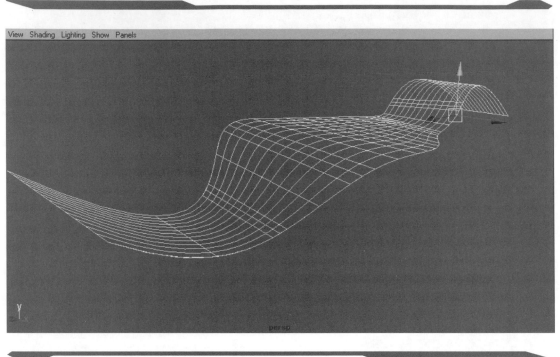

View Shading Lighting Show Panels

persp

Our mesh created from contour lines

low you to stamp or "instance" objects all over your map or level. This is where the modularity and prefabrication planning really delivers.

Think of a file reference button as a cookie cutter that lets you stamp pieces all over your map the way you would stamp cookie patterns into cookie dough. Once you stamp the cookie dough, you're committed. Once you stamp a model on your map, however, you have the freedom to move it. Oh, the beauty of digital tools!

For example, you might want to place a group of towers or satellite dishes onto one section of your map, and then place bridge pieces and rock walls onto another. This is accomplished by file referencing.

Suppose you've built an archway piece that will be used repeatedly throughout your level. We already know that smart asset design affords maximum reuse. We are always striving to get the most out of every asset created. You may create a placeholder archway piece while the final or "in-game" version of the archway piece model is being completed by a 3-D artist.

For our purposes, let's assume that you have the final archway piece ready to use. Once you have created a file reference button called "archway" that is associated with your archway mesh, you can place archways all over your map and move them around like a construction set piece. This method is very useful when building up maps and levels.

File referencing allows you to create plenty of detail and complexity by making efficient reuse of models. It is memory-smart, because once a referenced piece or model is loaded into memory, a game engine can place referenced models everywhere they are required, knowing how to draw the item in every instance based on the one instance. Go ahead, put the "archway" piece everywhere it is called for. Every piece is not utterly unique. Every piece has maximum reuse value, which we need for solid performance and for building up complexity.

Step Five: Start Checking Layout Details

After placing instanced items like archway pieces or columns with canopy pieces all over the map, your level geometry begins to take shape. You can follow your agreed-upon grid system to make early positional adjustments and start to move a character or temporary character (sometimes just a cube the grid size of an upcoming character). At this point, you are mainly checking for sizing, scaling, grid issues, and bad geometry (parts of the mesh that have errors or can be simplified).

GAME PROTOTYPING

One of the biggest current challenges in game development is *game prototyping*. How do you test out or "prove" game ideas from concept to execution? These days, before proceeding with actual game development, game publishers require solid proof that a game idea is fun, engaging, extremely play-friendly, and commercially relevant.

Publishers routinely require that game developers provide a sophisticated proof of concept (POC) that demonstrates a working version of their game. For most independent developers, preparing such a POC for submission to a publisher can involve substantial costs, and does not guarantee a publishing agreement.

There is no easy and affordable solution for testing a game idea. For example, suppose your team is interested in building a 3-D isometric combat racing game. The simple game heartbeat might be to combine traditional racing with car-to-car combat in an isometric setting. A three-quarters or isometric camera view allows players to view entire sections of the track at once, perhaps laying down hazards to thwart their opponent, and gathering power-ups to cause havoc on the racetrack for everyone around them. How do you test this game idea? If you don't have a complete game engine which can be customized quickly, and even if you do, considerable resources at a substantial cost will have to be thrown at taking a game idea like this through to the complete POC stage.

Short of complete actual engines, there is no way to test game ideas in any efficient way. Some game ideas, by definition, are easier to prototype than others. A game of environmental navigation and light puzzle solving might be fairly easy to prototype. One person could prototype a game like *Myst* using an application like Macromedia Director. Prototyping a 3-D update to an arcade action game like *Smash-TV,* however, would be difficult, because it would require considerable test programming and art resources to do it justice.

Prototypes are commonly used in other entertainment-oriented industries. Every large toy release produced for the market is rigorously prototyped, tested, refined, and tested again. As we've seen, this is not very easy to do in the world of game development.

Developers sometimes use tools from previous game releases to test new ideas for future games. However, if the next game a developer is considering doing is substantially different in genre from a previous game, using that previous game's established tools and code may be of very little help.

There is no "game construction" prototyping software used commonly in the industry. Testing a game idea often requires substantial code resources, which often must be custom-written in order to try to test a game idea to any degree of completeness.

POST LEVEL STUBBING CONSIDERATIONS

Using the combined power of file referencing, modularity, and prefabricated geometry pieces, you have now stubbed out your level basics. Awesome, isn't it? Hopefully, now you see the importance of the previsualization and level planning stages. As always, you're trying to transfer gameplay concepts and ideas past level geometry and into action. It's wonderful to have a visually stunning environment to navigate, but we need so much more. We need a stunning environment with tons of fun play. As exciting as the early level stubbing phase can be, it is really just the beginning of an extended refinement and cross-checking cycle.

From this point forward, we need to focus on adapting architectural and terrain features to support gameplay in the best method possible, and we'll need to check character flow (such as character navigation) throughout our new level. Are steps, items, and ladders positioned at the right heights for our character to step, jump, and climb? Do our environmental hazards show the right scale, purpose, and design intention? Is our level in total coming together size-wise on an appropriate physical scale? As you can see, there are many features and facets to check at this point.

We also need to check our concepts. Amidst these details, are we keeping the big game picture in view? The early evolution process in level development needs to maintain a certain amount of forward momentum, or ideas and goals tend to get lost or dissolve in the fray of details. Also, before we're too far along we want to be able to make large adjustments if necessary. This suggests the importance of getting early feedback from players and testers. Finally, as the level goals start to become more obvious, do they help to support and enhance the original game vision or heartbeat? We'll discuss each of these important considerations next.

Adapting Architecture and Terrain to Games

If you have done most of your grid planning correctly, you'll minimize the amount of immediate reworking necessary as you begin to adapt or alter architectural features or terrain features for your game. Remember that these features should always support gameplay! This is why it's so important for you and your team to have thought out and committed to paper what's really going to happen from a pure game-play standpoint. If you have ignored or shirked this mental exercise, and not gleaned the details that flow from it, you could end up with a very pretty architectural walk-through that has no play value. Now, there is nothing at all wrong with a beautiful architectural walk-through—if you're in the business of creating architecture for clients. However, we're building games! We need so much more than a walk-through.

Hopefully, you won't have doorways, windows, or pipe ducts that are too small for your hero character to enter or exit. You won't have bridges that are too small to drive two cars side by side over when you've called for such functionality in your design. However, even though you will have planned for certain geometry and architecture, and will have built a prefab system to account for your designs, you'll still find that you need to add to or subtract from your construction set new pieces. It's important to think of your level construction set as your arsenal. Experiment. Try to do amazing things with it. Hopefully, the transitions through planning from your paper sketches have translated into a great starting point for building up your level further.

It's not always the case, though. Maybe, despite your best individual and team mental projections, your paper floor plans are not working out that well in 3-D. You did the sketching, the concepts, and the gameplay notes, but the results didn't work out perfectly. That's okay! We're looking at basic traversal and navigation right now. That's what this phase is for! Remember, modern game design is largely about elaboration and refinement.

With modularity and file referencing as your allies, you should be able to make significant adjustments fairly quickly. These are powerful concepts. If you had built up this level geometry in any other way, you might find yourself making edits by hand to complex geometry. You might be trying to resize or trim geometry, somehow put it back together without errors or leaks—any number of problems may come your way. I can't stress enough the power of file referencing and modularity!

Architecture edits for gameplay purposes become much easier using a modular/prefab system of construction. For example, suppose that I've stamped 20 pagodas all over my map. If I wanted to make a change to the pagodas, and didn't use file referencing, I'd have to approach each of the 20 pagodas on the map and make the changes by hand. This is a killer. However, with file referencing on my side, I can adjust just one pagoda—the file referencing definition file for "pagoda"—and all 20 pagodas will be updated on the map. Wow! Much better.

Another example: suppose that I want to stamp terrain sections of a certain kind all across my map or level. Maybe I have a terrain stamp with some rock outcroppings on grass where the rocks are of a given height. Suppose I've used the stamp 43 times in my current level. What if I want to change the height of the rock outcroppings based on a gameplay decision? Maybe a character needs to get over them in a few instances and they are currently too tall on the grid to allow a character to step over them. Wouldn't it be nice to adjust just those few and not have to do it by hand? I can make a unique file reference and do the task much more quickly!

Checking Character Flow Throughout a Level

Character flow refers to how well a character fits into the environment. Can the character navigate steps, ladders, and jumps and reach switches? Are hazards or props coming together in scale with a character's size and abilities?

Once you have your basic level layout complete, you'll get to move a block around. Just kidding. Not really. Depending on your production planning, you may be moving around a 128-unit block (based on your grid settings) because the animation system support for the game engine is not yet complete, or character animation is not complete, or a combination of these factors. That's okay.

What we're now looking for as we move around throughout the level are any fundamental problems. Are there pure geometry errors? Is the construction "clean" (has no redundant or unnecessary geometry)? Can we simplify anything? Can we do something smarter, smaller, or cleaner? We're doing early checking for feel and overall scale. Are the pagodas and ponds the right size relative to our characters? They should be close, if we did solid grid planning. Still, there may be some changes required.

Do our transitions between interior and exterior spaces work out correctly? Did we forget about any pieces that we need to end or terminate a physical feature in the level or map? That lava has to flow somewhere, so where and how does it end? It doesn't just stop at the edge of the paper like it did on our topographic sketch! We may need to add some transition pieces here to our construction set.

Undoubtedly, our character or vehicle is going to do things in the environment, right? We want to start looking at these actions early on. The character might use door switches and will probably perform a wide array of interactions with the environment. Part of our grid system details should define at what unit height these operations occur. This is design information for the whole team that must be followed. Other designers might be building other levels, but door switch height, for instance, must be common to all. What unit height are drinking fountains in the world? At what height should a ladder be placed from the ground in order for a character to be able to grab it? How high, measured in world units, will the shutoff valves be located? These are the features we're starting to check in order to confirm character flow throughout the level.

We have to check everything level-wide as it begins to take shape. We want to check ramps and inclines, elevator access points, ladders, switches, and shutoffs. At this point, we might be riding on flat cubes standing in for boats or barrels across a pond or river, because the art for the boats or barrels isn't complete yet. This is also why it's very important for designers to have basic modeling skills.

Again, the level is only stubbed or blocked-out to the most complete degree possible at the time. Yet, we want to identify problem issues early on rather than late in the process. We will be required to make trade-offs and weigh play value. This is part of bringing the game concepts to a complete state.

Again, the power of file referencing: We can put in placeholder files for this stuff to simulate our game ideas quickly. When we get final art, we drop those in instead.

Jump Heights, Hazards, and Scale

We're all aware that there is endless jumping in many games. I'm not just talking *Frogger*. Jump heights are another good example of the multitude of character interactions with the environment. A *jump height* simply refers to how many units on the grid away from a starting point a given character can jump. This number of units can be tuned or changed in the game programming to make the character's jump higher or lower. Jump heights are important because, like all character interactions, they become a test case at the end of the level stubbing process.

A character will normally have a defined and generic jump height. If the player powers up the character with jet boots, "SuperJump," or "reverse plasma graft happy soles" (you get the picture), the jump height may be doubled, tripled, or more.

Suppose that the generic jump height is 64 units. That means that anything over 64 units high cannot be jumped. Maybe a character's step height is 32 units. This means that, for animation purposes, the character's stepping animation is created for a 32-unit-high step. You can see how important it is to follow your world's grid system if events that take place in it are going to look right. A character's "push switch" animation might be relative to a 96-unit-high switch. The character has an animated pushing motion at 96 units high. If those switches are placed in the world at 47 units high, that character is going to look pretty stupid thumbing the wall.

Jump heights, step heights, push heights, pull heights, catch heights, ladder heights—all of these height descriptors need to be checked as you begin to move past the pure level stubbing or breakout phase. Maybe a mission calls for an event with no height information determined. Now is the time to think about it, and get it in there as placeholder information.

As the stubbing phase comes to completion and the level starts to get locked down, we will want to start implementing *collision events* as well. When a character walking on flat terrain collides with a step, for instance, a collision event occurs. We'll want to use this event to trigger that character's stepping animation, for example. On the same event, we might also want to trigger a door slamming shut. Typically, dependent on your engine and toolset circumstances, you set or paint collision fields that generate data for the programmer.

Hazard areas like fire pits, bubbling oil pools, or acid pockets need to be checked for scale and flow. Are these environmental features working out in the transition from concept to execution? This is what you're checking. There's next to zero play going on right now, so it can be hard to tell. Later on, in play testing, these areas will need to be adjusted to build the perfect play setting. You'll learn more about the play test sequence in Chapter 7.

Keeping the Big Game Picture in View

Maybe you're building out or stubbing golf courses for a golfing game or working on a new vehicle-based combat game. Then again, maybe you're working on an FPS set during World War II or in the Old West. In all of these cases, it's important to keep the big game picture in view. Literally.

In other words, it's important to cross-reference your concept drawings, game heartbeat, and gameplay notes. Typically, of course, you're working from a game design document, which is the roadmap and "detail skeleton" for your game. It details the purpose, functionality, and approach to execution for your game. (Appendix A provides some reference information on design documents.)

Assuming that we have a well-crafted design document in place and have just completed building out our first level basics, how do we keep the big game picture in view? It is largely a matter of mental exercise. By starting with smaller sections of your level at first, using your documentation and reference material as a launching pad, try to picture in your "mind's eye" the game playing right there in front of you as you intend it to. Start with only a section of your game if it seems easier, and really try to flesh it out in your mind. Take more gameplay notes. Share them, and refine them, with your team. Remember, the process is all elaboration and refinement!

Picture in your mind the kind of character and environmental interaction you've been talking about, dreaming about, and obsessing about with your team or on your own. Try to see the defining gameplay itself. Is it a defensive mechanic? (For example, guard this pile of loot.) Is it a puzzle mechanic? (Work with these logical or physical limits to accomplish a solution.) Is it an offensive/defensive mechanic or game operation? (Attack enemy 1 and enemy 2 while protecting your pile of loot.) Work at it hard enough and you'll have a "That's how it will work!" moment. It's an exciting moment. Wonderful. Visualize how it will work. Try to visualize how the play mechanic you just saw in your mind blends into your level, arena, or playfield. See it right there on the big screen in your mind!

As you develop this ability, you'll be able to "move a camera" around in your mind, even view your levels at different strata sometimes. Believe me, it's okay if it seems hard at first. Trying to think in 3-D is hard for many of us (2-D was hard enough). I think you'll find this mental projection technique, for lack of a better term, very useful in "seeing" game mechanics and in "seeing" your levels. As you build up this ability, you will probably be able to "see more" at once than when you began. You'll see how the combat system details will work, or what might make for an odd, loveable, miniature golf course set along the spine of a whale—and most importantly, why it works for the game.

The Early Evolution of Levels

When I speak of "levels," for the moment, I mean everything from a 2-D platform shooter with a boss at the far right end to a fully robust 3-D first- or third-person level. In this context, I'm even talking about maps and missions for RTS and RPG titles.

Levels, maps, and missions start as concepts that aim to service an over-arching game vision. Conceptually, perhaps we are trying to re-create something historical, like a section of World War II's Battle of the Bulge. Maybe our level is simply driven by a twitch mechanic or fast-action mechanic. Our task is to try to build levels that support this fact in the best way possible, in the most interesting and challenging way possible.

I've mentioned and recommended the importance of planning. We have to know where we're going. In game development, however, getting there is a process of evolution. It would be nice to have the guarantee that we could simply execute the plans for a given level in a game exactly as conceived. It rarely seems to happen this way. Don't get me wrong, we still need every bit of our planning and concepts. Yet, game fundamentals spring out and make themselves apparent in a number of ways. Levels, as game components, evolve too—in a number of ways.

Technology forces shape design and establish the limits. As a design team, you can't do what the code won't. As a design team operating in a production environment, you can't do what you can't afford from a pure resources standpoint. There might be great "game support reasons" for implementing a certain ability or feature. The reality is that it might not make it due to technology limits, unmanageable frustrations, experience issues, or a number of other factors.

Levels evolve in two important ways. First, they sometimes evolve according to your game vision. This is the best possible case. They evolve the way you had hoped they would, given enough refinement. You test and reject or test and alter game ideas, based on pure technology support. Second, they evolve in ways you would not choose, in ways you would prefer they didn't. In these cases, you are sometimes not able to accomplish the kind of specific gameplay you seek due to soft factors like software tool constraints, editor constraints, engine support constraints, unresolved technology issues, and so forth. Outstanding levels, maps, and missions only have a chance to grow with good technology "fertilizer"—a robust bed of pure game engine ability and tools efficiency and integration.

A game engine developed for the PC, or next-generation console systems, is basically a large and complex set of C++ code modules that handle such things as player input/output, a draw or rendering system, an animation system, an audio system, and a big-ole main game logic loop, which tells these other systems what to do and how to do it. Software tools are what set up and sometimes control art, animation, and audio assets for integration into a game engine. The pure ability of these tools will often limit level evolution. Game-wise, a game development team can only build in as much gameplay as these tools and the programming team allow. Programmers have many simultaneous, dependency-oriented tasks to accomplish at all times. No one chooses to let gameplay fall on the floor.

The Importance of Early Feedback

Once you have laid out your basic level or world geometry and made any corrections based on checking the level thoroughly for space flow issues, geometry errors, grid problems, and size or scale problems, it's time to hammer home the importance of a communication feedback loop.

For most game development teams, there will be technical issues, tools support issues, and basic implementation issues that are best attacked early on. After the initial build-out phase, as your level begins to grow and take shape, it will be valuable for the team as a whole if relevant feedback from the design team can be communicated and shared with other team members involved in other areas of development that impact design specifics.

One of the common limiting factors for most teams at the design implementation level these days is software tools support. Perhaps you're working with a solid or semisolid game engine. (A *solid* engine runs without any significant errors. A *semisolid* engine runs with some or many known bugs or error points, which is a more common condition, because the engine is growing and changing in parallel with the game content you are trying to build.) Even if your team's programmers have built out solid game engine architecture and the artists have the use (and choice) of solid 3-D packages, game building requires so much more than simply getting your model and animation assets into the game engine (which also offer certain challenges).

The point is that design implementation or "building in" your game heartbeat is often heavily dependent on tools support. If your tools do not have the functionality to accomplish your team's game vision, you will probably miss the mark. Getting feedback to your tools team (if you are lucky enough to have one) is critical to getting the support in place early that will allow you to accomplish design objectives for your team.

Is Your Primary Mechanic Working?

As soon as possible at the beginning of your building phase, it's important to ask this very question. But, be fair-minded. Give your game a chance to get to the state where it's appropriate to ask this question. If it's not working, consider why it is not working. Is the concept sinking in execution? Are the software tools you're using simply not capable of executing your team's design ideas? Are the programming requirements heading into orbit?

Despite doing the mental work, the previsualization, the picturing of gameplay in your mind from the beginning, is the game simply not fun in the ways you assumed it would be? Every developer runs through these mental checks and challenges. You have to ask these questions early. If the primary mechanic, as defined by your game heartbeat, is not working, you now must make the decisions about instant evolution or rejection. Most teams, due to development pressure, must find a way to evolve the game toward success in every meaningful way possible, to fix those things that can be fixed to make for a better play experience. This is a best-effort situation.

Are Your Level Goals Enhancing Your Game Vision?

Throughout the game development process, a team is constantly verifying its goals for a game. Whether you're building maps, levels, or missions for your genre game, your team will benefit from taking a close look at how well the "meat" of your levels is helping to enhance your game vision, or serve your game heartbeat. If there are elements to your levels that are derailing the experience, you will want to cut them. This is why it's so important to try to understand, as a team, what your game is going to be … the defining elements.

Simplicity is a virtue in games and other places. If your level has too many subgoals— if every time the player accomplishes something another little subeffort is tacked on ("Now go do this …")—the effect of having goals in the level tends to be diminished. Keep the goals as clear as possible at all times. If you don't, players will soon feel disconnected and start to ask themselves "What was I supposed to do again?"

Don't break the experience into a million pieces by forcing the player to do things that distract from the fun they're trying to have. Most games hinge on an action element. If you're stopping the action every other minute, the game will feel jarring.

CASE STUDY COMMENTS ON LEVEL EXECUTION

In 1997, I was working on an action-oriented RTS for the Sony PlayStation. The game had many missions, with several pursuit goals per mission. At the time, it didn't feel like we tried to over-reach on the number of goals per mission. We definitely didn't have a large number of subgoals. In fact, we simply had a set number of goals per mission that needed to be accomplished to clear the mission and move on in the game.

Sometimes, in this style of game, it feels like you need to craft many goals in order to keep the player entertained throughout the missions. There's nothing immediately wrong about directing player actions with goals. In fact, most players gain a sense of comfort in knowing where they should direct their actions.

It's all a matter of balance. Many game-play decisions come down to balance scenarios. Your ally in making such decisions is combined player feedback. In this example, what started to evolve based on player feedback was the idea that players liked the action elements of the game the most. They still wanted to utilize strategy in executing their actions, but the action itself was key to their enjoyment. In short, they didn't appear to need an elaborate goal system. They didn't want extended mission briefings. This is partly due to the fact that the RTS genre is abundantly more popular on the PC, and this console title tried to capture that enthusiasm while boosting the action elements.

Knowing this to be true, we didn't add any new goals, and in fact we got rid of a few and focused our final efforts on the part of the game people seemed to like the most: the team-oriented action elements. We didn't lose the strategy side at all. We still had basic fundamental strategy concepts employed in every mission. We just tipped the balance of the game toward refining action items, like creating several new flavors of radius projectile weapons and enhancing our team-based combo attacks.

Another big negative for our team was the "pain" involved in making changes to our levels. Our tools were unstable, and we had a convoluted process for editing levels, rebuilding them in the game code, and then checking our results. I can't stress the power of tools enough. Bad, buggy, or poorly planned tools can literally kill a game before it has a chance to live.

INTERVIEW WITH JOHN KRENG

John Kreng was born the son of the Cambodian Ambassador to the United States and is fluent in Chinese, Vietnamese, and English. He has been training in the martial arts since he was a child and holds 3rd Degree Black Belts in Tang Soo Do and Te-Katana Jujitsu. For two years, John was the #3-rated tournament fighter in the United States, and was a member of the U.S. Professional Karate Team that toured South America. He has also graced the covers of Inside Karate *and* Karate Review *magazines.*

In stunt work and fighting for film, John has worked with Steven Spielberg, Debbie Allen, and such Hong Kong luminaries as Tsui Hark, Jet Li, and legendary wire-fighting master Yuen Cheung Yan. John has served as stunt coordinator/fight choreographer for the films Enter the Grill Master, A Party Called Earth, Hard As Nails, The Haunting of Slaughter Studios, Shakedown, *and an* LA Times *profile commercial featuring Yuen Cheung Yan.*

His style and approach in choreographing an action/fight sequence is to find out more about a character's personality, strengths, and limitations, and then tailor the action to the character's personality traits. By doing this, the choreographed action scenes will operate within the structure of the plot line and also tell a nonverbal story that supports and strengthens the plot and does not take the viewer emotionally out of the picture.

With his extensive knowledge and love for martial arts films since he was a child, John has conducted and written in-depth interviews with action filmmakers and actors who are at the forefront of the field, for magazines like World of Martial Arts, Kung Fu/Qi Gung, and Impact. His interviews include Jackie Chan, Sammo Hung (Martial Law), Jet Li, Michiko Nishiwaki (My Lucky Stars), Yuen Woo Ping (The Matrix, Crouching Tiger-Hidden Dragon), and Ronny Yu (Bride With White Hair). He was also the coordinating editor, project supervisor, and author of the Bruce Lee 25th Anniversary Tribute Issue published by TC Media.

John is also an accomplished stand-up comedian, with four national TV appearances, the subject of a PBS documentary by Academy Award nominee Renee Tajima, and the first non-African American to appear on BET's ComicView. He performed regularly at The Comedy Store in Hollywood, La Jolla, and Las Vegas for ten years, and opened for Eddie Murphy, Louie Anderson, Roseanne, and Pauly Shore.

John is also an accomplished stand-up comedian, with four national TV appearances, the subject of a PBS documentary by Academy Award nominee Renee Tajima, and the first non-African American to appear on BET's ComicView. He performed regularly at The Comedy Store in Hollywood, La Jolla, and Las Vegas for ten years, and opened for Eddie Murphy, Louie Anderson, Roseanne, and Pauly Shore.

TM: How do stand-up comedy, world-class competitive fighting, and vast amounts of martial arts film knowledge influence your game designs?

JK: Let's start with how I got into video games. I was in San Francisco visiting my friend Jeremy Cantor (whom I got my black belt with and also went to art school with), and I was talking with him about what I was going to do with my comedy career during the early to mid '90s. This was because 95 percent of all the comedy clubs across America closed down and I lost almost all my bookings for the rest of the year and it was only June! I was also going through a divorce and needed some stability in my life to think things through. Jeremy was working at Sega at the time and he asked me if I ever thought about being a game tester. I never even thought of it, let alone knew that a position like that existed! He thought I was the perfect candidate because, first, I was a martial artist and a huge fan of Hong Kong action films ever since I was a kid, and every game has some sort of action element involved, so I knew what would make an action sequence look good and how it could be executed. Second, being a stand up comedian, I knew what would make something funny in almost any situation. Third, my writing experience would be useful. On top of knowing how to write jokes, I was already taking screenwriting classes at UCLA Extension. With this experience, I was able to write and convey the experience of what my game would look and feel like. Finally, my art background; by being an art major, I was able to quickly notice what looked wrong with a drawing or animation and help the artist make it more effective in a game.

When I came back to Los Angeles, I went to a computer store and looked at the back of all the video game boxes for an L.A. address. If you were a game company in L.A., you got an enthusiastic letter from me telling of my skills and my eagerness to work in the industry. There were a few. I had two interviews, one of them hired me, and the rest is history.

As a matter of fact, these skills that I mentioned were what got me out of "QA hell" and into my first design assignment as assistant game designer for The Mask on [Super Nintendo Entertainment System] SNES. I was walking past an artist's office and I heard him cussing up a storm. I asked him what was wrong. He told me that he was having a hard time with an animation of a character that was throwing a kick. I asked him if I could look at it. So he showed it to me. It was a character that was throwing a jump spin hook kick. He told me that it needed to be faster and it did not look powerful. So I told him to eliminate a couple frames at the point where the character is about to make contact, extend his hips more so his body will look more elongated, and tuck or bend in the nonkicking foot to give the illusion of height. He didn't believe me since he thought I was a lowly tester. So I demonstrated the technique for him in his office and showed him the points I was referring to. I left him alone so he could digest all that I was tossing at him and thought to myself, "He won't listen to me. I'm just a lowly tester in his eyes." Not too much later he comes to grab me to go to his office. He showed me what he corrected and asked if this was along the lines of what I was explaining to him. Wow! He took my advice. The artist showed the other artists what changes he made and they all liked it. The artist was nice enough to tell the rest of the team that I helped him out with it. Not much later, other artists were coming in to ask me for advice.

I remember when I was first picked up as a regular performer at The Comedy Store, which was like a comedy college, and I would just hang out just to listen to stories that the comedians would talk about. I was like a sponge and would just take everything in. Comedians like Sam Kinison, Arsenio Hall, Damon Wayans, George Carlin, Richard Pryor, etc. And what I got from listening to them was that all you need do is experience life personally and first hand, no matter what you do in life. This way you can recall your experiences first hand, and it resonates much clearer and stronger when you express it. If you are going to create a world or environment for your game, how are you going to make it truly effective if you haven't really experienced life yourself?

TM: What general "method of attack" would you suggest when building up a game design?

JK: I ask myself the following questions: What do I want the player to experience? How is the player going to experience these emotions? How do all these experiences fit into a single game? What makes this game different than the rest of the games that are out there? What elements will totally immerse the player into your game environment? What will keep your player coming back for more? Are you creating a subculture with this game? What are the rewards for each level or victory? Are the rewards worthy of the journey the player has to go through, or are they a letdown? I like to go at my designing process this way, by asking these questions, because you build the game around the emotions you want the players to experience. I feel this is a more organic approach.

TM: You've done plenty of work in the fighting genre (no surprise), what are some primary design considerations for fight games? How do you bring your expansive fight knowledge to gaming?

JK: I bring a certain understanding of techniques that a normal person would not know about. I have seen, read about, and studied many different systems that are out there throughout my 30 years in the martial arts. After a while, you have developed a mind that sees things that you know will look effective on the screen. To others who do not know martial arts, it is simply a way to kick someone's ass. There's much more to it than that.

TM: What do you like most and least in the next-generation (modern) fight games you've seen?

JK: Unfortunately, they are all the same. It seems as if everyone is extracting from the same Jackie Chan and Yuen Woo Ping films. Graphics are nicer and much smoother than from the 8- and 16-bit days. I see them adding more grappling moves into the game, which adds more dimension to it, more like in the UFC and Pride Fighting contests, but you cannot control the grappling move on the martial arts games. Right now they are just animations. You cannot do turnaround/reverse moves if you are about to get slammed.

TM: As a fighter in body and spirit, what would you like to see as the future of fighting games? What excites you most about future fighting games?

JK: To be honest, I don't play that many fighting games right now, simply because I'd rather go to the dojo and experience it myself through free-sparring. It's much more fulfilling and a great workout. I observe and watch a lot of games. Unfortunately, they are all the same. I'd like to see a game that is based on real fighting strategies, understanding more of a strategy in fighting and how you can manipulate an opponent by seizing the centerline. Different types of footwork, throwing fakes, and diversions mixed in with punching and kicking combinations would be nice. There is also an issue of conquering yourself—the inner game—in order to get the upper hand on your opponent. I'm talking about a person's thought process, which can either break you down or build you up, and this changes in varying degrees throughout a fight. That is why you have to develop a strong yet flexible mind to overcome yourself. Even though you might overcome yourself, it does not always mean you will always defeat your opponent because he might be much better than you. These are some of the things I'd like to see in fighting games, some extra dimensions.

TM: You've said that working with Japanese game developers is considerably different from working with U.S.-based game developers. How? What are the advantages and disadvantages in your experience as it applies to game design execution?

JK: With the Japanese developers, they plan everything out—even down to the sick days and bereavement days for a death in the family. With many here in the U.S., usually most producers don't have such a certain game plan. It's a "run and gun" mentality. Especially, it does not help when marketing runs their "drop dead" deadline schedule because they have an end cap open date or a film that the game is tied into. Unfortunately, marketing does not know what is involved in making a game. And taking them for a tour of the QA facilities and/or production staff really does not let them have the total experience. It doesn't let them understand what is really involved. They really have no idea. Many times the game itself suffers, because the producer is forced to take out elements in the game that are showing problems in the testing phase, because they cannot meet the deadline.

TM: In your opinion, what might U.S.-based game designers learn from Japanese game designers based on your observations of each?

JK: The Japanese designers and production teams that I have worked with are very meticulous in what they are doing. Everything is scheduled out in precise detail. They had a game plan that they would live by, so we would not have to worry so much. Most of the time we had weekends and nights off, whereas with productions here in the U.S., we were always running around putting out fires that would not have occurred if they planned things in advance.

TM: What negative trends, if any, do you notice in games these days that might be addressed via better design?

JK: I feel marketing runs the game industry too much. Unfortunately, they pigeonhole the games. Either it's a sports game, fighting game, shooting game, or something based off a movie that they are "projecting" to be a blockbuster. There's a certain formula that most games follow, and it can make it pretty boring. They like to clone ideas off existing games: "I like that hot new game that's sold a gazillion units. So let's ride that premise and do something just like it ourselves but different so we can make money off of it." I'd like to see more diversity in the gaming experience.

TM: Game design is a competitive field; how does one diversify and prepare?

JK: Know what games are out there. Develop an intuition about those games, where you can play it while also having a critical mind. You can spot the weaknesses and strengths of each game. Bruce Lee once said something that I still use in my life. He said something like, "Absorb what is useful; reject what is not; add a little of yourself and make it your own."

TM: A powerful statement. You performed as a fight coordinator for many games. Now you do fight coordination for TV and film. Can you briefly talk about the process for each?

JK: In film, I get with the director. I ask them what type of a fight scene they need for the scene, whether it be comical, serious, etc. I read the script and learn more about the characters involved in the fight. This way I can tailor the action so it will complement and support the characters. For example, if the characters were emotionally distant, I would not have them do any grappling or close-contact fighting. Unless it was part of the story or character arc, I'd keep them at a distance and fight with Korean style kicks, long jabs, and crosses. So, once I find out what characters are involved with the fight, I put together a fight in my mind to visualize how the different styles will contrast onscreen. I also have to find out how the characters will change after the fight.

In order to make a fight scene effective, you have to start with one emotion and end with a different one. By the time I meet with the actors, I have a general idea what is supposed to happen. When I first meet with the actors, I run them through a basic workout to assess their physical skills. I can tell within the first five to ten minutes if they actually live in their bodies or their heads. If they live more in their bodies, they are usually easy to train because they have all their sensory skills turned on. If they live in their heads, it's an uphill battle because this type of person uses only one of their senses, and the mind-to-body connection is not communicating properly, or is too slow. About one out of three people live in their heads. By the first meeting, I usually have them understanding a basic version of the fight. My goal is to have the actors feel good about what they are doing. Then, by the time we get to filming, I have to make sure that they are in the moment with the moves, because they might have been practicing the moves so much they do not look natural and spontaneous anymore. That's how I generally work with actors or stuntmen on a fight. There are much too many other details that I have left out; these could fill a thick book.

In games for motion capture, I have to audition the martial artists and look at their basics to see if they have a solid foundation and structure with their art. Then I see how they react to punches and kicks. Then I see them put together a combination of moves and see if they are able to flow from one technique to another. When you do motion capture, it gets really repetitious because you might have to do the moves over and over again. Fortunately, the danger factor is pretty low here because I only have one person do the moves at one time. The only thing that sucks is that you spend a lot of time capturing all the moves for the motion capture camera. In film you do the stunt a few times (depending on the stunt), then you leave.

What I don't like about the game industry is the hours are pretty hectic, but you do not get to reap any of the benefits once the game is finished. In film and TV, we have SAG (Screen Actors Guild) and AFTRA (American Federation of Television & Radio Actors) that protect us, and we get residuals every time an episode or show airs on TV. You don't have anything like that in games. The only thing you might get that is close to it is a bonus check.

TM: Why are well-crafted fighting games so appealing to large numbers of players?

JK: It's a way of getting out your frustrations. It's also a way of living out your fantasies of beating someone like what you see in the movies. Because a real street fight is over in seconds and it's not real pretty to watch. It's pretty ugly and there are a lot of emotions involved. What a lot of fighting games do is create a subculture, because if a kid is able to perform a special move with a certain combination and timing, he's all of the sudden the popular kid of the group of kids who play and follow the game.

TM: What tips or suggestions do you have for game designers just getting started?

JK: Find a well-written game design document to get an idea of the elements that are involved. Learn as much as you can about all the other aspects of game production. Most important is to get experience by getting into a game production and see if it is something you really want to do. Be persistent and never take no for an answer when seeking a job. Design mock game design documents and add what you feel will make the game better than the games that are out there, and get your gaming friends to honestly critique it.

TM: In your experience, what fundamental game design rules should always be observed?

JK: Know what is out there, and use that as a foundation to build upon. Learn the rules of what makes a great game, and then learn how to effectively (not carelessly) break those rules.

TM: What skills and abilities should new game designers focus on? How about fight game designers?

JK: With fight game designers, I feel they should think out of the box and bring on other elements that would make the game more compelling. There are too many fighting games that are very similar yet still the same.

TM: Do you think working as a game designer requires preparation outside of technology (learning scripting and 3-D packages)?

JK: Yes. Everything you know helps makes you a better designer.

TM: Where are the best next-generation games likely to come from?

JK: Any place that lets the production team come up with something different, that is outside of the box, that is relatively easy to play, has rules that are consistent, can completely immerse (or should I say addict) the player in the gaming environment, and support the structure of the gameplay at all times.

TM: Does the industry need change to support game design growth?

JK: Yes. Like Hollywood, they have formulaic tendencies and are concerned with making money, but do not take the time to research and develop new ideas.

TM: John, thanks for taking the time to talk!

MEGA TIPS

1. Use and reuse prefabricated geometry by designing level pieces or "level construction sets" with modularity in mind at all times. If you are building your own toolset, make sure that it allows for this ideal.

2. Keep a level journal as you play your favorite games. Make notes in your journal about what works, what doesn't, and why a level or play idea

succeeds or fails in the games that you play. Remember that design is a process of elaboration and refinement.

3. Before geometry construction begins, establish agreed-upon team guidelines for all major construction issues (for example, scale, grid sizing, and character heights).

4. Prototype game mechanics where possible, before committing large development resources.

5. Complete the level stubbing phase with a complete test pass through the level, identifying all known problems or issues. Communicate these quickly and early to appropriate team members.

6. Work with the big game picture present in your approach.

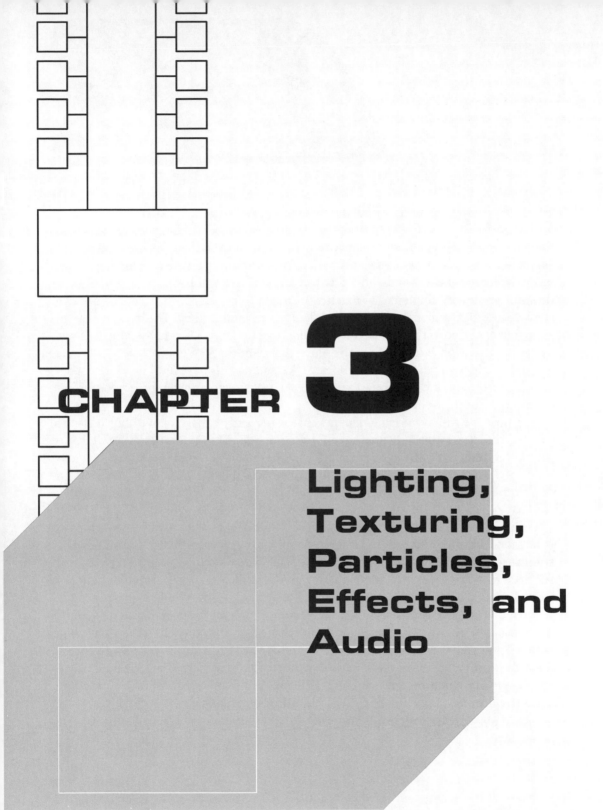

CHAPTER **3**

Lighting, Texturing, Particles, Effects, and Audio

FOR

a game to be competitive these days, its game environment must be visually enthralling. We want to connect the player's emotions to the play via their eyeballs and their twitchy fingers (or even their not-so-twitchy fingers for slower-paced games steeped with character building, resource management, or environmental exploration filled with clues and cues). However, a visually enthralling game environment is so much more than just eye candy or sweet visuals. Eye candy is just that ... momentarily sweet, but ultimately unfulfilling. The best use of visuals in games supports interesting and meaningful gameplay. During the time we have a player's attention, we want to grab hold of their emotions. We want to provide new levels of excitement and "connectedness." We can do this in several ways, often depending on the specific emotional experience we're trying to transfer: panic, confusion, impending doom, wonder, and so forth.

Is it possible to have great gameplay that is perfectly satisfying without utilizing state-of-the-art graphics technology? Of course it is. Many great games reduce to simple yet addictive actions or motivations. (Shoot that thing before it eats you and survive!) However, when games call for rich environmental immersion, we want to deliver in that area as well. We want to melt the player with mood. Mood transfers emotional cues.

From an environmental design standpoint, some of the most powerful weapons in your mood-altering armory are lighting, texturing, particles, effects, and audio. The application to games of each of these elements continues to evolve with technology. We need to try to keep pace, remembering all the while that we're trying to build on shifting sands.

Each of these elements—lighting, texturing, particles, effects, and audio—can be studied in great detail in its own right. We're going to survey the use of these elements as they apply to building up game environments. Most importantly, we need to understand their use at the conceptual level so that, no matter how they evolve, we understand their application in principle, enabling us always to build better games. In this chapter, we will survey and explore each of these areas with our goal clearly in sight—to understand how these elements are used to create mood, which in turn supports gameplay.

LIGHTING

There are several lighting parameters we can normally adjust to light an interior or exterior environment. How we accomplish our lighting goals exactly is dependent on many factors, such as our game engine software tool specifics or the tool system we have built into a common 3-D package. We'll talk about several kinds of lighting control in this section. First, let's take a moment to look at the high-level concerns for designers starting to light a game scene:

❯ **Source number**   This is always confined by performance issues, so it's best to start with what you believe will be the minimum number of lights required to accomplish your lighting objectives.

❯ **Type of light**   Your choice will depend on the scene details and your plans for handling those details.

❯ **Intensity**   This is frequently adjusted, but you should light for your game scene environmental details (for example, external sunshine, early dusk, internal office fluorescent lamps, and so forth).

❯ **Falloff (dissipation)**   Relates to tuning and dialing in your lighting, so at this early stage, you will want to consider where falloff might be applied across your level to benefit your lighting goals.

❯ **Color**   Comes from color concept drawings, if you have them. If not, you'll set up a starting point for the color palette of your lights and adjust these as required.

We should also consider some of the more particular aspects for lighting our world:

❯ **Location-to-location lighting details**   Inevitably, sections of your map will be lit differently. Considering the lighting for your map on a location-to-location basis makes you aware of how lighting requirements will change from section to section. Don't change the lights just to change the lights. Change the lights to change the mood.

❯ **Emphasis points**   These are props, clues, or visual payoff points for your lighting that you want to highlight and accent for the player. Don't miss this!

❯ **Special-case light animations**   Consider whether you want to do any special-case light animation. For example, will there be rotating siren lights? Lightning strikes? Searchlight sweeps? These fall under special-case light animations for the sections of a map that call for these effects.

❭ **Matching the scene with other lights that will be present**   Think about how your scene will have to match added lights. For example, if you have your lighting set up brightly to begin with, and a character enters that's going to fire off a huge nuclear weapon with a light blast all over your map, it will blow out your lighting. When the weapon fires, all that light will be added to the light present and make it too bright. You'll have to pull your light back or turn down the weapon lighting effect.

Whether you're building a snowboard racing game, another kind of sports game, or a medieval action/fighter game, lighting specifics and capabilities will vary on a case-by-case basis. What won't vary so much is the idea that you are using lighting to transfer a feeling—the kind of feeling you're trying to build for the player. You are trying to support gameplay emotion using lighting.

In the case of a snowboarding game, a night track might be lit with minimal point lights (discussed later in the chapter, in the section "Lighting Strengths or Multipliers"). Restricted lighting might, in fact, be part of the course challenge. Another track might be a brightly lit sunshine love fest, with lens flares (the "ring" generated by looking at a bright light source quickly) and plenty of rim lighting (provides hot light accents on object edges). Both help set the mood.

The gameplay for a track racing-oriented snowboarding game will come down to smooth execution and delivery on stunt kicks, flips, ollies, and jumps, and avoiding track collision with objects (like trees or other snowboarders). This "smooth execution" factor is often a matter of subtle controller tuning (adjusting programmatically how the game controller reads user input—like hitting that triangle button to perform a skate/snowboard move such as an ollie). How the game responds directly is a matter of controller tuning.

There is also a practical application to lighting. You don't want your players stumbling around in the dark, unless that's your point! It will grow old fast. Several disciplines converge here as you "build up your eye" for lighting and its effect on emotion. It will require study of various kinds.

Studying lighting through the refined visual experiences of cinematographers is a great idea. They work every day in the language of light and composition. Studying photography to build eye recognition and sensitivity for light values, contrast, saturation, hue, and accent lighting is also very helpful. Studying color theory, including the emotional connection and human reaction to colors, is also very valuable. The color of light itself has been demonstrated to alter human physiological responses, and thus shifts our mood. Becoming a better game designer is built on studying many related areas. I like to think of game designers as "specialized generalists." Game developers are eternal students.

Here's a quick sketch example. Figure 3-1 represents a small room displayed at full brightness ("World" light at maximum intensity). Obviously, this room's lighting is

FIGURE 3-1

World light at full brightness

flat and emotionally unattractive. The lighting doesn't really serve any purpose other than a practical one—we can clearly see our way around.

As a workflow point, I actually leave the lights on "full-bright" when doing the layout and basic construction phase (described in Chapter 2). Compare this very simple example with Figure 3-2, which shows the exact same room with a single light added; its brightness factor has been altered. This room transfers much more feeling, and is only beginning to transfer a mood factor. All we have done is change brightness values! This breaks up the uniformity of the single flat light that we started with. We have so much more control at our disposal than just brightness factors.

Cutting-edge game engines are starting to feature dynamic lighting. This opens up entirely new ways to use lighting in games. Lighting will soon have an even more immediate and direct effect. Dynamic (or real-time) lighting allows characters and objects to interact with light and to cast shadows as they would in the physical world—not by precalculating the light and "faking" shadows to imply a real light source. However, dynamic lighting, as you might imagine, is very graphics processor-intensive. It requires substantial graphics hardware assistance. Very soon, however, it will be used in many games.

FIGURE 3-2

Single light with altered brightness

Now, let's look at how we might control lighting with the intent to transfer mood in support of gameplay. In the following sections, we'll look at the various ways that you can control lighting, all of which are intended to transfer mood in support of gameplay.

Position

The placement or positioning of your lights in a scene must serve several simultaneous goals: practicality (for example, illuminating the player's way), aesthetics (transferring mood to support gameplay), and performance (managing trade-offs between desired lighting effects and performance-ready lighting effects). Always try to engineer a level for both maximum visual results and maximum efficiency. To that end, use only as many lights as you require to achieve your objectives, and no more. Don't add lighting that isn't needed. Don't add what doesn't move the scene along. Don't add complexity for the sake of complexity. It's easy to want to go goofy with lighting. It looks cool. However, throwing lights around like a holiday party at your Christmas tree doesn't get you very far. It won't work out in performance. Be ready to pull lights out for performance reasons.

In general, you want to position lights to replicate their real-world positions or source points. If you're replicating the lighting for a mob boss's office, players expect certain kinds of lighting. Maybe you are trying to simulate track lighting. You wouldn't light it like a space hangar, which again speaks to the importance of having solid visual reference material. You'll also want to position lights in new and unique ways to achieve your intended effect. For lighting interiors it's often useful to clip out lighting configurations from architectural magazines to use as reference. I have a file cabinet full of them.

I've found that a good exercise to build your lighting skills to the point where you can begin to accomplish your intended effect is to take a scene photograph from a fantasy movie scene (*Cinefex* magazine is a perfect resource) and try to rebuild or re-create the lighting in your software tool. Then, feel free to experiment. Lighting is fun, and it's all about discovery. Light the same scene using only sidelights. Challenge yourself. Next, use only overhead lights, and then use only floor level lights. Now mix and match them all. Doing this will help build up the tools in your lighting toolbox.

Light Color

Your scene lights will commonly cast off a color determined by an RGB value (the amount of red, green, and blue in the light's color). You can use this to great emotional effect. Apply a little color theory here. If you want to infuse the scene with tension, or reflect a cold emotional setting, or just create a "cold" character's lair, throw in a heavy blue value to your lights. If you want to accent a fireside chat scene within a 12th century hovel in Ireland, warm up the lights with heavier doses of orange, purple, and yellow.

As previously mentioned, human emotional reaction to light color is a research topic unto itself. For our purposes, it's easy to understand why it's so important to learn about how we all respond to color, and then try to apply that learning to your game scenes. There are some basic rules, but you should investigate their boundaries. You should feel free to experiment with these ideas, and to try new things. Sometimes you might want to use a certain amount of juxtaposition. Experiment with throwing in light colors that do not correspond directly with mood and see what happens. Pay attention to how cinematographers use light color in films. You will probably find that they gear the color or tone of light in the scene to support the emotional context of the scene. Pay attention to how stage lighting designers use light color in theatrical settings. Above all, work toward forming your own comprehension and understanding of how light color can be used to transfer tone and mood in environmental settings.

Basic Lighting Types

Generally, to compensate for the various tools and technologies you might find yourself using to build games, you have several types of lighting to draw from in most game development situations.

Point or Ambient Lights

Point or ambient lights are often used as "world" lights since they throw off light in all directions from a single source point. This is the kind of light you use to fill physical spaces, to simulate sunlight, and in large part, to set the overall lighting feel for your ambient or "available" light in a scene. Refer to Figure 3-2 for an example of using a point or ambient light.

Spotlights

Just as in many physical situations, such as on theatrical stages, spotlights are used in game scenes to feature or highlight certain props or characters—in short, to make objects or characters stand out from the rest of the scene or the background in some way. You can also use spotlights to indicate gameplay.

Spotlights can suggest exits, unexposed passageways, clues, and damageable items, or simply lead the player's eye to "don't miss this" features in your game scene. Maybe you are using spotlights to accent statuary like our frozen beast in the cathedral example in Chapter 1. It will be a visual treat to see a spotlight on a transfigured, steaming frozen beast as you help to tell the curse backstory for your level.

Spotlights take the shape of displaying light in cones, and you can control many of their display properties to get your desired effect. You can adjust the radius of the final light, blur out the edges of the spotlight, and so forth. Figure 3-3 is a two-light scene demonstrating a spotlight on a prop with additional lighting support coming from an overhead ambient light.

Directional Lights

Directional lights are soft fill lights. They can be used to bring out detail. Directional lights can be aimed or targeted in your scene at props or items to provide fine detail and highlights. Figure 3-4 shows the effect of adding a directional light to fill or detail an object. Again, this is only a two-light scene with one ambient and one directional light.

Lighting Strengths or Multipliers

The strength or intensity of your light, regardless of type, can be adjusted for the kind of lighting intensity effects you desire. The specific way this is controlled varies according to the software tool you're using, but the end result is the same. You will want to adjust light intensity for your scene on an individual light basis and global light basis. Lowering the lights will almost always add drama and suspense to your scene.

A little warning: don't go overboard with lowering the lights. Some games pull back so far on lighting that it is difficult to navigate a character through the scene. You don't want to sacrifice "playability" or create player frustration ("I can't see anything!") just because you like the look of extremely sparse lighting. This kind of

FIGURE 3-3

Spotlight example

FIGURE 3-4

Directional light example

lighting might work in a stage scene, where character voicing is being emphasized, and the passive listener is asked to focus on the interchange of dialogue. It doesn't work well in an active game environment.

You don't need to make players stumble in the dark constantly in order to transfer mood and achieve your lighting goals. If you don't have lighting contrasts and variety (light to dark) to support the mood based on level actions, areas, goals, and scenarios, you're probably not using lighting to its best advantage anyway.

So, how do you find the perfect balance for your level lighting? Perhaps you want sections that are very dark, with only soft lighting, and sections that have more vivid lighting. This usually is accomplished by finding the right balance between your local ambient lights and your point lights. I've found that by setting the ambient global lights slightly lower than seems appropriate and then building the light back in using point lights and spotlights, I can achieve consistent results in reaching dramatic lighting.

Lighting Falloff

For visual effect, you will often want to simulate light dissipation as it leaves a light source. We all know that light fades as it leaves a source, commonly called *falloff*. Controlling light falloff is simply a matter of controlling how fast or how slow light will dissipate from a source (your light in the scene). If you want immediate falloff, you won't let light leave the source for very long. If you want it to dissipate slowly away from the source, you'll adjust the intensity of the falloff range. Falloff is commonly controlled for floor lights pointed upward along a wall surface and for streetlamps.

Three Sample Lighting Setups

Let's take a look at how to approach lighting for three sample setups: the somber castle, the happy forest, and the scary forest.

First, consider how you might light up a somber castle. As a starting point for lighting a room in a somber castle, I would factor in one global or ambient light and two spotlights. Accent the ambient light with heavy purple (RGB: 128,128,255) to make the room look cold. Aim the spotlights in each corner, pointing in opposite directions: one pointing up, one pointing down. If the ceiling is high enough, you can imply that the light is coming from a number of sources in the scene. Figure 3-5 shows our setup results. You could experiment with this simple process to light all the other rooms in your castle.

A starting point in lighting a section of the happy forest would include one or two bright ambient lights tuned for distance (in other words, experiment with the distance and height between these global lights over the section you're lighting). Balance the color of these ambient lights with large doses of orange and purple. We want what I call "cereal box" sunlight—warm, magical, and glowing. (As a visual reference point, recall Gandalf's arrival at the Shire in the horse-drawn cart in *The Fellowship of*

FIGURE 3-5

Somber castle

the Ring movie from *The Lord of the Rings* trilogy. The magical sunlight and color treatment in the scene really helped transfer the emotional ideas of wonder and enchantment. I would then use two strong spotlights to highlight terrain features, like an animated flower patch, a talking tree, or a happy creature's hut. I would also scatter some light shafts coming from the direction of the sun using a directional or tunnel light. You could also add some dust particles in the light path. That would look very cool. We'll see how you would begin to do that in the section, "Particles," later in this chapter.

How might you light the scary forest? Again, for a section of the scary forest (I normally light section to section), use a single "choked" or minimal ambient light. Weight the ambient light color toward blue and orange. Since I've only used one global light, I'm going to use three spotlights. I would orient them toward red and blue and place them at the base of gnarly trees or other fantastic props in your scary forest. Use the spotlights pointed toward the sky at the base of your gnarly trees (or other props) to create drastic and intimidating shadows. Fear lies in the shadows, right?

ANIMATING LIGHTS

Depending on your software toolset, animating your environmental lights can be used to accomplish several kinds of effects. For instance, you might want to simulate local firelight in your 12th century hovel as characters are gathered around the hearth telling backstory points or gearing up for a mission. To do this, you can animate changes in intensity for your point or ambient light to approximate firelight flicker. You simply set up an animation cycle or loop (in other words, frame-to-frame values) of intensity values that replays over and over until you determine it should stop.

Another obvious use would be in the creation of lightning flashes. Simply set up a cycle or loop with high-intensity "burst" values, and then randomize its playback. Maybe it only plays back every 30–40 seconds and has a chance value included, which determines whether or not you get a flash.

In another example, you might animate your lights to coincide with a jump to "light speed," creating a light-streaking or "strobing" effect. There are many possibilities for light animation. You might use a form of light animation to simulate power falters in an aging mine shaft where lights buzz and flicker while trying to stay alive. You could even set up some of your lights to burn out over the time the player spends in the scene. It's always a helpful exercise to think about how you might use one technique in another way for a future effect in a future game. This is part of building your idea inventory.

TEXTURING

Textures (or "skins" or "surface maps") are like the label on a soup can. They are images that wrap over a surface. We can make a box look like a rusty box by using a texture map image of a rusty box surface. Whereas an object's position is identified in terms of an X and Y coordinate location (like on a grid), the "position" of a texture on the surface of something is identified in terms of a U and V position. This is simply mathematical terminology. U and V take the place of X and Y.

Creating textures is an art form unto itself. Great texture artists are very valuable on a development team. Without texture maps in our games, we would have only flat, shaded surfaces to look at. This wouldn't be very interesting, would it? Flat, shaded surfaces do not look weathered or stressed or give off any of the visual cues and clues that can be accomplished by using texture maps. Further still, by using a bump map, we can imply that a surface has volume and depth, is bumpy, corrugated, or etched. The bump map changes the surface to have pimples or rivulets for instance. We can imply that the surface has some dimensionality in this way.

Textures are usually created so that you can tile a surface with them. Tiling is like laying down a floor made from a tile pattern. We want to reuse patterns, but we don't want to see the seams along their adjoining edges. If we were tiling a snow surface, for instance, we wouldn't want to see tile-edge lines where the tiles mesh against each other.

Textures that can tile are textures that fit together like jigsaw pieces along their own edges. Figure 3-6 shows an example of a "tile-able" texture. This type of texture might be used as a floor surface or a wall surface.

Other kinds of textures are more use-specific and are not used to fill large, open spaces like floors or walls. They tend to be used to imply physical environmental details like sewer outlets, stained-glass windows, or piping systems. Figure 3-7 shows an example of a use-specific texture.

Depending on the scale system you are using, textures can be created at different pixel sizes, resolutions, and bit depths. Each of these is determined by your game engine's requirements. Each game engine is custom-written to handle surface or texture information (sometimes in new and ever-changing ways). Quite commonly, however, most handle only textures of specific sizes and resolutions.

For instance, repeatable textures created to cover large surface spaces like walls and floors might be created at 128×128 (128 pixels wide by 128 pixels high). A "detailing" texture like a door trim pattern, a texture that would fit nicely surrounding doorway edges, might be created at 64×64. Determining the appropriate size for your textures is usually a matter of intended use. Knowing how a texture will be used in a scene is an important consideration when constructing it.

FIGURE 3-6

Tile-ready texture

FIGURE 3-7

Use-specific texture

It is kind of tricky sometimes to create a texture that will tile well (without showing any seams or edges). When you are creating tiles based on complex or interlocking patterns (think lava flows or Mayan temple inscriptions), it's important to utilize the skills of a texture artist. Quite often, in the production process, placeholder or temporary textures are put into a scene until the finalized textures are handed off by a texture artist. It's important for world builders and level designers to at least be able to construct and make basic modifications to these placeholder textures or to create their own "basic" textures. The more you can learn about texturing the better!

When a texture doesn't work (or isn't made to tile properly), you will know it immediately. You'll see an unwanted repetitious pattern emerge immediately. This means that the texture in question doesn't hook up seamlessly on an edge.

Using Textures Well

Part of creating your asset breakdowns (recall the simplified version described in Chapter 1's cathedral example) includes identifying which textures you will need to complete a scene or section of your game. From your concept sketches, you'll need to work closely with your texture artist to extract and build a texture set that you can use to detail your scene or level. You should give considerable forethought to creating your texture set. You'll want to build the right texture pieces in the right ways to accomplish your visual goals. For example, your 128×128 textures might look great on floors and walls, but if you attempt to use them in another way, you may run into trouble and need to resize them or even create custom versions.

As previously stated, textures are placed onto a surface using a U, V coordinate system to locate a map on a mesh or geometry surface. When you stamp textures on a surface, though, they may not line up correctly. You will want to "shift" or "slide" them across the surface to line them up correctly. Most game engine tools allow you to accomplish this by changing the U, V values for the selected texture. This is very helpful in lining up textures in the way that you would like.

In some cases, you might want to actually change the draw scale or draw size of a certain texture to make it fit the scene better (in other words, at the correct scale relative to everything else in the scene). You can do this by changing the U, V draw values, which will stretch or shrink your texture in those directions according to your changes. Be careful when doing this, because you may get unintended results. You can only stretch or shrink textures so far, before it becomes totally obvious that you have done so. It will blur out or compress your textures to the point that they cannot be used. Again, this is why, at creation, you need to know how you intend to use your textures.

PARTICLES

Some of the most interesting, complex, and processor-intensive visual effects being created for games (and movies) are using particle systems or dynamics. When you think of particle systems, think of naturally occurring behaviors, such as the flocking of birds as they fly together, forming a larger single unit out of many individuals, or localized rainfall dropping from a single cloud onto a scarecrow. In a flock of birds flying together, each bird becomes a particle in the system. In a simulated rainfall from a single cloud, each drop of rain becomes a particle in the system.

Here are some other effects you can build with particles:

❯ Fire from a torch

❯ Exhaust from vehicle tailpipes

❯ An attack formation of angry mutants

❯ Swarms or clusters of objects

❯ Sports dynamics (skater's ice chips, shattering baseball bats, dirt clouds from slides, divots from bad golf swings, and so on)

Developers have many choices to make in building up effects for games. You can create fire as a sprite animation, flipping individual frames like traditional animation, or modeling the behavior of fire using a particle system. You must make many trade-offs to maintain game performance speed. You certainly can't use elaborate particle systems for everything just yet. They are simply too tough to compute. Where you can use them, and where their output can be optimized, they offer dazzling visual possibilities.

Using Particle Emitters

Just like a light or an actor (a character or prop), you can put emitters in a scene. An emitter emits particles. (Think of a sprinkler on your front lawn as an example of an emitter.) You define how many particles an emitter will emit. It's generally best to start with very low numbers, because emitters are processor-intensive.

Suppose we start with 50–100 particles. Particles can be emitted from a point or from a surface. For this example, I've chosen an omni-oriented point emitter. Figure 3-8 is an example of a point emitter sitting on top of a cylinder (like a smokestack, for instance).

You can see the result of particles being emitted from this point emitter in all directions in Figure 3-9. I have set the particles to render or draw as circles so that you can see them easier. This is a very basic beginning to starting to shape the behavior of your particles toward your intended effect.

The behavior of particles is influenced and shaped by forces, called *fields,* applied on those particles. You can use fields in hundreds of combinations and create many

FIGURE 3-8

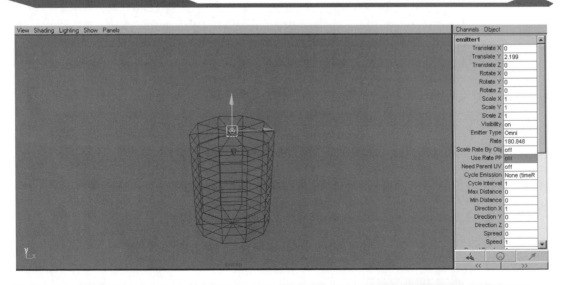

Omni-oriented point emitter

FIGURE 3-9

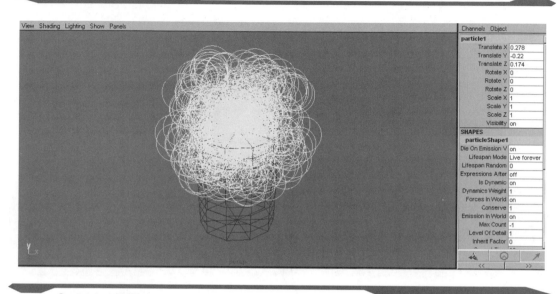

Omni particles emitted

visually interesting results. Gravity is an example of a field you can play with. You can create attraction and repulsion factors for your fields.

In Figure 3-10, I've simply added a turbulence field to start to shape the particles toward something resembling smoke or steam behavior in my animation sequence as particles begin to billow away from a source point.

After you begin to learn how field forces affect particles, you can build up more sophisticated behaviors. Maybe you want to create bee swarms, or create ice chips blasting and streaking off an ice skater's blade. There are endless possibilities, each with certain visual impact. Very cool stuff.

Now for a little game development reality check. How a specific game engine or engine toolset handles particle system data and particle assets depends entirely on *which* game engine or toolset it is. Each has unique hand-off or asset import/export challenges.

Exporting Particles and Dynamics Information

Game developers have several choices to make when working with and utilizing particle systems and dynamics. There are a couple of common pathways:

❯ Build complete particle systems and manipulation tools into your own editors.

❯ Import particle system data from Maya or 3ds max and then re-create it within the game engine.

FIGURE 3-10

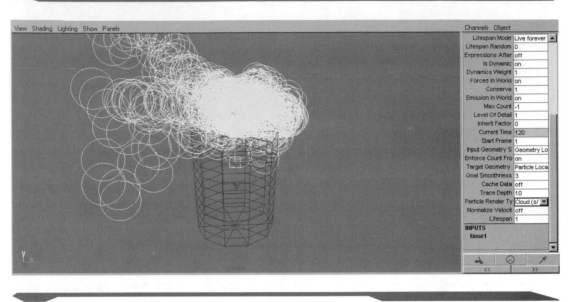

Turbulence field added

The first option offers the benefit of load-sharing some of the particle effect creation work, but also presents a tool-specific learning curve.

As you might imagine, many current games feature a variety of particle effect elements: spell casting, magic glows and curses, water fountain spray patterns in a mystical garden, vehicle exhaust, projectile weapon bursts, and so forth. All of these effects can be handled using particle systems. Each of these individual elements becomes an asset that must be created uniquely for your game.

Many games feature hundreds (approaching thousands) of these kinds of elements. If you have a solid tool to quickly create and refine these elements in a format that is game-ready, or a tool that works within the game engine itself as you create them, you remove any import/export hassles. Still, in this case, artists and designers have to learn how to use the custom tool quickly. This isn't always easy or efficient.

Many developers, however, have not built custom tools to create particle effects. They rely on the strength of the particle system features built into 3-D packages like Maya and 3ds max. These particle systems are well tested and established. But how do you use particle effects created in these packages within your games? Your development team will have to make a couple of choices.

Suppose that you want to create a particle-based fire for the hearth in your 12th century hovel. One option would be to dynamically export your particle information out of your 3-D package. This generates a file with data about each particle's position or behavior over a given period of animation frames (for example, from frame 1 to frame 30). Using this method, your game engine can read in this data file and re-create the particle system effect that you built up in your 3-D package.

Another option is to render out the particle behaviors as an animation sequence, and stamp this onto a polygon surface. You can give your computer a real headache doing this. I've crashed many of them. When you start to ask your computer to render particle system output, keep the numbers low. To begin experimenting, keep your number of particles reasonable (less than 100) and your number of animation frames manageable (roughly 30 frames).

Once you have your particles behaving like fire and colored like fire, you create a render sequence of your fire. Next, you could create a simple polygon plane and map your fire render sequence to the polygon plane. Finally, you parent (or associate) the plane with the fire on it to the kindling in your hearth and move the plane into position. You now have a particle-based fire effect for your hovel!

To extend this idea to another example, if you were building vehicle exhaust, you would follow the same procedure and parent your exhaust plane to the vehicle's tailpipe.

Ideally, it's nice to have a toolset that allows you to simply position emitters in a scene and then tweak the particle behavior in real time. Figures 3-11 and 3-12 show scenes constructed using the WildTangent Studio (WTStudio) tool. This tool enables users to create emitters and adjust particle behavior in real time.

FIGURE 3-11

Use of emitters for steam effect

FIGURE 3-12

Use of emitters for fire effect

Many types of particle-oriented effects (like lightning, snow, rain, waterfalls, lava streams, and disease clouds) can be built using particle systems. Getting the right look for these effects involves tuning the behavior using fields and applying colors and textures (or sprite maps) per particle.

It should be clear by now that there are many choices and methods of operation for working with particles to create in-game particle effects. The current generation Unreal engine, for example, has a powerful built-in system to generate effects using particles and emitters. Effects generated this way can add visual interest to your environments, help tell story points, and transfer lots of mood.

EFFECTS

Now that you understand a little of the process involved in creating particle-based effects, let's take a quick look at their application. As we've seen, particle system effects are a great way to accomplish many visual details. However, they can easily burn up system performance, so their use must be planned, refined, and often optimized.

Sometimes an effect can be accomplished by using a simple sprite effect instead. A *sprite* is typically just a 2-D graphic asset that can be moved, scaled, or rotated. Sometimes a trade-off occurs between using a sprite effect and using a particle effect. If the sprite effect looks convincing, you can save some processing power by choosing to use it over a similar particle effect. If the sprite effect simply doesn't look right, you might be forced to build the effect in particles, or to not build the effect at all.

There are even emitter types that emit sprites instead of particles. The sprites behave like particles. These are less processor-intensive and can still be used to create interesting effects, like magical spells.

Figure 3-13 is an example of building a magic effect using sprite particles from an emitter attached to the drone insect. You can see clearly from the bitmap outlines that these are sprites being emitted in the animation sequence.

As you build up your environments, you will introduce props into your scene via file referencing. Maybe one of your props will be a warrior skull and a faction flag mounted on a pike weapon. These props might be scattered about and stuck into the ground to warn players that the enemy is near.

You'll want all of your props to fit the visual style of the game you're creating. You accomplish this by doing crafty, low-polygon modeling and making great use of textures. A particle effect added to a prop can make it stand out from the others and say something. Plus, it just looks so cool! Maybe you would like to create a sinister magical glow on a totem at the center of your pike props. The point is that you can add visual detailing to your props by using particle effects efficiently. Try using them as

FIGURE 3-13

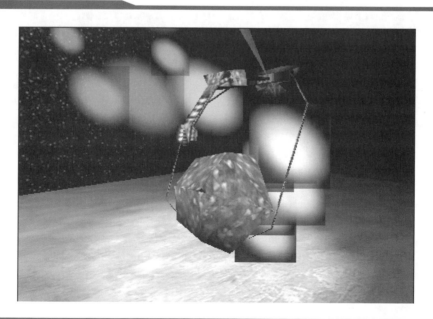

Sprite emitters for effects

signifiers. Tell the player something with the effect detailing that you add to a prop. Don't just use an effect to use an effect. You must use effects sparingly so that you don't diminish performance.

You have to learn to manage how often, and in what ways, you add effects to props. In the end, again, it's all a matter of balance. If you use the same effect on every prop, it quickly loses any impact it might have otherwise had. You have to learn to use prop effects to highlight and emphasize. Every prop is not deserving of emphasis. Setting some props out ahead of others by giving them special qualities helps to keep your universe diversified, and will definitely help to reduce visual boredom.

AUDIO

It has almost been a tradition in game development to ignore audio until the very last minute, and then cripple the chances that audio can make an important contribution to a game by providing audio developers with nearly nonexistent resources. The importance of audio in games has been vastly underappreciated for far too long. However, thankfully, this handling of audio is changing for good. Game audio has reached a new era. Audio will have to continue to evolve if game publishers and developers want to deliver competitive game entertainment content. The change toward supporting audio fully and completely can't happen quickly enough for me. Audio is not merely an "add-on" tacked to the end of a project; it is a critical aspect of delivering exciting game content.

Some of the design tools mentioned previously allow you to attach audio events to models or to place sounds in a scene. Some go further, letting you tune the "range" within which the audio event is perceptible to your hero character, for instance. This setting determines from how far away your hero character (or player's avatar) can "hear" a given audio event.

Game audio is sometimes used as a clue element. I've found that an audio clue works best when used together with another kind of visual clue (such as bloody tracks). Knowing that you're near a waterfall because you can hear it, for example, helps to keep a player oriented.

Next to visuals, audio is your best ally in transferring mood in support of gameplay. The following are some types of audio that you can use to support gameplay:

❭ Audio that scores cinematics (movie snippets), segues, and level transitions

❭ Ambient or environmental effects audio

❭ Special effects audio

❭ Music to accent dramatic points in the game

❭ Character dialogue

❭ Interface audio

Audio for games is usually done by a small in-house audio staff at a game developer or by independent contractors set up to provide game audio. The level or mission descriptions in your design document, described in Chapter 2, should specify your audio requirements and intentions. Your development team needs to ask itself the following question: How are we going to use audio to support gameplay? The answers to this question range from the obvious to the not so obvious.

Typically, audio is used in games in one of two ways: music is "streamed" or played off the CD or hard drive to accompany a scene, or audio effects or music segments are loaded into your hardware RAM. The gaming consoles and PC sound cards have processors dedicated to handling audio processing. This fact has allowed game developers to do more than ever before. Audio-specific processors and RAM have helped open up the field.

In general, audio events that must happen rapidly or in real time, such as kicks, punches, gunshots, and gear shifts, are loaded into audio RAM for immediate playback upon button or key input from a game controller or PC keyboard. Audio that accompanies cinematics or segues might simply play off of the CD or hard drive.

From a design standpoint, pay attention to when and how audio is used in your favorite games. How much or how little of which types are used? Huge crunchy gunshots and hollowed-out beam-weapon sounds definitely support gameplay, but don't forget about ambience! A character's footstep sound alone is not ambience. Some "greater" audio cue should always be setting the tone and prickling the scene. Maybe something is breathing. Maybe you hear distant chimes. Footsteps aren't enough. Ambient audio should close you in and give you a sense of perspective and immersion. As a goal or ideal, aim for multilayer audio at all times. Personally, I always try to find new ways to keep the player on edge by using audio, or to deliver a new audio experience.

For a baseball game I was working on, I thought it would be interesting to localize the audio to players on the field. In other words, I wanted to simulate baseball game audio with a sense for position on the field. Playing in a major league baseball game "sounds" different if you're a catcher versus a center fielder. This particular game allowed players to play specific field positions (for example, catcher or infielder) and to "grow character attributes" for each position on a baseball team. I wanted the audio to reflect this idea.

The field of game audio has plenty of room to grow. It hasn't become very dimensional yet, partly because developers have assumed that players' speaker systems (for all but the diehards) are marginal at best.

If you know that several weapons' sounds will be playing over your ambience or your music soundtrack, you should try to fill the audio spectrum from low bass sounds to higher frequency sounds. For a variety of reasons, this isn't always accounted for.

Design planning also plays a crucial role in implementing audio. These days, many licensed games are in production. Licensed games are those based on well-known characters and universes like *Scooby Doo* or *Star Wars*. If you are going to record character dialogue using actors' voices, your in-game character dialogue better be ready and tested. You might only get one chance to get the dialogue you need, and you might have 30 minutes to do it.

Pushing Game Audio Further

We all probably have a pretty good idea how audio is used commonly in games. New standards and technologies are pushing game audio further. Game publishers really only start supporting features and functionality after they are present in a large number of players' homes. These days, some game audio is Dolby-encoded for expanded stereo and surround-sound setups, but the enthusiasts who have such setups constitute a small subset of the general gaming audience. Hence, it's hard to make the argument to a game publisher that this kind of support is necessary or is a competitive advantage.

Huge areas of game audio possibility remain commercially unexplored. Putting a cricket sound in a scene is one thing, but attaching a sound to a missile ripping by the player's head that creates real positional audio feedback for the player is an exciting and almost entirely untapped area of game sound development.

Doppler shift, the rise in pitch frequency as an audio source approaches and its immediate lowering in frequency as soon as it passes (think of an ambulance whizzing by you), can be modeled in game scenes. Quite honestly, though, construction tools are only starting to get this sophisticated. SoundMAX (www.audioforgames.com) is trying to change this scenario. Plus, many of the most interesting audio phenomena would require the player to use headphones. Many players simply don't wear them when playing.

Many environmental designers are excited by the possibilities for positional audio, and are just starting to explore these avenues. Implementing innovative audio and using audio in games in new ways becomes, yet again, primarily a software tools issue. It is a content-innovation issue. Game programmers routinely have plenty to deal with in coding and expanding state-of-the-art game engines and toolsets. Only fairly recently have the tools become powerful enough to allow developers who are focused on game content alone to be able to experiment to a greater degree than was previously possible.

DESIGN TOOLS SHIFT

Developing lighting, texturing, particles, and audio for games means more than creating these particular assets in commercial 3-D packages. It isn't just a matter of writing an asset exporter from a 3-D package into a game engine, either. It's all about how much control you have over these kinds of assets once they are running in a game scene via a game engine. Designers are hamstrung by tools every day.

At this point, it's important to understand that one of the critical design, layout, and execution challenges faced by most game developers involves what I call "tools shift." This term simply refers to a present working reality in game development: you don't necessarily know what tools you are going to use to make this game for this platform, versus what tools you are going to use to make another game for a different platform. After you finish a game and move on to creating another game, you may need to rapidly learn another toolset to support the current title you're working on. You may even be learning and exploring the toolset for the following project while you're finishing up your current project.

For most independent developers, creating a custom toolset is an expensive proposition. It's expensive to build, to support, and to document. Maybe the tool will only have use in the creation of a single genre game, and you'll be moving on to another title, possibly in another genre, which may or may not be able to take advantage of the tools framework you've created. Ouch! It happens all the time.

The tool you are currently using might be a large MEL (Maya Embedded Language) script written into Maya. MEL lets you customize Maya in an open-ended and flexible way to suit your own development needs. Then again, maybe you'll use a MAXScript written into 3ds max. There are similarities, and also striking differences.

Perhaps you will use a stand-alone editor written as a tool for a specific game engine—each of these editors has performance and use nuances all their own. Each of these possibilities (as well as others) contributes to tools shift. Tools shift can make it extremely difficult to accomplish meaningful, hopefully powerful game editing on a tight schedule with limited resources.

If you're working in a constantly evolving development environment, my advice is to get to know well one 3-D package, one FPS editor, and one RTS editor. It's also important to be able to move around between scripting languages that are C-based (structured/object-oriented languages) or conditional (like Python or Visual Basic).

Many of the tools used to build games are quite complex and are not mastered overnight. Mastery is often as elusive as those particles wafting away from an emitter. It's like trying to catch a flock of birds in the dark wearing handcuffs. Most of game development is a gradual and sometimes excruciating learning process. If you are learning to model low polygon objects, or learning to model environments, don't beat yourself up if you're not building the Taj Mahal in 15 minutes during the commercials. Persistence alone is omnipotent. Just like many crafts and disciplines, you have to stay at it to improve. You will improve. It might not be according to the schedule you are demanding from yourself, but you will see progress.

CASE STUDY COMMENTS ON CORNERSTONE ELEMENTS

From our discussion in this chapter, we have seen how important lighting, texturing, particles, effects, and audio are to building game worlds. These categories are regularly drawn from when building convincing game locations. With the advent of 3-D gaming came something closer to real lighting (today's move toward dynamic lighting sets the bar even higher!), particles, and true environmental modeling. In the 2-D games of the recent past, lighting was simply "drawn" into sprites, particle systems didn't formally exist for game developers, and flat "environments" were created using nothing but tiled sprites.

It's important to recognize how much 3-D has brought to gaming. In addition to new capabilities and a wider palette of action, it has brought about a slightly different kind of workflow for game developers.

As games have moved from 2-D to primarily 3-D, software tools have tried to keep pace. In the days of 2-D game development, all game assets (art and audio) were handed off to game programmers, who installed them and created their behaviors. This is still the case, yet the scope and complexity of the games being made have skyrocketed. A game today is no longer a novelty or a marvel in its own right (although there is plenty to marvel over in today's games). A game today is made within the confines of a highly competitive business, where content is king. Developing great content requires having the time and ability to focus on content. Most independent developers, quite honestly, can't focus on great content if the development team is fighting to get a game engine and toolset into working shape. This has encouraged many publishers and developers to move toward using licensed game engines (such as Quake, Unreal, and so forth).

For the working game designer or level builder, becoming very familiar with each of the cornerstone areas (lighting, texturing, particles, effects, and audio) is essential. Keep in mind that this role on a development team has many forms of challenges. For example, perhaps you've constructed all or part of a level according to a set of team guidelines, using a new or emerging toolset. Unfortunately, game development is an often-hairy evolving beast, so these guidelines may change. Guideline technologies tend to change at the most inopportune moments of your game project's existence. This frequently happens mid-development. All the while, you will be expected to demonstrate progress to your game publisher. Occasionally, you will have to redo work and basically end up re-creating a level, yet again, according to another set of guidelines or to serve the needs of a critical game engine adjustment, enhancement, expansion, or new technology demand.

It's important to remember that, when you're building games, you really are innovating along the way. Having confidence in your cornerstone elements is the first step toward jumping into the fray.

The Moonlight Forest Example

Now it's time to go for it! Choose an environmental editor from your favorite game (for example, *Unreal 2* or *Jedi Knights 2*) or download a free one from www.wildtangent.com (visit the Developer Central section and download WTStudio and the WTStudio Sample Project, so that you have some assets to work with). Try to construct a simple scene using the assets provided. I built a very simple forest under moonlight with a tree smoking in the background from a lightning-bolt hit. The following are the areas to focus on:

) Understanding basic lighting concepts

) Applying, shifting, and scaling textures

) Creating a basic particle emitter

) Adding a sound

) Loading an actor into a scene

Figure 3-14 is a quick example of how to get started learning more about each of the areas we've discussed in this chapter. The following are the steps that I used to put together this example using WildTangent Studio:

1. Start with a default room and resize it to make it a little bigger.

2. Put a space texture on the surrounding horizon walls.

3. Put a grass texture on the ground.

4. Create two cylinders. Scale one down as a cut, and sink the smaller one into the floor and put a water texture on the surface and stone textures on the sides.

5. Load some "tree" actors and size and scale them into position.

6. Create an emitter and assign it a sprite smoke bitmap.

7. Create two point lights and a spotlight. The first point light is the ambient global light and is positioned in the upper right of the scene in the position of the moon. The second point light is on the surface of the fountain to simulate a reflection from the water. The spotlight is targeted on the fountain from the moon's position.

FIGURE 3-14

Moonlight forest

INTERVIEW WITH RICK SANCHEZ

Rick is an extraordinary artist with a long and diverse background in games and other forms of entertainment. His previous clients and employers include: Activision, 3DO, Sony Pictures, and Disney. He has worked on Battlezone, Vegas Games 2000, Might & Magic VII, and Heroes of Might & Magic III for the PC, and Jasmine's Bazaar, The Toontown Avatar Project, and various other games for Disney Online. Rick has also worked as a character designer, art director, and storyboard artist on various film and television projects, like Jumanji, The Magic Mill, Cybercop, and Health Nuts, with many freelance credits on various commercials.

TM: Hello Rick! How important is lighting in a 3-D scene? What role does lighting play in games?

RS: Lighting is probably the single most critical and important aspect of 3-D. Good lighting sets the mood or feel of the game or scene that you're working on—it's what every art director is usually trying to capture in his vision. With today's incredible games like Halo, one of the main things everyone notices is the lighting and how it interacts with the environments and textures to create a certain ambiance.

TM: You've built many textures! How do you build great textures?

RS: Well, that's kind of a complicated process. I build them mainly through techniques I developed by experimentation with the greatest 2-D graphics program ever ... Photoshop! That's my opinion, anyway (no, I'm not being paid or sponsored by Adobe, just in case you're wondering). I just "calls them as I sees them." Back to the textures. In a nutshell, I usually look at real-life textures. I pay special attention to details like how light reacts to a surface; also, colors, and the contrast in the pattern of the object, etc.

A couple of points to keep in mind are, keep your textures tileable! Don't have extreme areas of contrast (some game engines create strobing or flickering anomalies from a distance in the game ... quite annoying and unattractive!). Maintain some reference conceptual art for the proper color palette to help coordinate the 3-D lighting to come later. There are tons of little details. Just maintain the basic principles of color theory and harmony.

TM: How much of a game's visual style is controlled by texturing?

RS: Definitely 110 percent! Let me be clear ... it's in the lighting and textures.

TM: What mistakes have you seen made in producing texture work?

RS: Repeating patterns, strobing, textures that are too saturated, textures that have too little contrast and look washed out, the overuse of canned textures from texture CDs and texture libraries. There is nothing really wrong with using them, as long as you can modify them to acquire the desired effect or look. I've seen the same textures used in a variety of games. The truly great ones always have their own special textures created from scratch.

TM: How does texturing, lighting, and effects come together for you in a scene?

RS: No matter how good your textures are, if the lighting is not right, they will not have the effect desired and you'll have created a mediocre-looking game that will only be saved by the actual structure of the game—the gameplay (how well the game flows, its storyline, and most important ... the programming of the game engine itself). Everyone knows that these days eye candy is more than half the battle.

TM: What three tips would you offer for improving your texturing skills?

RS: Master Photoshop! Pay attention to detail, no matter how seemingly insignificant (sometimes the smallest of scratches or grime can sell your textures and pass them off for the real thing!). Of course, you should always have plenty of reference books, photos, and paintings, etc. I recommend Birn and Maestri's Digital Lighting & Rendering. This is excellent resource material without having to understand complicated rendering algorithms and advanced-level mathematics.

TM: What are some of the team production challenges in coordinating lighting, texturing, and effects work?

RS: Well, to be frank, I've not had a really difficult challenge as far as the production, coordination, and distribution of assets for games. It all boils down to having and giving the right support to your fellow animators, texture artists, modelers, art director, and, yes, even the programmers are invaluable to giving you vital information, suggestions, and insight as to what can and can't work to sell an effect or shot in any game. Communication is vital in a team environment. Regular creative and trouble-shooting meetings are essential to maintaining the overall vision of the game—keeping it alive and fresh, solving any glitches or issues that need to be addressed. It is during these meetings that some of the best (and sometimes wackiest) ideas come to fruition. It's a collective effort; that's how great games are made.

TM: How do you develop as an artist while working towards building games?

RS: You really can't help but to develop and grow as an artist while working on a project. The daily tasks and challenges that arise as you encounter artistic dead-ends will force you to reach for answers, find solutions, to be creative and develop so-called visual cheats to make an effect work, or to sell a shot—to give the textures or lighting the right effect. All these things allow you to grow as an artist and as a creative individual.

TM: What specific art skills help you most in your work?

RS: Definitely, my drawing and color comp skills. Everyone can learn to use a computer in a few hours, learn a software package in a few weeks, master it in a few months … but it takes years to develop your drawing and artistic skill. Furthermore, you have to maintain them every day. It's not like riding a bike … once you learn, you'll never forget. With art, it's a daily regimen; you must draw every day or you'll lose your skills.

TM: What do you enjoy the most about working in games?

RS: It's a fun environment, you don't have to dress up, and sometimes you get free food and ice cream … you can't beat that!

TM: What do you like the least about working in games?

RS: My only issue is the commute. I hate driving … anywhere. That's why I love working freelance. I only have to come into the office every once in a while for meetings, to hand in some artwork or something like that. I love telecommuting. I wake up … I don't even have to comb my hair or dress up. I usually just get up, make my pit-stop, sit and eat breakfast at the computer desk as I work. Before I know it, it's time to go to bed. I'm at least 85 percent more productive this way.

TM: Agreed. How has the impact of new technology changed your work over time?

RS: It's only gotten better and more fun to work in this industry … we now have fewer limitations than just a few years ago. Faster CPUs, affordable graphics cards, better software, better hardware, online gaming, broadband, etc.—I could go on and on.

TM: What practical advice would you give to aspiring digital artists?

RS: Don't do it! (Just kiddin'.) No, really, I would push myself to develop all the skills of my craft, but concentrate on the industry you love. Is it film and broadcast? Is it special effects? Is it character animation? Which area within these fields do you want to get into? Modeling or animating? Particle effects?

Obviously, you must master all the basic facets of 2-D and 3-D art, but specialize in the one area that is best suited to you. Don't try to do it all. If you like to animate, focus on character rigging (forward kinematics, inverse kinematics, setups, and envelopes) [forward kinematics refers to the use of joint rotations to pose a character; inverse kinematics refers to controlling a number of joints using an IK handle; and setups and envelopes refer to slider-based motion control of joints or vertex groups, and so forth] and animation. If you like modeling, then focus on a particular part, like polygon modeling. Build the cleanest models you can. But don't forget to still work with NURBS [Non-Uniform Rational B-Splines] and splines, since the new technologies are allowing us to do more amazing things. Don't be surprised in the near future to see full-resolution film-quality characters. Oh, and most important, try not to master more than two 3-D software programs! Don't be a pig like me and use a great deal of your precious time learning every program out there and then end up never being able to use half of them … better to be great at one than to be good or average in a couple of them.

TM: What are you excited about in the near future for digital art?

RS: Man, that's a question I was hoping you wouldn't ask. I'm excited about so many things and I can't really talk about a lot of them (signed NDAs [nondisclosure agreements], you know!). It's such an amazing future! The bar is constantly being raised. The effects are so incredible now. Technology is allowing for more and more creative/expressive freedom. Artists are only limited by their own imagination. Heck, man! I'm excited about everything!

TM: How important is it to specialize your art skills these days?

RS: The working environment is always set up as teams of specialists in every area of production. You have conceptual design (some people call it production design), or art direction, then modeling, animating, environments, particle effects, compositing, and textures. You have to specialize.

TM: What kinds of games would you like to build in the future?

RS: The most wicked, mind-blowin', intense, sensory-overload, knock-your- socks-off action and graphics ever!

TM: What games still excite you?

RS: Halo, Tom Clancy's "Splinter Cell," Mech-Assault, Commando … to name a few of my favorites.

TM: How do you compare working in games with working in TV or film projects?

RS: Well, working on film is the most demanding art-wise. You have to be the absolute best at what you do. Film graphics are satisfying due to the end result, which is usually amazing when it all comes together. Everything is done in layers for ultimate control when compositing. TV is not as intense, but is a little more high-pressure due to the time and budget constraints. You're usually expected to crank out an episode of animation per week—not a whole lot of time to be tweaking an animation or redoing a character.

Working in games is a lot of fun, though you still have the deadlines to meet. It's usually a lot more relaxed atmosphere. You're able to work at a steady pace, and you don't have anybody breathing down your neck. If you do, it's usually some other dude just admiring your work or comparing notes, cool things like that.

TM: What's the best way to revitalize your art skills over time?

RS: Always look at other artists and notice what they're doing. Believe me, there is nothing more humbling than that. It forces you to push yourself harder. Either that, or it can make you want to quit out of frustration. You have to believe in your vision, be persistent, and always ask yourself: "How did he do that?"

TM: How has working in art changed over your career?

RS: It's only gotten better and easier due to the tools you now have as an artist. I still remember doing paste-up for advertising ads, magazine layouts, coloring by hand, stick-on lettering, etc.—especially stick-on lettering. Man! What a pain!

TM: Thanks for taking the time to talk it over, Rick!

MEGA TIPS

1. Learn as much as you can about how the "cornerstone" elements function in games. Remember that game worlds are built as hosts for gameplay—not as visual grandstands.

2. When you begin lighting your level, use only as many lights as it takes to achieve your objectives, and no more. Use your savings to finalize other level details. Weigh the trade-offs before putting in more lights.

3. Build up a wealth of environmental lighting references by clipping architectural magazines.

4. Study how light color relates to emotion.

5. Study photographic and stage lighting books. See Appendix A.

6. Study with a master texture artist like Eni Oken or Rick Sanchez (www.oken3d.com).

7. Finalize a texture's intended use before its creation. Leave final texture positioning until all environmental details are locked down.

8. Build as many effects as possible using sprite emitters rather than particle emitters (they are less processor-intensive!).

9. If you will use particle effects in your game, and they are not part of your engine tool system, decide early on whether you will export data or create particle sequences attached to polygon planes.

10. Use particle-based effects to highlight props or features only when truly necessary. Don't diminish your effect by overusing it.

11. Make sure your design document's level or mission descriptions specify a clear plan for making the most of any intended audio effects. Don't make audio a tacked-on detail. Experiment with ways to use audio more to drive players through your mission or level.

CHAPTER **4**

Actors,
Props, Items,
and Camera
Details

YOU now understand the development sequence from previsualization all the way up to starting to detail your levels and maps using lighting, texturing, particles, and audio. Different map/level/mission/world builders have different working styles and like to order their work in different ways. Your personal work style needs to mesh or meld with your team style. After all, to handle the complexity and scope of today's games, you are normally working with a team to build your game. Certain work elements that you depend on to complete your work as a team member may be ahead of or behind the overall development schedule. Usually, it's the latter.

You may find yourself waiting for tools to be built or technology decisions to be made. In such cases, a "dependency" exists—your own ability to do meaningful project work is dependent on another variable, factor, or resource issue. You should use this "dependency" time wisely, to further other team goals and solve or predict other problems. For example, you might use this time to extend the functionality and stability of your level or scripting software tools, or to document the tools you are currently using. Maybe the model exporter tool, used to bring models into the game, is not working correctly—don't wait for a fix; move on to perfecting animations or making better textures.

Personally, I concentrate first on functionality and flow. I ask myself, "Is this map starting to look like it lives up to our gameplay intentions in building it?" I don't worry about lighting or texture details too much yet. That comes later. A large part of building maps and levels involves problem solving of the following form: "How will I accomplish this or that level goal?" Before you start to lock down more final lighting, texture, and particle details, try to work on making sure that the map or level operates mechanically.

During the building phase, many new assets are coming your way—new character models, new props, new items, and so forth. A large part of the process at this point is building in these new parts of the game. There are often multiple refinement loops taking place simultaneously as the game begins to come together here.

As stated in previous chapters, often you have to use placeholder graphics to stand in for game elements. For example, a cube becomes a placeholder for a fountain spitting acid. When you get final art (model and animation) for the fountain spitting acid, you replace the cube with this final art using file referencing. Again, you're still trying to lock down the operational features of your game at this point. Part of locking down these features involves placing actors (hero, enemy, and NPCs), props (environmental features like chairs, boxes, and altars), and items (like power-ups and collectibles) and tuning specific camera details. Your camera details determine how the camera or player view will move or function in a scene. Thus, in this chapter, we're going to take a closer look at the placement of actors, props, and items, as well as camera considerations.

PLACING ACTORS

Once you've built up the world or environmental shell (the environment that will host your game) for your level or mission by the process described (or something quite similar), much of starting to make your game take shape involves placing objects and then testing or scripting them. We'll cover approaches to scripting in detail in Chapter 6. For now, let's take a look at what it means to start placing different kinds of common actors.

Hero Actors

Your hero actor is typically the star of your game. Mario, Crash Bandicoot, and Samus (*Metroid*) are perfect examples of hero actors. Not surprisingly, hero actors often have the most extensive animated abilities, and the most complex range of interactions with the environment. Since the hero actor will be controlled by a player throughout a given level, the placement of a hero actor normally begins by placing the hero at a default start point in the map or level (such as a garden at the center of the level). This is commonly called a *spawn point,* because the character is born or brought forth from this physical point on the map. This is where the player begins his or her adventure with the character. It also might be the point that a character returns to in order to start playing the level again if all the character's lives are exhausted and the player has not reached a "save point" further into the level.

The point at which you place your hero actor or actors (for multiplayer games) becomes the origin of action. There is a natural domino effect of action that occurs as the hero character traverses the level in any direction away from the start point.

Different tools handle the placement of a hero character in different ways, but essentially you load the actor into the scene and define a physical starting position as the birthplace of your hero character. Often, the player is guided through a level or mission introduction and/or cinematic, and then the game scene cuts to the character's wait-state animation, showing the hero character waiting to be controlled by the player. Maybe the character is folding his arms and tapping his foot.

Characters often have several wait-state animations. Which wait-state animation is played can be controlled randomly so that the player sees a different one from time to time, or a particular animation can be set as a fixed feature from the spawn point. In the hero character's actor properties, you might determine which wait-state animation is to be played when the character is born or spawned.

A hero character may have only one spawn point in a map, or several spawn points based on saved game information. These points can, of course, be tuned and customized.

Enemy Actors

Inevitably, you want your hero character to encounter and be challenged by strange beasts and beings in a number of ways. These strange beasts and beings are your enemy actors. Keep in mind that "actor" does not necessarily mean "human." Enemy actors can be plants, exploding blobs or pods, hot potatoes, crazed machinery or car parts, and possessed silverware.

Just like laying out a real haunted house and determining which beasties will pop out of the walls, jump down from the skies, or grab up at the visitor's ankles, you will be setting up your hero character to experience the all-digital version.

After you place enemy actors in a scene, you can modify their attributes or properties. How much damage do they do to the hero? How hostile or aggressive are they toward the hero? Will they become hostile to characters or NPCs of another class or faction? Will they fight till the death, or fight until they are 80 percent injured and then flee? Answering questions like these can help determine how to edit attribute and property settings for your enemy actors. You can see how important your editing tools are in this process.

How you set up enemy actors for your game is dependent on several factors. In general, setting them up well is a matter of play intuition (gained from those thousands of hours you've played games!), play testing, refinement, and experimentation. Setting up enemy actors varies to a great degree by the game genre you're working in and your team's own game goals for the gaming experience you're trying to provide.

Two primary factors to consider when you start to place your enemy actors are difficulty ramps and risk/reward value. *Difficulty ramp* refers to how quickly a game becomes difficult over time. Just like you (most likely), I've played too many games to remember and for countless hours. I'm still speechless when I get hold of a game that won't give me a chance. Personally, I get no enjoyment out of being crushed into oblivion in time for tea.

Most games feature a recognizable overarching difficulty ramp for the whole game, ranging from early simpler levels to very difficult later ones. There is also a difficulty ramp on a per-level basis. Some levels become very difficult rapidly, whereas others pace the difficulty to increase more gradually over time. As a builder, you want to be constantly aware of where your level or mission fits into the overall game. This is a matter of regularly tuning the number and strengths of your enemies. Of course, many games feature difficulty settings, and you will tune your map or level accordingly based on test feedback from players. Remove your ego. Listen to players openly and honestly.

Risk/reward value simply refers to the premise that a player must take a risk or be exposed to a hazard in order to receive a reward. This gives the reward value. However, you must carefully build in balance. If items are too easily obtained, the player gets no sense of earning or accomplishment. If items are next to impossible to obtain, the player is not rewarded for their effort and becomes frustrated.

Figure 4-1 illustrates a simple plotting of the risk/reward concept. A small amount of life or health energy (L) is available to the injured player without confrontation. The payoff for taking the risk to confront three enemies (E) in an enclosed space is a collectible (C) and a weapons upgrade (W). This is the classic scenario. You can extrapolate this idea to numerous scenarios of your own invention. Be sure to use a legend to plot out these elements on your topographic map, and remember that play-testing your game will be the ultimate guide to many placement issues.

Risk/reward scenarios set up classic game conflicts. The idea from this point is to extend conflict vocabulary into new and interesting avenues. Every game developer is hard at work trying to do this all the time. You can see the evidence in games all the time with more complex NPC behaviors, more intelligent enemies, and partially destructible world geometry that allows players to create their own passageways by demolition. In this case, we have a way to avoid conflict. Need an escape route? Blow a hole in the wall with a grenade. This creates added play-test issues if a number of wall

FIGURE 4-1

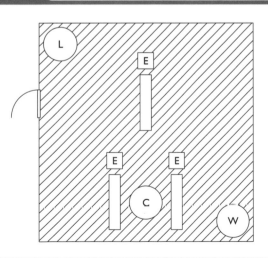

A risk/reward scenario

sections in your world can be tunneled through. You simply can't predict where the player will choose to do it! This is why many games have taken the approach of allowing only certain sections (identified visually for the player with special markings or details) of level geometry to be destructible by the player. In that way, you *do* know where a player will be able to blow a hole in the wall, and you can play-test for it and build and stage your scenes around it.

Enemy Hazards and Blind Data

An area related to setting up enemy actors involves setting up "enemy" hazards. Hazards can take many forms: lava pools, acid pits, boiling hot generators; we've seen each of these in many games. We want to be able to determine and edit how lethal these hazards are to our hero characters, or to any characters we want affected or injured by a hazard. This is often accomplished using what's called *blind data*.

We can tag or mark areas or items in our scene with blind data that is then exported from our art package and read by our game engine. We can create blind data definitions in the blind data editor of our 3-D package of choice. Usually, we give the blind data a name and ID number like Damage024. We might take Damage024 to mean "lava pool surface damage." We might be even more specific and create a blind data type of lava_pool_d024. It's important for your team to have file and data type naming conventions (agreed-upon file-naming rules) so that everyone can understand a type by looking at its name.

We also want to attach the blind data to construction elements in the scene, like polygon faces, vertices, or objects. For our lava pools, we want the lava pool surface to deliver damage, so we will attach our blind data to polygon faces (which make up the lava pool surfaces.)

Next, we can associate our Damage024 blind data with a paint color. Usually, it's best to try to keep these consistent by type. For example, try to use similar colors for similar kinds of damage (such as surface damage = red, items that cause damage = orange, and so forth).

Figure 4-2 shows the blind data editor open with selected faces being "tagged" or marked to be associated with our damage type of Damage024 (lava pool surface damage in our example). We can then customize the values of the tags we have set down or painted on polygon faces. We can edit them to cause more or less damage to our hero character on contact.

NPC Actors

In previous chapters, you have seen nonplayer character actors used in games in a number of ways: to tell backstory points and prompt the player along a certain pathway through the game; to serve as a reference point; or to teach players game controls and reveal specialties. More commonly, NPCs are becoming part of the minute-

FIGURE 4-2

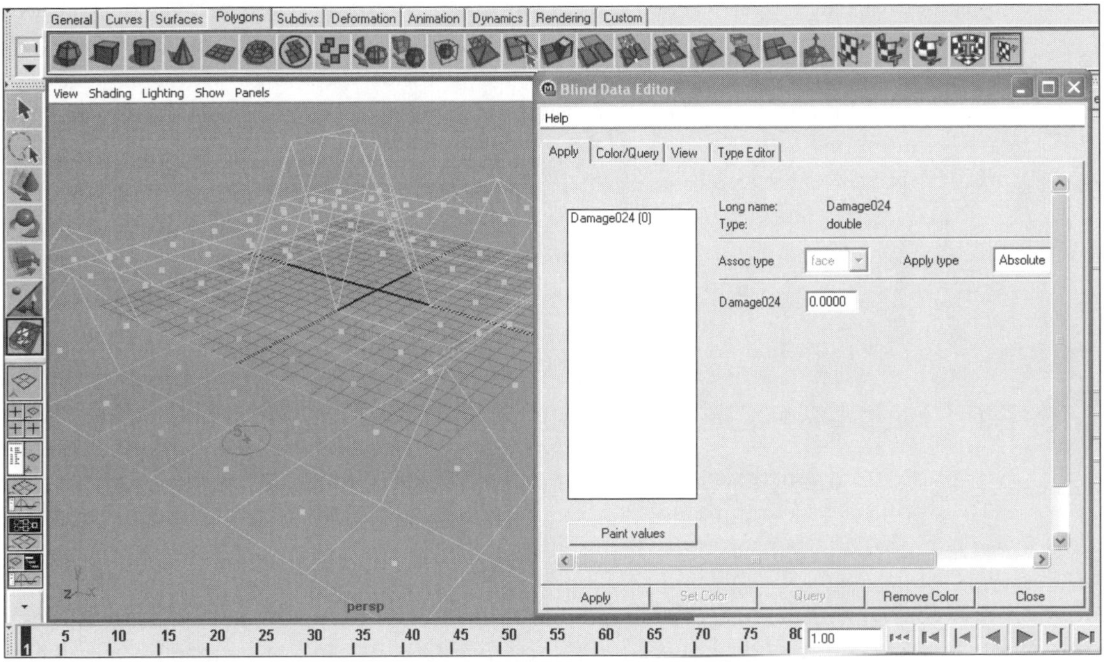

Blind data editor

to-minute action. NPCs can partner with players to achieve limited objectives. They can become an ally through a single-player game.

NPCs are put into a scene just like any other actor. Their model, texture, and animation data is loaded and created at a spawn point. Their properties, hostilities, and abilities can be set as attributes. Their behavior can be extended by a control script (a script that defines their behavior) or handled programmatically. Getting an NPC to behave in the way you intend, and perform the role you have envisioned, normally comes down to plenty of script writing and tweaking or editing. We'll look at this more closely in Chapter 6.

Boss Actors

A boss is a "payoff" bad guy. The boss idea comes from the days when games were rigidly level-driven, and the payoff for completing a game was defeating the ultimate boss or ultimate bad guy. Beating smaller bosses (minibosses) was a form of smaller payoff as players made their way through the game.

We still use boss actors, they're just not necessarily at the far right-hand side of the screen anymore! In 3-D games, we still use minibosses and bosses all the time. Minibosses can be used to accent certain high-octane parts of a level or mission. Maybe one level is a battle through an order of vampires in their infested lair, and defeating their leader is a miniboss experience. Ultimate bosses are still used as an action highpoint, a game climax, and the capstone to your experience in the game. They are handled just like any other actor, except that they tend to be greater in size and ability than anything you've seen previously in the game.

Making great boss actors that behave in interesting and challenging ways depends on the power of your *script pipeline*. In other words, your script system must be dynamic and powerful, and your game engine must be able to read and convert edited scripts into action.

TYPES OF PROPS AND THEIR USE

Props are used functionally in many ways throughout our game scenes. Any item or artifice that litters or populates your game environment is a prop. There are three basic categories that props tend to fall into:

) **Static props**   Props that don't change and can't be damaged, such as tables or chairs in a bar scene, or cots, toilets, and sinks in a prison cell scene. They just litter the world to make the game look (hopefully) more real in the ways you want it to. Environments not only have furniture pieces, but also have debris, clutter, and disarray.

) **Damageable props**   Props that have multiple potential states in the environment. They are not static; they change dependent on circumstances. For example, a potential damageable prop is a ceiling support column. If it can be destroyed and reduced to rubble (by a rocket, for example), you need a particle effect (dust clouds), a destruction animation of the column collapsing, and a new final state for the column (chunks of the column on the ground). This prop, when shot, transforms from a solid state to a collapsed state. Think of the hundreds of examples of damageable props in the games you've played: boxes shredded to splinters, gas cans exploded, and so on.

) **Scripted props**   The most complex props, since they generally require everything damageable props require and more. Let's say we're going to shoot an alien incubator with a gelatinous beast in it. We want this event to provoke outrage and begin an attack on the shooter. We need everything required for a damageable prop (glass explosion particle effect, broken incubator, dead beast), and we also need to write a script to create the onset of the resulting attack.

Using Props

You can do very cool things with each of the three kinds of props. You can use them together in a multitude of combinations. Here are just a few of the ways to use props:

> **Litter a scene**   For many scenes, such as parking lots, interiors, and sea floors, to make them look right, you have to litter them with props.

> **Target practice**   Some folks enjoy breaking things as a hobby. For them, target practice on damageable props is just what the doctor ordered. There is often little payoff (you might spawn something), but it does help players learn to use their weapons—especially if the prop is moving.

> **Destroy and reveal**   Use damageable props to expose hidden treasure troves or secret passageways to the player, or to create a shortcut through the map or a hiding point.

> **Invoke a script action**   The destruction of a prop might launch an attack by the player's enemies or cause any number of other kinds of fallout results.

> **Facilitate a puzzle**   Props can become part of light puzzle-solving to reach higher spaces (moving a ladder prop), or become counter balances (moving a counterweight prop on a see-saw item), or trip switches (a valve prop), or block enemy invaders (destroy something to seal off room entry blocking out invaders).

> **Serve as environmental markers (landmarks)**   Props can take the form of imposing statuary, a fountain of molten lava, or any utterly unique level feature that reveals location information to the player. These props help the player realize where they are in the level context.

> **Supply humor or emotional elements**   Props can be used for humor, as cool gimmicks, to evoke emotional reaction, and to help settle or unsettle the player.

Placing Props

Within defined technical restraints, you can place a large number of props in a scene these days. How you place them depends on their use and function. As you can imagine, plenty of change and iteration go on with prop placement in most cases. You can experiment with placement when you're littering a scene. Always keep character and enemy traversal in mind. Actors have to be able to navigate freely. You can use props to guide a player through a level, too, by creating pathways with them.

TYPES OF ITEMS/POWER-UPS AND PLACEMENT

The items/power-ups category includes several other elements present in most games, such as the following:

❱ Health or life energy pickups

❱ Weapons upgrades

❱ Weapons ammunition

❱ Save points

❱ Collectibles (for example, rings or stars)

❱ Special items (for example, a telecommunications device)

❱ Specific ability power-ups (for example, ability-specific increases like shooting distances)

❱ Special powers energy (for example, mana for spell casting)

❱ Special move pickups (for example, pickups that enable a character to perform unique actions)

How are these items placed? Normally, the planned placement for these objects is described in your topographic map's legend details and design document. You place these items based on how you see enemy conflict and support for your hero character(s) working in the map. For the most part, these items support and challenge the player. Sometimes the planned placement ends up working quite well, whereas others times it misses the mark completely.

Finding the right item placement is largely a matter of making many refinement passes on your map. It's a matter of feeling. Common sense is the starting point. If you have areas of high conflict, you'll want health or life energy pickups nearby. You may also want to help the player face difficult enemies with a local weapons upgrade and enough ammo to be satisfying. Build some "discovery" into your map with hidden treasure troves. Make the player earn special items and special power-ups. The player gets little sense of accomplishment if the special item is sitting on the floor in front of them. Make it a challenge to get and keep these items, but don't make it an insurmountable challenge.

It sounds obvious, but make collectibles "alive" and meaningful in the world, and make sure they are hooked into the game. Nobody really wants to pick up mindless objects that have little or no perceived effect on your powers in the game. Items have to count for something.

Also, keep in mind that the way you approach placement is different for deathmatch, team play, single-player, and co-op maps. Study your favorite maps in each of these areas, find out what other builders are doing, and then elaborate and refine. You will see patterns. Try to grow them in new and interesting ways. If you've made the player fight through sections of your level and risk something, offer a save point (for the consoles).

CAMERA CONSIDERATIONS

Three-dimensional games use camera systems handled programmatically (in the game code) to manipulate views within a 3-D scene for the player. The camera, like any other object in the scene, can move in three directions (X, Y, and Z). As the type of action changes often, so might the camera view. For instance, you might want to enable the player to zoom in for close-combat (hand-to-hand) melee action, zoom way out for field-based unit movement, and then zoom in or out in between extremes to any number of distances from the camera to the subject.

Sometimes players don't want to track (sweep the camera following something) between these positions, but rather simply want to jump. This is done often as the camera is forced to jump to another position by an action script or by player control. A good example of jumping the camera would be jumping from a first-person camera position in the driver's seat of a racecar to a third-person camera position tracking or following that racecar.

These camera motions or camera jumps are typically handled by camera scripts that can be edited to tell each camera in a given scene how it should move or perform. Getting the camera right can make all the difference in playability, and it is a complex undertaking in a real-time environment. If you come in with the camera too tight, you get no sense (or view) of surrounding action. If you back out too far, you lose contact with your characters. If you force the camera to zoom in and out too much, you jar and distract the player.

Pay attention to how the cameras behave in all the games that you play. There is plenty of camera tracking (following a subject) and camera dollying (smoothly moving the camera from point A to point B) involved. But the camera often makes more jumps and shifts than these two basic motions account for. Tuning the camera view for action is often a considerable part of building up a level or mission. Let's take a look at some common camera modes and discuss their use.

Interface Detailing

Camera sweeps are often used to add visual pop to the user interface (UI). For example, a player can see the camera sweep across the front of a racecar, or sweep around the front of an impressive selectable fighter character at a low angle, to emphasize that fighter's dominance. You can edit camera sweeps to set the camera's start and stop position and the speed or timing factor for the sweep (how fast or slow) to suit the camera performance required. In this way, you can give the player a solid and engaging view of a character or vehicle, which is far more dynamic than a flat image alone.

Character View Example

Another example of using camera work to detail an interface would be to use a camera for an NPC character view (a close-up front shot of your commander, for instance). With the advent of advanced lip-sync ability in 3-D facial animation, you can set a close-up camera view for an NPC and use the in-game model (or a custom model) to "talk" to the player. In many game settings, NPCs chime in to comment on gameplay, to give clues, and occasionally to help prompt and guide the player. With a camera set up to handle these NPC conversations, you can extend and enhance the role of the NPC as desired. You might even create an NPC studio (for example, a set to host NPCs in camera conversation with the player). Gone are the days of the flat-pasted NPC image it seems. Going even further, with a simple camera script, you could pan from one NPC to another (like two ship commanders on the bridge giving direction) in your NPC window.

Floating Cameras

Many games are starting to offer players the opportunity to locate or position a dynamic camera that can be moved from unit to unit or location to location at the player's preference. This allows for a quick jump into a melee scene at the unit level, for example, and a quick jump out to see what is happening across the battlefield.

Sometimes these camera moves, which are intended to allow flexibility and immersion for the player, are preconfigured and simply selectable by key or button input. If you're going to allow your player to customize a floating camera view (or several), you should at least provide some default camera setups for play—camera setups that have performed well for play in your own enjoyment of the game. Those players who appreciate this amount of granular camera control and want to edit camera position further will have a starting point. Those players who don't care will have selectable defaults.

Be considerate with camera moves. Too much camera jumping and camera distraction can cause players to become easily disoriented and confused, and breaks the game fun experience by making it a chore for players to return to the view that they are comfortable with.

Fixed Cameras

The fixed camera view is the mode you're probably most familiar with as a player. A fixed camera for a first-person game is an eye-level view from your character's perspective. Of course, this calls for the camera to be placed at the "relative" eyeball level of your character as he or she travels your map. If you run your character into a corner or crevice, that's exactly what you'll see.

Managing the camera for a third-person action game, however, provides unique challenges. Many third-person action games, where you view your character as if you're disembodied, have a fixed camera tracking the hero character above and behind their head at roughly 45 degrees elevation or greater. This works perfectly in wide-open spaces, but can cause considerable problems in tight, walled interiors or closed physical spaces.

When you're playing a third-person game (a game like *The Mark of Kri* for PlayStation 2 is a great example of excellent camera control), notice how the camera behaves when you move your character into a tight corner. Normally, the camera will try to automatically adjust to provide you with a better view of your character. Determining just what that camera position should be to insure character view in a real-time setting is quite challenging—yet several titles make it look easy. It isn't. For our part, the challenge on the design side is to make sure that a player's view is never totally obstructed and that the camera supports game action to the highest degree possible. This regularly is a part of the designer's efforts to tune the camera system details.

Special-Case Cameras

Sometimes, for the sake of visual diversity and gameplay, you will build special-case cameras to do something specific in your map. Maybe you want the player to be able to ride along while moving a droid that is six inches tall. Maybe you want to create a bungee-cam for a jump off a skyscraper. Maybe you just want to create a unique viewing perspective for some particular part of the game-play action details. Depending on the specifics, these special-case instances can be fairly easy to implement … or complete nightmares. Also, as a designer, the ability to perform radical camera customization is largely a measure of the power of your camera editing tools, and how they interface with the game code. If the special-case camera is fixed, you eliminate some problems, but at the cost of added functionality.

The power of your editing and scripting system to handle camera details is of large importance here. Many tools handle only basic or limited camera-move editing. Getting cameras to perform in a sophisticated fashion often requires intervention at the game code level.

Common Camera Problems

A host of problems can crop up with respect to your camera system—in fact, too many to list them all here. Instead, I've chosen to focus on two major problem areas for many camera systems.

The first problem is when the camera gets "stuck." As you might imagine, when you're moving a camera or multiple cameras all around a scene, they can collide with objects (and not know how to handle the collision). This creates a situation where a camera gets stuck in a physical location in the scene or jumps away and freezes. There can be several causes and several fixes for a stuck camera, but it is a common problem worth mentioning. The best approach I can offer to avoid this problem is to start by keeping your camera edits clean (well purposed and intentioned, don't try and do too much at once, allow your camera behavior to grow based on simple script steps rather than try and get to the desired end-effect immediately). Also, make sure that old and/or irrelevant camera position information is cleared out in the camera control code.

The second common problem occurs when the camera's view of game action is obscured by something. In a third-person game, when the character is deep in the corner of a walled or catacombed section of a level, they are often hidden from view. Some games try to account for this by having the walls go transparent when a character is obscured, enabling the player to see the character with X-ray ability.

Some players use this to their advantage by positioning their character in a corner pocket deliberately, which causes the adjoining wall to turn transparent and gives them a view of enemies waiting in the next room. This is a functionality trade-off you may be forced to give the player, since the transparency region needs to cover a certain scope or breadth to be effective in all possible cases where the camera is obstructed by corners or pockets.

Other games, rather than build in an automatic transparency to the walls, make an automatic camera move to get the character back into view in some fashion. Both of these solutions can be difficult to build in, but can indeed provide a solution. Along the way to creating a solution, these fixes can also create serious testing issues, since every deep corner in your map has to be tested for either transparency compliance or an auto camera repositioning, or for some measure of both.

It's best to plan for these issues at game creation. It sounds simple, yet in the heat of development, along with any number of other sizeable details, it can be duly identified and ignored.

If you're building a third-person game with enclosed or tight spaces, try to figure out up front what camera problems you will likely encounter. Use this identification process to influence the early building process. Assume that you may not have the time or resources to be able to provide radical solutions if you make a bad move here.

Camera problems, among many others, are why constant communication between designers and technical leads is so very important. If you're going to start building environmental assets (like the wall pieces that form the deep corners), you need to agree on camera implementation early rather than late.

CASE STUDY COMMENTS ON ACTOR LOADING AND CAMERA TUNING

You now understand that actor loading (the process of importing characters, props, and effects into your game) is the pathway for constructing your games. As such, it's a vital part of the game assembly process. Most developers, as we've seen, build their low polygon characters, props, and items in Maya or 3ds max. We've taken a look at texturing, animation, and applicable lighting too. Now we have to export these out of a 3-D package and into our game engine (either licensed or custom-developed in-house at a game studio—also called proprietary).

The software exporter (from Maya or 3ds max to our game engine) is a piece of tool code that reconfigures our assets to be set up appropriately to be "understood" by the game engine we're using. Maybe our engine requires us to set up polygon faces a certain way, or orient animation joints a certain way. The software exporter will have to account for this fact, and sometimes try to adjust for this fact (with mixed results!).

Frequently, our export tools are under development in parallel with the game we're making. This means that the software exporter may itself be undergoing a rigorous debugging phase while we're attempting to build things using it. It shouldn't be a surprise that this fact alone creates considerable challenges. Designers need to provide quick and useful feedback to the tools programmer(s) to get the exporter working well enough to serve the game. Often, game-ready assets constructed using these tools are due to your game's publisher at the same time the tools are under development.

During many game development cycles in my personal history (and I won't single any out; they share common factors), it wasn't necessarily building game engine functionality that slowed game development and affected gameplay development goals—it was the tools. To be precise, it was the lack of tools. How do you start building up exciting play if you can't get reliable assets into the game scene? You can't.

Many times, these software exporters fail. What looks perfect and functions correctly in your 3-D package of choice is destroyed in translation to the game engine. Consequently, you find that, for example, polygon faces are flipped, texturing information is lost, lighting information is missing or severely altered, animation data is lost, and local rotation axes on joints (joint position information for motion) are ruined. This adds up to a frustrating situation for the team as a whole.

Similarly, once actors can be loaded reliably into the game scene, if there is no powerful camera-tuning system, you cannot make game-dependent edits to camera moves. You need to be able to edit and refine camera moves by some pathway in the game engine in order to build up the kind of gameplay your team has as a goal.

This "challenge point" in game development highlights again the importance of powerful tool development. It is an area virtually every developer struggles with—large or small.

Planning and considering carefully your tool development choices is absolutely critical in building exciting and competitive games for today's gaming market. Although the scope and complexity of game titles continue to ascend, the amount of time to delivery and budget support have leveled off or even diminished in many cases. As a result, developers need construction tools of incredible power and diversity.

You can already see that this idea is becoming a development reality, as many game developers now specialize in a certain game genre (sports, RPGs, RTS, first-person, and so forth). It's becoming quite difficult to jump genre because of the unique development requirements (technology support down to tool specifics) for each genre.

INTERVIEW WITH NATHAN HUNT

Nathan Hunt is a lead engine programmer at The Collective, developers of highly acclaimed titles like Buffy the Vampire Slayer *and* Indiana Jones and the Emperor's Tomb *for Xbox. His past game credits include* Virtual Pool 2 *and* Virtual Pool 3, *among others. Currently, he is hard at work building game technology for next-generation game consoles. He earned a B.S. in computer science from UCLA.*

TM: Hello Nathan! Can you briefly describe your role as lead engine programmer?

NH: My role is to co-supervise and manage a multiplatform, multigame game tools and technology code base and help oversee a department of more than 20 engineers. This involves technical design, coding and maintenance of many core technology systems, and, from a management capacity, helping to ensure that our games are shipped in a reasonable time frame and with a competitive feature set.

TM: Full-time "game design" oriented positions are relatively new in the industry. In terms of workflow, how can designers best collaborate with programmers and technical leads?

NH: One of the key ingredients to creating a successful game is effective communication between the game designers and programmers. The most important factor to achieving this is for the design department to make sure they have a decisive, unchanging vision for the game in its entirety. Another key element is that designers must be able to provide low-level, functionality-driven documentation to the programming staff upon demand—documentation that is vague or subject to interpretation is very likely to be either implemented wrong the first time or be road-blocked before implementation can even begin due to lack of information. Finally, a designer has to be willing to compromise. A designer may be "perfect" when implemented to a spec, but when the technology development time could be halved while losing only 10 percent of the coolness factor, this is often a trade worth making.

TM: Strong game content is directly related to strong software development tools. Some developers build tools into 3ds max using MAXScript, others use MEL/Maya, others write their own proprietary tools as "stand-alone" software tools, yet others must use the tool associated with a licensed engine solution. This contributes to what I've called "tools shift" and makes for a fractured experience as developers move around in the industry. What do you see in the near future for design tools implementation?

NH: I don't see this fracturing of tools as something that is likely to go away in the near future. To date, there still isn't even a general consensus among engineers from one game development company to the next about the most efficient development tools. However, a designer can still survive and be strong in this environment if he/she is flexible and willing to adapt. Creative world-building concepts can generally be applied independently of the specific tool, provided that the tool capabilities are at a certain minimum level.

TM: How important is it for designers today to understand scripting languages? Which ones would you suggest new designers learn? Python? Visual Basic? Others?

NH: Similar to programmers and artists, the field of designer is becoming more specialized in the industry. And the level of knowledge and hands-on skill expected from a designer is also rising. While it isn't a requirement that a designer learn a scripting language, designers that have no production trade ("paper designers," as they are sometimes described) are quickly becoming obsolete. The two most common areas of production work for designers are world building and scripting. Assuming scripting is the chosen path, I'd say that the specific language is almost irrelevant. Because each game is likely to be scripted in a slightly different way (and potentially with a different language) than any other game, it's most important that a scripter/designer first understand the workflow of scripting, then be willing to adapt (and possibly even help co-design) to any scripting system that most suits the game being developed. So learning any off-the-shelf language package will lay the groundwork for proper training.

TM: With the time to game delivery limited, and the demand to satisfy the gaming audience with content regularly increasing, what do you think of the idea of "modularity" in tools design? Do you think most developers will build their tools to allow for game content to be constructed like a digital-Lego system?

NH: This is what nearly every game development house aspires to achieve. Of course, they all fall short to some degree—when tools become general enough to make cutting-edge games using a building-block type system, then programmers may become obsolete! But I think solid, intuitive tools design is absolutely essential to making a high-quality game in a reasonable amount of time. The earlier in development the tools can be stabilized, the more time the design and art teams will have to create and refine content.

TM: Let's say we were building an action-oriented RPG. We desire a drag-and-drop construction system with easy (and full) scripting support. Would you be inclined to build it into Maya (for instance) or write a stand-alone editor? Why?

NH: The "ideal" development tool is still not widely agreed upon. As with many things in game development, each choice on this issue is all about pros and cons. If a game is to be laid out and implemented primarily by designers or has a significantly large scope, it might make more sense to write a stand-alone editor that stresses easy world and game event construction rather than sophisticated modeling capabilities. On the other hand, if the environments were to be stylistically complex or intricate, this would be difficult to achieve without using Maya or a comparable program. I suspect that in general, as games continue to compete more and more heavily on aesthetics, we'll see more and more developers go the route of integrating into Maya (or even 3ds max).

TM: What would you say are the three greatest challenges in building tools that work seamlessly with game engines?

NH: Challenge 1: Tools must be finished (or at least able to allow users to create production-quality work) relatively quickly in order for the development team to have enough time to create game content. But achieving this can only be done with very solid planning and teamwork from technology and design.

Challenge 2: Maintaining a solid communication channel between the design and technology department is a must, and is where the process has a tendency to break down. This has to be an open collaboration, and both groups have to be willing to compromise and be very goal-oriented.

Challenge 3: Team members must recognize when a tool or tool feature isn't working or needs to be improved, and just as important they must be able to recognize when a feature is "good enough." If tools continue to change too late into development, then there's likely to be a crazy, unpleasant rush at the end once designers have their full toolset. On the other hand, if the tools are locked down too early and therefore end up being too limited, designers may not be able to create the game without great pain and difficulty.

TM: Do these challenges differ greatly by platform (Xbox, PS2)?

NH: I believe that these challenges are universal regardless of development platform.

TM: In building a game as a technical lead or director, what do you expect from a game or level designer on a daily basis?

NH: Any designer has to realize that game development is driven by design. The most dazzling game technology in the world can't make a great game without a good design behind it. And because a bad or uncertain design can end up wasting many man-months (or in extreme cases, man-years) of programmer time working and reworking content, this responsibility absolutely needs to be taken seriously. No designer is perfect, and neither is any up-front game design—however, a designer at any level should always be striving to improve his or her planning skills, and must recognize as early as possible when a slight alteration to a game's development path could end up making the game better or the team more efficient.

TM: How do you debug tools during content development?

NH: In the early days of tool development, the team needs to realize that creating ideal tools is a learning process, and that the first few efforts at using a tool to create production work are likely to only be partially successful. But once full game development is underway, the process of altering or debugging tools has to be done with great caution, and is more costly both because it must be done with more care and because mistakes can undo a larger quantity of usable work.

TM: In building up gameplay, is it helpful to have designers tweaking behavior or performance scripts all day long?

NH: When a scripting pipeline is set up efficiently, it can be a very powerful tool in the hands of a strong designer. Because scripting from a high level can control the quality, feel, and personality of a game, it absolutely makes sense to have some number of designers working on such scripts in a full-time capacity. The number of designers needed for this varies by the demands of the project.

TM: Can you tell us about some of your goals in game technology development?

NH: For me personally, great games are more important than great technology. So in the end, my number one goal is to create the tools pipeline and competitive technology to facilitate the design team to make a truly great game, with broad appeal. Technology is a means to an end, and ideally will be used effectively within the scope of a finished game.

My secondary goal is to be able to implement a game based upon a well-laid-out initial plan, and complete it on time, on budget, and to the full satisfaction of the development team. Creating games is a business, and while game quality is extremely important, so is the bottom line!

TM: What would you say are the main "categories" of scripts (camera scripts, prop behaviors, enemy behaviors) a designer works with today?

NH: This definitely varies widely by game. However, I imagine that the most commonly used form of designer-based scripting is to define character behavior. This can range from animation sequencing to high-level character AI thought processes. To a certain degree, event triggering and object interactions can also be thought of as a form of scripting, even if they are set up in a visual tool such as Maya as opposed to being defined by a scripting language, and this is how a huge percentage of game designer time is spent in game development today.

TM: What are the elements to tuning the "feel" of a game? What attributes are important in a game designer to do scripting?

NH: Being a good scripter is definitely a talent, and not every designer has an aptitude for it! First, a scripter absolutely must understand the overall vision of the game. What is the desired end-effect in terms of style? Will it be consistent with the work of the other scripters? And how will the implementer know when it is done? Second, a great deal of patience is required. To get something just right often takes seemingly endless repetitions, play testing, and fine-tuning. Last, and this is mastered by only a very few designers, the scripter should recognize when a system or feature just isn't working out sufficiently, or when a sensible, global change would most dramatically enhance the overall feel of the game—this type of global decision-making needs to be collaboratively worked out with the programming staff.

TM: What advice would you offer to aspiring game developers interested in making games but not sure where to begin?

NH: First, play lots of games. It can't hurt to know what you will be competing against. Attempt to identify elements in games that you feel are weak, and elements that you feel are strong. Second, make sure you continue to educate yourself about the latest thinking in game development. There are numerous web sites that contain a wealth of information about all facets of game making, and news sites will help point out industry trends and noteworthy events. Third, make sure you refine and hone your communication skills. Written communication is becoming more critical in game development every day, and of course being able to communicate concisely with team members verbally is an absolute must. Last, once you feel you can contribute to game development in some capacity, take the plunge and start interviewing! There are lots of companies out there willing to train people who are eager to learn, open-minded, and show aptitude.

TM: Is it possible to "prototype" game ideas or game mechanics without having access to sizeable programming and art resources?

NH: This is a tough one. In many cases, some form of prototyping is possible. For example, there are simple game construction kits. Or, some games lend themselves to making test versions in other mediums (for example, it's possible that for an RPG or a turn-based strategy game a paper-based version could be made to test out some of the game elements). However, a great game is more than the sum of its parts, and it is difficult to tell if a game is going to have the real magic that will set it above its competitors until all the elements can be seen working together as they were intended.

TM: What misconceptions do you think people outside the game industry have about working in game development?

NH: Misconception 1: "I like to play games, so it's a no-brainer that I'll like to make games." This is a misconception for one simple reason. Creating games is fun and it's entertainment, while making games is work and it's a job. That doesn't mean a person can't love the job, but it does mean that there will be times when a game developer has to work on something that is unappealing or painful but simply has to be done as part of shipping the game.

Misconception 2: "I can only be happy making the types of games I like to play." Most people are pretty picky about the types of games they play. In fact, an average gamer probably would really like only less than 10 percent of the games on the market chosen at random. But each game has its appealing elements that its creators can take pride in, and every well-done game will appeal to someone. So an aspiring developer should go in with an attitude of "what can I learn?" and worry about making the perfect game at a later, more experienced point in his or her career.

Misconception 3: "I know good game design when I see it, therefore I'm a designer." Pointing out when a game design is weak or doesn't work is a valuable skill in game development. But it is only the beginning of being a good designer. While suggesting solutions is the natural next step to identifying problems, not everyone can consistently take this step.

TM: What misconceptions do you think people inside the game industry have about working in game development?

NH: Misconception 1: "I'm too experienced to be working on tasks of type X." Elitism is unfortunately all too common among game developers. In many cases, people refuse to work on tedious work, considering it beneath them. But while a more junior or less qualified employee may be able to carry out a particular task that is given, someone with pride in their work will still be willing to do a great job and in a timely manner.

Misconception 2: "I work long hours, so I shouldn't have to play by any rules of conventional professionalism." It's true, game developers often work long hours, as deadlines are all too frequent. But game making should still be a professional environment, where individuals make their best attempt to adhere to a schedule and a plan, to respect and support their co-workers, and to be dependable to the rest of the team. When an individual pulls an all-nighter and then disappears for the next two days for recovery despite the rest of the team, it is not the best way to ship a game.

TM: What is the best way to build your gaming intuition?

NH: Different individuals have a different level of aptitude for this. However, people can continue to refine it and enhance it in two ways. The first and most obvious is to play many games. Knowing how other games work is a great way of becoming ingrained with this type of knowledge. The second just comes from experience at developing games. Occasional setbacks and failures are great tools for educating a person about what is "right" in a game and what is not.

TM: Any "nameless" development stories you'd like to share?

NH: I can't think of any!

TM: Can you share some insights with us about your own path to becoming a leading-edge developer?

NH: One of the key lessons I've learned in being a game developer is that team building is perhaps the most important aspect to creating good games. Teams dominated by individuals as dictators—no matter how strong—rarely produce the same quality of game as teams that are universally collaborative and supportive. Team sizes have continued to grow over the last decade, and this trend isn't necessarily going to stop anytime soon. I believe that the game development companies that will most dominate in the years to come are those that can come to grips with how such team members should interact with each other.

I've also found that while much of game development is about creativity, inspiration, and innovation, the vast majority of time is spent doing hard, often stressful work, sometimes to hours that seem inhuman. I think that one of the keys to becoming a very valuable contributor to game development is when a person fully accepts that every task on a game has to be done by someone, and each of us has to be miserable for a time in order to get back to the fun stuff!

One more lesson learned—I feel that the most important attribute for any individual game developer, and perhaps what should be prized above all other factors, is the ability to consistently be level-headed and sensible when faced with challenges. The field of game development changes with a remarkable frequency because it is still such a young industry. The people who will continue to remain on top are those that can quickly break down and solve new, unforeseen problems.

MEGA TIPS

1. Plan your tool requirements early and dig in to the details.

2. Do your first pass placement of all actors, props, hazards, and items on your topographic level map using a symbol legend. Conform to this legend across the design team.

3. Include "camera notes" with your level specifications in your game design document. These notes should attempt to predict possible problem areas for camera motion and camera scripting.

4. Plan your NPC use early and try to be flexible. Leave room for building in behavior adjustments, new or better ideas, reworks, and tuning to improve the NPC-to-player contact experience.

5. Make sure any sophisticated boss behaviors can be accommodated by your toolset.

6. Identify and categorize your prop types as static, damageable, or scripted. You might even build this identity into their filenames (for example, s_barrel for static types, d_pillar for damageable types, and sc_altar for scripted types).

7. As much as possible, work up front to lock down tools stability. Make sure the game asset pipeline from 3-D package to engine is functional as early in the development curve as possible.

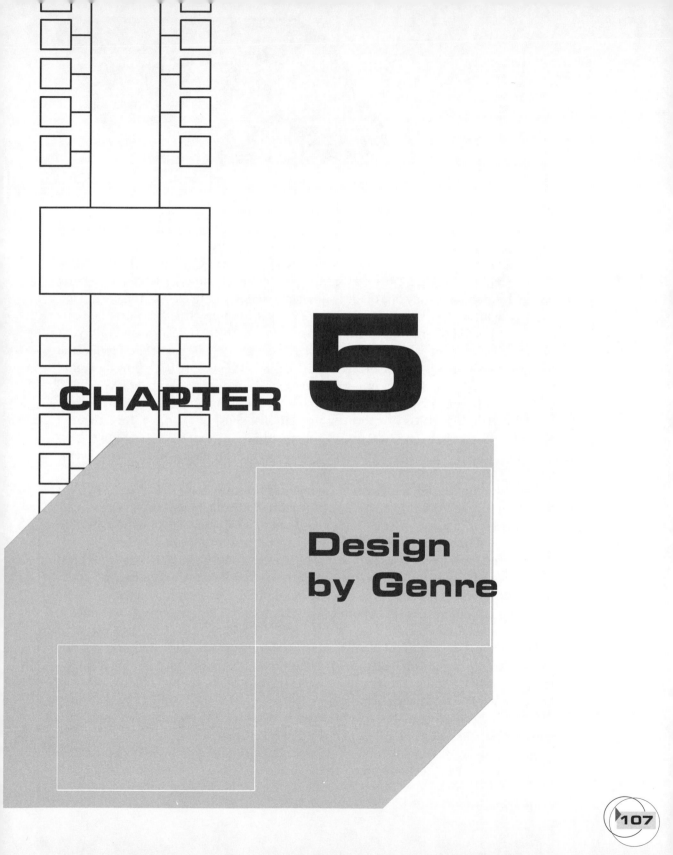

CHAPTER 5

Design by Genre

UP to this point, we've covered a sizeable amount of material in the practice of building up game worlds. A large number of the elements discussed so far will apply to building games across genres. Yet, every game genre has particular design nuances and requirements combined with specific and unique challenges. A thoroughly entrenched "genre-specific" game designer could write an entire book on design specifics for any one of the major game genres, and in fact some have (for example, *Swords & Circuitry: A Designer's Guide to Computer Role Playing Games*, by Neal and Jana Hallford published by Premier Press, 2001). I encourage you to explore more deeply, in every way possible, the genres that hold a particular fascination for you. As you saw in Chapter 4, even developers themselves are becoming more and more genre-focused. Keep in mind that, regardless of genre, every game you build will teach you something important about how to build some aspect of the next one.

Maybe you love RPGs or sports or simulations (sims) or shooters. Investigate. I started out by writing text adventures and arcade-style shooters. No designer is an expert in every game genre. Every designer/developer brings a collection of diverse design experiences with them to each and every title.

In an attempt to provide you with the widest possible view, this chapter surveys the major genres from a design perspective. I don't include every known or possible genre; rather, I include several of the major ones. We'll look at the highest level, at some of the factors that influence design particulars for each of the genres.

There are many game titles that don't fit easily into any one-genre category. This is for the best. There is nothing wrong with game genres having blurry edges, or games from outside a traditional genre borrowing more genre-specific concepts or play ideas and presenting these in new and engaging ways. I'm not a genre purist, and I'm not an obsessive categorizer.

Normally, you won't find me sitting around arguing about whether or not a title can "truly" be dubbed an RPG, for instance, or whether it simply contains RPG elements mixed with any number of influences from other genres. I don't measure games by categories. I measure the game experience itself, and nothing else. Mix it up anyway that you choose—I'm only interested in the taste of the soup. For me (and for many others, I suspect), it's all about the game experience.

Simplicity is occasionally deceptive. Does it work and is it fun? Do I have that warm game "buzz" feeling boiling over? Wonderful. Will I be stuck on the couch playing until I hear the morning paper delivered on the doorstep? Perfect. Uh oh, I need to run some laps.

As this chapter unfolds, we'll survey some of the major design elements for major genres, and finish up by looking at creating cinematics, backstory, and dialog. In the big picture, these can be applied across genres. We'll conclude our game genre survey with a summary of the game designer's everyday work tools.

SPORTS GAMES

Some players hate sports titles; others can't get enough of them. One thing is for sure: they have done more to promote console gaming than any other genre. Football, baseball, basketball, hockey, soccer, track and field, volleyball, rugby, racing, surfing, fishing, skateboarding, tennis, BMX, golf ... they've all been treated as electronic games. Hang around the game industry long enough and you'll probably work on a sports-related title. The following list focuses in on some of the relevant design aspects of sports titles:

) Motion capture versus hand animation

) Established rules

) Simulation versus fantasy

) Licensing

) Heavy tuning

) Defense scripts

) Player and arena look and feel

) Statistics

Sports games frequently require that game characters (based on well-known professional athletes) perform both elaborate physical moves and utterly unique signature moves. This can take the form of a particular batting stance and swing, a particular pitch delivery, or a one-of-a-kind slam dunk on the basket. Players expect and appreciate the ability to "control" these moves within a sports title. This makes fluid character motion a design requirement.

Developers have to either "hand" animate this motion, by moving joints and bones attached to the 3-D character model, or use motion-capture technology (sometimes they even employ both methods). Motion-capture sessions outfit an actor/athlete in a suit with small light-reflective balls or points attached to it, which are then read into a computer via a scanning system that tracks the movement of the ball points. This data must then be significantly processed into useable motion data for the game. So, one of the first big design hurdles for sports is making player motion look accurate and familiar, while working functionally in the game. Figure 5-1 shows an athlete wearing a motion-tracking suit with the reflection points visible.

FIGURE 5-1

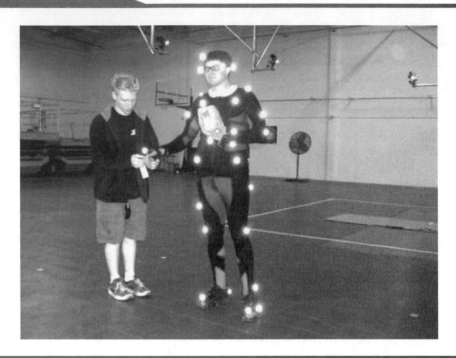

Motion-tracking suit

Sports games have established rules. In many other genres as a designer, you are tasked with creating the rules. Typically, for standard sports titles, you will be translating the rules of a particular sport into your game. Design-wise, in an effort to maintain the best game experience, you will have to consider how the flow of a typical game and its rules affect the player. You will frequently decide to provide the player with options to disable parts of the officiating rules of a game that breaks the "action feeling" for the player (for example, turning off "icing" calls in a hockey game). Every effort will be made to bring the full set of rules of the given sport into the game.

A point of design balance is frequently called for in the "simulation versus fantasy" area as it pertains to sports. A hardcore simulation that attempts to re-create every minute detail of a sports game experience in real-time may find an audience among die-hard simulation fans, but lose the action player in the mix. For example, a baseball game may simulate the catcher sending signs for pitches, to which the pitcher either agrees or shakes off the sign before pitching. For brevity and less distance between "action points" in the game, you would probably cut sending pitch signs altogether. Simply put, you want plenty of condensed action points if you are trying to appeal to the action player. This is why it's so important to keep in mind your "target player" when making design decisions. You make decision trade-offs based on your intended audience.

The fantasy aspect of the sports experience flies in the face of sports simulation. A purist baseball simulation might have you spending nine years playing AA/AAA ball! Players want to proceed quickly, get better at both offense and defense quickly, and challenge the pros by lunch. This is part of the pleasure in the experience. If players are stifled by an extended or cumbersome route, with bad physical play controls, you will lose your audience.

Licensing, the ability to use known professional teams, players, and stadiums or venues, will affect the "reach" of your design. In the recent past, you could make sports games without a major sports league franchise license from, for example, Major League Baseball (MLB) or the National Basketball Association (NBA). Technically, you still can, but most game players prefer the game that has access to and utilizes the familiar talent of the sport they prefer. Again, part of the fantasy is putting yourself in control of the teams and athletes.

Sports games require heavy tuning. *Tuning* refers to editing into perfection moves, functions, or data until an action or event "performs" properly in the game. Animation transitions from move to move are complex, yet must perform seamlessly. Sports games usually require editing minutiae like ball scale (the size of the ball at different performance points), passing zones (when does the ball transfer ownership from player to player?), and catch zones (how big is the zone for catching or dropping the ball?), among many other detail-specific functions.

Most sports titles include a player versus CPU mode, so the computer has to be programmed to compete against human players in offensive and defensive actions. These require complex scripts and programming. Here's a quick example. If you have two defenders and a goalie guarding a hockey goal, with two wingers and a center coming at the goal on offense in some unique formation, how does the computer best position the defenders? It's hard to program a player's intuition.

This is why sports games build rules into their scripts ... rules that can be discovered and exploited easily by human players! The rules in defense or offense scripts generally take up a straight conditional form (for example, if the puck is in this quadrant or area on the ice, with this number of players involved, then set up the defense like this, and modify it slightly in this way based on opposing player orientation).

Another challenge for sports game designers is getting the player and arena look and feel correct. People spend hours staring at these players and locations. They know what they look like. You want these to be pleasing to your audience, and you have to present the players and arenas in the best possible light to your licensor (the party giving you permission to use known players and arenas). This often requires plenty of work and revision to get player models, textures, and facial detail correct.

Getting "signature" moves to look right can be a real challenge. Stadiums and venues get the same treatment. They undergo considerable modeling, texturing, and lighting revisions to bring them into the game.

You want to ship your sports game with the latest statistical information for that sport. However, just like game development, sports do not operate in a vacuum: players get traded, players' stats change every other night, teams change logos, stadiums get new corporate sponsors, mascots get revamped, and so on. In an attempt to bring the player the most exciting and "realistic" experience, you have to try to accommodate these changes as best you can. It requires considerable detail tracking and is rarely easy to do.

FIGHTING GAMES

Fighting games of all flavors continue to be popular, with standout titles like *Tekken 4* and *Mortal Kombat: Deadly Alliance* leading the way. Let's look at some of the design details that influence the fighting genre:

> Motion-captured fight performances

> Controller tuning

> Fight arenas

> Fighting performance and combos

> Prop utilization

> Multiple fight settings

> Expanded fight modes

Similar to sophisticated sports moves, fight games include elaborate physical performances from fighters. Again, for the sake of motion fluidity, these performances sometimes begin by utilizing motion capture. Design-wise, every single move required for motion capture needs to be planned and accounted for to build the moves required by your fighting game. Motion-capture sessions can be very expensive, so you must undertake serious session planning to insure that you will motion-capture *all* the moves required by your game design. Figure 5-2 shows a single spreadsheet sample entry. There can be hundreds of these motions and in-betweens (motions between motions, or motion segues). You can learn more about motion capture by visiting the House of Moves web site (www.houseofmoves.com).

Many teams extrapolate each move destined for motion capture from the game design document into a spreadsheet such as Microsoft Excel, or they use asset-tracking software like NXN alienbrain (www.nxn-software.com) to build a motion-capture

FIGURE 5-2

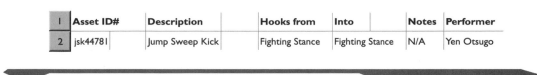

	Asset ID#	Description	Hooks from	Into	Notes	Performer
2	jsk44781	Jump Sweep Kick	Fighting Stance	Fighting Stance	N/A	Yen Otsugo

Sample spreadsheet entry

list. You will probably want to consider planning a "make-up" session to capture moves that were omitted, changed, or replaced from your initial capture sessions.

A large part of the "feel" of a great fighting game is in the game-controller processing; namely, how quickly button presses "fire off" or "translate" into controlled fighting moves. The game controller gets "scanned" for input by the game engine repeatedly many times per second, and building flash fighting response times often comes down to tuning the controller and animation handler code to minimize any lag in move execution. Fluid fight character control becomes a performance-engineering issue for the game code as it reads in controller input and translates this information into character movement. Next comes animation tuning in making sure that fighter model animation transitions (from one move to another, such as from a fighting stance to a torso grab) can be made without interference, dropped frames, or bad animation "hook-up" transitions (how motions end and begin; how they flow one into another).

Fight arenas have expanded in modern fighting games from the very popular fixed-view scrolling fighters, to fight games within complete environmental arenas built upon more elaborate camera systems and environmental interaction. This has opened up the physical fight space and made fight games seem much "larger," but it has also made new demands on background resources, challenging artists and designers to create a wide variety of compelling fight arenas. Fight arenas now allow for fighting characters to "wander" through the scene from area to area as the fight progresses. This has compelled designers to build up far more sophisticated fight scenarios incorporating multi-area fight scenes, weather effects, and so forth.

Fighting performance has become more complex, while staying true to the idea of multibutton combo attacks and unique character abilities. Fighting strategy has continued to challenge players to "last through the long round" as they must learn to balance high-power attacks with life energy loss and damage taken over ever-larger fighting fields. Fighter characters are capable of large numbers of attacks, each of which must be polished for performance.

Grabs, throws, weapon use, and special-case moves must be carefully planned as their execution on opposing characters can be tricky when you have characters of vastly different physical sizes fighting each other (for example, think of Yoda fighting Count Dooku in *Star Wars Episode II*, or a dwarf fighting a giant). A dwarf punch or grab hits a giant's shinbone. A chest-high grab for the giant versus a dwarf collides with nothing.

Programmatically, and as part of your toolset, you will be tuning collision boxes or collision areas to trigger certain events. Collision boxes determine where the two fighting actors or characters "collide" with each other. This occurrence will trigger an event. Among other uses, these events trigger physical animation reactions to punches, kicks, grabs, and weapon use, or display events like blood-spray particles, sweat sprays, or tooth chips. Ouch!

Fighting games are starting to incorporate more prop use. Fight characters can grab items in the scene (such as bar stools) and use them as weapons. This kind of action calls for the same kind of scripting that you might use in any other third-person action game.

Multiple fight settings have created a demand for much more elaborate fight levels, as the fight drifts or wanders through an environment. Gone, it seems, are the days of the relatively fixed-view fighting game as the genre continues to grow.

Expanded fight modes allow fighters to pair up with computer-driven fighters in tournament modes, and bring single-player action elements to fight games, rather than just a one-on-one setting or a simple tag team. The fight genre remains a very popular genre, yet it reserves plenty of room for growth into the future. Fight games with far greater dimensionality loom on the horizon.

PUZZLE GAMES

Sometimes it seems like puzzle games or "puzzlers" get forgotten. How many times do you see huge ads for a new puzzle game? It's happened, but it's rare, and it depends on your definition of "huge ads." *Tetris* is a landmark game title, and a point of pop-culture history at this point. Some of the most popular games for the so-called "casual" gamer are straight puzzle games or puzzle-related inventions.

At this moment, many people the world over are playing and enjoying puzzle games. You may be called upon to try to create or rethink a puzzle game. The game audience by age might be young kids, teens, middle-30s, or seniors. The puzzle game you are asked to build might not be focused on age at all, but they tend to be.

It's no secret that puzzle games can be highly addictive and, therefore, very successful. Some attributes of puzzle games to consider include

❯ Light on art assets

❯ Deceptively simple game mechanics

❯ Focused experimentation and revision

❯ Draw on assembly or "crunch" behaviors

One thing I love about puzzle games is that they are typically "light" on art assets. This is not to say that a puzzle game cannot have complex art requirements. It simply means that, compared to many other genres, the laundry list of art requirements is generally shorter in length. Figure 5-3 demonstrates a simple yet highly addictive puzzle game built for a cell phone.

Put another way, you need fewer art assets to build a simple puzzle game. This is very good news for small developers, and for those just starting out in gaming. One or two people can build a world-class puzzle game. It would be next to impossible for one or two people to build a world-class third-person action game from scratch (and be finished by the end of the millennium). Puzzle games generally require puzzle pieces, such as blocks, widgets, shapes, or gizmos of some kind. Once you have built

FIGURE 5-3

Puzzle game for cell phone

these objects and have them working in code, it's easy to make new ones, and you don't need complex organic character designs or advanced 3-D modeling techniques to do it.

Most puzzle games hinge on a "foundation" game mechanic—a spine, a heartbeat! Think about the simple beauty of *Tetris*: shapes and colors. We are challenged to arrange these shapes in an optimal way to accomplish something. It's like playing with building blocks as a child. That exact kind of natural childhood play is a fertile field of puzzle game ideas. Time to wax nostalgic and harvest those ideas. Why *did* I like digging in the sand for hours and watching ants carve out tunnels inside a plastic cage?

Puzzle game mechanics can be deceptively simple, and we always risk overthinking our ideas. Game designer 1: "That's stupid, we shouldn't just pop something; we should give the player the ability to grow their own popping characters. People like to grow things, not just pop stuff." Yep. Game designer 2: "If they're going to grow their popping characters, then we need to develop a balanced or weighted system to determine how they grow up or progress through the popping ranks." See what I mean.

Some very successful games rely on matching and popping. There is no secret mystery here. They simply feed our desire to match and pop things. Why we have a fundamental need to match and pop things, I don't know. I like to twist bubble pack to create the "machine gun" effect myself. I also like rocket launchers. Would any rocket arena freaks admit to playing *Puzzle Bobble* or *Bubble Bobble*? I will.

Developing a puzzle game, then, usually requires some focused experimentation and revision. You start by experimenting with a particular idea you believe "captures" one of these fundamentals of play. You define the way you believe the game will work, and you experiment. There will be plenty of code tweaks. In time, players might like an "unanticipated" aspect of your game that isn't even what you assumed would be the main point of the game. That's okay. Go with it. Experiment. Listen. See where it leads—quickly. It's through this revision process that you improve your game.

As I've said, for the focused part of your puzzle game experimentation, you have to be willing to draw on assembly behaviors and what I call "crunch" behaviors (those addictive, repetitive, and satisfying behaviors like popping, squishing, smashing, breaking, matching, and mixing). Take these assembly and crunch behaviors and set challenges for your player. Experiment until it becomes obvious that the game is working. Bring it home!

REAL-TIME STRATEGY GAMES

Building a real-time strategy (RTS) game is an immensely complex undertaking. From a design standpoint, there are many decisions to be made in "planning" an RTS game title and many more to be made during its development life. For popular reference, *Starcraft* and the *Age of Empires* titles are well-known examples of RTS games.

Most RTS games utilize groups of vehicles, humans, and/or creatures available for player control. The player can control groups or individual units and direct their efforts in a number of ways. Frequently, these groups of units are run through missions with objectives that require the player to apply strategy to resolve or conquer a given objective or scenario, or to topple another player. Let's focus on some of the topical challenges for design in creating an RTS-style game:

> Requires heavy art asset design and creation

> Unit definitions

> Unit behaviors

> Interface hazards

> Pathfinding

> CPU opponents

> Simple or complex strategy

RTS games are extremely asset-intensive. They require tons of custom art, code, and tools support. It takes a sizeable team, working well together, to deliver the amount of raw assets required to build a competitive RTS title.

These player-controlled groups of humans, creatures, vehicles, and mobile weapons require precise definition. For every unit, lowly and mighty, what abilities, weapons, affiliations, motives, strengths, weaknesses, and tendencies will they possess? Each of these specific unit details tend to come together for designers in data tables.

Here's an example of an extremely simple, generic, character-unit table with an arbitrary value system that has a maximum of 30:

Strength	20–30
Speed	5–18
Intelligence	5–15
Luck	10–20
Endurance	20–30
Attitude	20–30
Hit Points	20
Dexterity	5–20
Vision	8

You can see that the table specifies a character's common traits with numbers you can alter (shift up or down) if need be. For an RTS, you will build tables to specify in great detail your characters, vehicle offensive and defensive abilities and dependencies, resource system dependencies (for example, gold, water, oil, gas, wood, spice), general weapons abilities, research systems, trade systems, political relationships, and so forth.

You might have a similar table to define a unit vehicle—let's say it's an armored troop transport. You'll need concept art and a description of this vehicle. It might have three flavors: Standard, Super, and Mega. It might have both a projectile weapon and radius weapon. It will have a certain number of hit points (places where it's able to take damage) and a certain armor rating. It will have a certain capacity to carry troops. Every single unique unit requires definition. It will look different as a Mega transport then as a Standard transport.

Once the unit definitions are solid, you will want to describe unit behavior. Okay, we know something about the units—now what do they do? Do they auto-fire if an enemy is detected? Do they seek something? What do they seek? What is their default movement pattern? Can it be altered by the player? How can it be altered? How does this impact code and interface?

Carrying through with our troop-transport example, we need to determine this unit's mobility (for example, it drives from point A to point B; it can be set on patrol on a square or circular perimeter; and so forth). Also, our troop-transport vehicle has a projectile and radius attack. How do they work? Is it just a straight projectile? Does it heat-seek or curve in flight? From how far can it attack (how many grid units can it cover)? Can this projectile weapon be enhanced? How? We need answers to similar questions for the radius attack. Is it a ring or "shockwave" attack? What does it look like? How far does it extend or how many grid units will it cover? Can it be enhanced? How? If these are rechargeable weapons, how are they recharged? Does the unit have to return to a resupply base? Will a resupply droid fly in and recharge the unit? Is the "fly in" automatic or initiated by the player? Now we need to go through a similar process to define and describe the resupply droid.

These are just a few of the many questions to answer in starting to define unit behavior.

There is plenty of information coming at the player in an RTS. What's the state of my units? What's the state of the enemy's units? What's the state of that particular unit (the one that's on fire)? Likewise, players are able to direct large amounts of information back at the game. Go build this. Try and protect that. Harvest this resource. Patrol this area. Are the trade routes open? Are my fishing vessels sinking? You get the idea. How does this information flow back and forth between the player and the game? It flows via the interface.

The *game interface* is the operational shell that surrounds the game. Building an interface that is sleek-looking, comprehensible, and powerful is not easy. Certain "interface hazard" exists everywhere you look in the construction of an RTS title—true for other genres as well, but especially true for an RTS. Multimenu systems that you have to drill down into are slow and irksome to the player. You lose people when interfaces are too deep. If you sacrifice interface comprehension and navigability for complexity or a multitude of features, you are burning your audience.

I try to pay very close attention to game interfaces. I study even closer the ones that don't lose me. I keep a journal of what works well in an interface for me, and some notes on why I believe it works so well. Was it a layout factor? Was it a customization feature that made it easier for me?

Unit behavior must interact with the terrain or environmental setting of the game. In various formations, as individuals and as groups, units must navigate terrain. They need to find their way around objects on the terrain (such as buildings, rivers, and other units). The code used to control their movement from point A to point B is called *pathfinding code*. There are several algorithms that programmers can use to create the control code that describes how units should move and conform when confronted by obstacles. How do you move a large group formation through a narrow passage? Units get stuck, hidden, and clumped together. It's a bottleneck of ants trying to get into the ant hole.

In creating CPU opponents to challenge the player, your scripts and game code will have to be balanced against an "average" human player (it's hard for all developers to determine exactly where the median or average game skill level is for any kind of title).

The human player might make better strategic moves, for example, but be slower at building up a large fighting force. The CPU can build forces quickly by constantly creating new soldiers at an optimal rate, but will probably make some bad strategic moves. You have to balance all of this with the play experience in mind. If the CPU quickly and effortlessly builds a huge army with the most-advanced soldiers, vehicles, and weapons available in the game and devastates the human player immediately (and repeatedly, if your player grants you another chance to entertain them), you're going to have a frustrated and humiliated player. This is the exact opposite of the experience you intend to deliver. Yet, many games continue to make this mistake.

Since we're building a game with strategy at the core, how much strategic thinking will we demand from the player? When building up strategy scenarios, we can use either simple or complex strategy. Simple strategy might imply doing something to counter your enemy. That's not enough, though. Does it make for an exciting and addictive play experience?

Requiring players to use complex strategy, where the player must be thinking several moves ahead of their own current position (like the kind of strategy and concentration chess requires) can make for a very difficult game. This will narrow the number of players for your game. Most games build scenarios around simple strategy. This strategy element regularly takes the form: "use these weapons or these vehicles in this way to overcome a common type of obstacle or attack pattern on the part of the computer." In other words, use these "things" strategically.

Once you have the basics operational, an RTS title requires copious amounts of final tuning as you improve unit behavior and tune or dial in the difficulty curve for the game. The difficulty curve for the RTS is extremely important if you want your title to have the best possible chance of reaching the largest number of players. You simply can't tune the game difficulty for an RTS wizard. You will lose many potential players in the process.

ROLE-PLAYING GAMES

Along with every other genre we've discussed, role-playing games (RPGs) have really entered an exciting new age, and are gaining new fans everyday. There is plenty of genre-sharing between RPGs and other game forms these days. Role-playing games allow players to "become" a character, take on that character, and perform and survive in a world *as* that character. Popular examples include *Everquest*, *Neverwinter Nights*, and *Dungeon Siege*.

Let's take a look at some of the relevant design factors for RPGs:

> Emphasis on character building and character relations

> Asset-intensive

> Developing a character system matrix

> Melding characters with action

> Female gaming audience/emphasis on social interaction

> Story intensive

RPG players are challenged to build many physical, mental, magical, and alliance-oriented traits and leanings for their characters, and to then build relationships with other characters as well. There is a natural design emphasis on how characters are built, and what building a character then means in the context of that character's world.

RPGs can be heavy on asset creation in art, because multiple character types, features, unique abilities, costuming, settings, props, items, and specialized interfaces are required to build a meaningful world for characters to operate in and carry on exchanges with each other.

Building a character-system matrix helps you create characters that have "complementary" powers and abilities. Different designers do this in several unique ways.

You want to encourage players to experiment with building up different character types, although many players have favorite character types based on their own personal preferences.

You might have close-range-melee fighters, and encourage them to band with magic-based-projectile fighters, for instance. You might have trench bombers, whose work needs to be protected by archers. In short, you'll be working to find ways to have a wide range of character abilities that have certain slight dependencies on each other. It can be a vast and complicated undertaking.

Many RPGs are successfully fusing character building with action elements in exciting new ways. Based on a foundational character-building system and character types, characters face all sorts of action challenges as characters grow. This also becomes largely a matter of player preference. Some players are content with simply "growing" characters by making choices in their confrontations, akin to their paper-game roots and love for games like Dungeons and Dragons. Others prefer to "grow" by participating directly in a character's actions. Here the action element itself takes the lead.

Female players, not necessarily interested in rocket arenas, often enjoy playing RPGs that focus on building, nurturing, and communication. Everyone knows that the game market, from a content standpoint, doesn't serve female players very well. Role-playing and character development that weaves a personal story might be one of the bridges to bringing many more female players into gaming. It's critical to the growth of the game industry that game developers find ever more ways to build the female gaming audience.

Many RPGs are story-intensive. They require and invite elaborate story details for their characters to experience on the game path. "Story" itself is always a topic of great debate among game developers. Several RPGs have done a wonderful job with story, and used story elements to great effect. Questions like the following are common topics of discussion among developers: How can story best be utilized in games? Is story ultimately very important in a nonlinear experience? We'll talk about this some more at the end of the chapter.

FIRST- OR THIRD-PERSON ACTION GAMES

First- and third-person action games continue to be quite popular. Many players feel let down by a glut of these kinds of titles based on the enormous popularity of a few. Standout first-person titles include the *Quake* series titles and *Unreal Tournament 2003*, among many other great titles. A personal favorite of mine in the third-person action area is *Heretic 2*.

Just as a reminder, "first person" refers to viewing the game from your character's own eyeballs, and "third person" refers to viewing your entire character's body as if disembodied (for example, the common "chase" camera view that follows your character around).

Here's a summary of the design factors for first- and third-person titles:

❯ Modeling- and texturing-intensive

❯ Level detailing requirements increasing

❯ Require heavy bot and script refinements

❯ Performance-intensive

Plenty of modeling is required for the large number of characters and props that populate most first- and third-person games. Depending on the complexity of the in-game models required (all optimized into low-mid polygon versions) and how your engine handles level of detail implementation, there is a considerable amount of custom modeling work to be done for these games. They also require plenty of texture work to make eye-popping characters and environments. Level of detail (LOD) implementation is the process of displaying a higher-resolution model of a character when the camera is close to a subject, and a lower-resolution version at a greater distance from the camera.

In some of the current titles, animated textures and multitexture surfaces are helping to create effects like light bouncing off a pool of water in motion. You can also see some bump-mapped surfaces that give depth to a surface area (for example, wall etchings or the unevenness of a brick wall surface).

Level detailing requirements are increasing regularly. There is more emphasis on complex lighting and animated lighting. There are much more sophisticated props. Many of these "landmark" props require custom particle-effect elements, too. For instance, it used to be enough to have a statue of Horus as a landmark in your Egyptian city level. Now, Horus needs lightning emanating from his eyes at regular intervals, burning the floor before the player's very eyes. Chances are, you'll have to play around with both the look and the behavior of the lightning effect for some time before it works right and looks fantastic.

Bots, computer-controlled players, have improved their "abilities" in recent years. This is due to the hard work on the part of developers in building complete behavior-scripting systems, and then working with those systems to try to "replicate" some of the more advanced playing styles of advanced first-person shooter players. While not perfect, the results are very impressive.

Many of the operations that help build gameplay in these titles depend on triggers and scripts. It regularly takes very long hours and many work passes to achieve the kind of prop behavior or action element you desire. This affects design, because everyone wants to push hard, achieve more, and do what hasn't been done previously. If you spend too much time on any one prop or action behavior, you risk not having enough time to complete another one later in the level or later in the game.

This game genre is particularly performance-intensive. It regularly requires some pretty serious hardware on the player's side. This genre is known for "upping the bar" in machine requirements for graphics cards, memory, and CPU speed. These requirements can be used to great effect for many titles, but from a commercial standpoint, making the argument to your publisher that an average player will need the absolute latest "everything" can be a very tough sell.

SIMULATIONS

Many popular simulation-oriented games let the player experiment with a growth process of some kind. You might be growing a zoo, an amusement park, a futuristic city, or a record business cartel. Some developers don't even consider these kinds of titles to be games at all, but rather something closer to a digital or software-based toy. They certainly allow a player plenty of room to experiment with the experience at hand.

In any case, this genre continues to hold serious player appeal. Most of the successful titles to date seem to focus on growth and the shaping of a growth process. A player's decisions have impact and show positive or negative results. Raise the taxes or the ticket prices too high, and suffer the consequences. These games teach players to strive for a degree of balance in their dealings, and to find *edges*, or ways to maximize a process without overloading it. They have been used by some as an entertaining teaching tool.

Let's look now at just a few design considerations:

> Unit-intensive

> Open-ended or "blank slate" beginnings

> Easy to expand

> Passive in a positive way

> Rule- and definition-dependent

Simulators are unit-intensive. They require hundreds (even thousands) of art assets, which form the play pieces (such as buildings, roads, animals, ride pieces, snack shacks, people, and vehicles). These titles can be extremely heavy in art asset requirements, which becomes a design and production trade-off point. Your time and budget only allow for a limited number of assets. Which to build to serve your game idea?

There is a natural tendency to over-commit, and to over-design (extend the scope of the game in too many simultaneous directions). Design-wise, similar to an RTS, you need to specify in detail all of your unit pieces, their functionality, and their behavior. Most important, you need to define the rules that govern how they live and change together.

Simulators often start with a "blank slate" beginning for the player. This is the beginning of a somewhat open-ended process, although the game may end with a certain objective reached (for example, a certain sales record, attendance record, or physical size). These are really akin to digital construction sets with the ability to track player-edited values and decision points. This is a very appealing aspect for those who like to see choice or action results played out before them.

Simulators have the advantage of being relatively easy to expand. Once your art specifications are solid for creating new "pieces" (provided they don't require complex code components on the behavior side), many new units can be added to re-theme the game, extend its replay value, or to specialize it.

These titles offer a more passive and cerebral experience for players who aren't necessarily looking for fast-action overkill. It can be very relaxing to build up or to play a simulation scenario, start adjusting values, make changes, and watch the results unfold.

A large part of the design backbone for simulation-oriented games lies in defining and implementing a rule system that will guide or govern the growth process. At the most basic level, this can be modeled in a standard database program or on paper. From a "numbers" standpoint, this can be a simple or horrendously complex undertaking. It can be tempting for aggressive "computation excited" developers to try to do amazingly complex data models of economies, behaviors, attitudes, and the like, bringing the results of these computations to bear on the simulation for the player.

Commercially speaking, developers regularly run out of time and end up forcing rules into the code that sound like "A measure of dissatisfaction results when taxes outweigh services" or "A measure of dissatisfaction results when admission prices outweigh perceived value." I know this is very general, but these are the starting points for shaping rules that might guide or govern a simulation-based play experience.

Basically, it becomes a bunch of data table comparisons. Do visitors to your complex recognize that there aren't enough bathrooms or exciting rides? It becomes a table comparison, and I think you can see the idea behind it. That's exactly how you begin to build up your rule set. The rules cascade and have priority. You have your "driving" rules that are checked first in comparison, and then the rules that are peripheral or supplemental to the driving rules.

CREATING CINEMATICS

Game *cinematics* are simply movies created to enhance and help define the player experience. Creation of game cinematics is commonly handled in one of two ways: either a complete rendered movie sequence is compressed to an MPEG format and played back by incorporating a playback codec (encoder/decoder) into the game code, or the game engine itself is used to render and play back a movie cinematic.

In the first case, a video codec like DivX (www.divx.com) or Bink (www.radgametools.com) is built into the game engine to handle the playback of an MPEG movie. These movie or cinematic elements are created expressly for the game in a commercial 3-D package with add-ons, and since these are prerendered (versus real-time) they can take advantage of higher-resolution models, textures, and dazzling special effects. *Warcraft III* had some jaw-dropping cinematics of dazzling beauty created for the game, handled with the use of a video codec.

In the second case, a developer might choose to use the game engine itself to build cinematics. Game assets like character models and pre-existing or custom environments can be used directly in the game cinematics. They simply use the game engine that draws the game itself to draw the cinematics. Custom scripts are routinely used to "stage" the cinematics and control character and environmental details.

In either case, your cinematics (included in this general category are introductory movies, segue or transition movies, special-purpose or insert movies, and end movies) are used to tell the story elements behind your game, and to bring your player emotionally into the action by engaging the eyes and mind.

Cinematics are storyboarded with shot breakdowns (or shot contents) divided up into scenes. Storyboarding skills are an extremely helpful addition in the transition from written or verbal conceptual ideas into a visual story logic that makes sense to the player. It shouldn't be a surprise that considerable resources are required to produce complex cinematics. Here is another place where developers, in a frenzy of completely understandable excitement for their title, can simply over-commit. Before you know it, not only are you building a very complex game, you're rendering complete movie sequences. Like so many other areas in game design, it all sits in the balance.

DEVELOPING BACKSTORY

There is plenty of discussion among game developers about the role and status of story in making games. If you look at the games themselves for evidence, some genres seem to require almost no story at all. Is anyone really enthralled by the "story" behind his or her favorite shooter, simulation, or puzzler? I tend to doubt it.

On the other hand, other genres, like RPG or RTS games and many other action/adventure titles, employ story-telling elements to great effect. But I don't really want to create story demarcations based on genre (in other words, I'm not going to state that certain genres have great stories in their games and other genres do not). Is it possible to have gut-churning story elements wrapped inside an epic shooter? I'm not going to say that it's impossible.

I take a very pragmatic approach with story requirements and games. In my experience, it seems beneficial that game designers should be motivated students of story-telling techniques and story formatting. They should, at a minimum, understand the traditional dramatic story arc and how it works in practice: call to action, conflict, and resolution. If the story arc is unfamiliar to you, that's okay; fortunately, there is an abundance of great reference titles in this area.

Telling story and backstory in games is supposed to support and extend the game-play experience, not replace the movie industry. Where story heightens a player's enjoyment and feelings of liberation within a game, I say use it! To this end alone, every trick in the proverbial book should be used.

Games are, by definition and inclination, different from movies in a number of ways. These days, as we all know, there is mutual inspiration of sorts between games and movies. Yet game designers are not screenwriters, and screenwriters are not game designers.

Developing rich story lines, accessible story logic, and complex characters is no easy undertaking for screenwriters. Similarly, developing innovative, replayable, highly addictive and lasting play mechanics is not easy for game designers. So, on the point of telling story or backstory in game titles, game designers need to be able to provide solid and entertaining story support for their games. They don't need to compete with the Coen brothers or Steven Spielberg for their next job.

CREATING DIALOG

Creating dialog for games is a tricky, multivariable task. First of all, you should never write dialog until you have your story details locked down. How do the characters know what to say in telling a story if they don't yet know what story to tell? Remember that your story arc and story details should support, not compete with, your gaming experience. So, think about what kind of story adds dimensionality to that gaming experience as a possible source of influence for your story details.

Let's assume that you've managed to get the story details locked down. Among many development teams, this is an accomplishment in itself, as people react to story ideas in vastly different ways. It takes a strong personality to combine the many ideas coming from a team, to synthesize and process them, and then to make decisions and act on these ideas as a creative spur.

You will probably either have several kinds of dialog to write yourself or work with a contract professional writer, depending on budget and team style. Characters will provide voiceover narration to accompany intros, segues, mission endings, level endings, and game endings, and will sometimes make directional or guidance-oriented commentary. Characters might even teach the player to play the game.

The following are some more practical considerations for creating and using dialog:

▶ When you display dialog (and you still want the game playable with audio turned off or inaccessible), how will you present it to the player?

▶ Will the dialog need to be localized or translated for worldwide audiences? This can have a practical impact on interface design, because the symbols and lettering for certain languages require a minimum pixel dimension display space in order to be legible onscreen.

▶ For localization purposes, all language functionality should print to the screen (not be embedded or "drawn into" screen graphics or interface elements). This is done by planning for localization early in development so that your display system for languages can be switched in the game code.

It's important not to leave all the writing details on the floor to snowball at the end of the project. In fact, you really can't, because placeholder or "close to final" dialog will be required along the development path to gauge effectiveness and to help build up game details.

Like motion capture, planning to record dialog takes intensive preparation and planning. Again, you want to try to avoid needing massive redos. You may not get the chance! Depending on several production factors, you may be recording "audio as you go" through the process of building your game. In other cases, you might be recording 90 percent of all the in-game audio over a few intense days, or a single week.

Add to these constraints the fact that many games these days are built around licensed properties (like *Terminator 3* or a *Star Wars* related title). Characters from these well-known properties that appear in the game may require the voices of the actors who performed them in the movies or on TV. The amount of interest and participation for recording game dialog from these actors and/or studios can be very high or very low. I haven't found anybody in the middle yet. The demands on time for these actors can obviously be a critical factor as well. In short, unless you've done considerable planning and shown some good old-fashioned project foresight, you might very well miss the opportunity to get an actor to deliver the line that will put your game over the top.

Add to this bubbling stew the fact that actors may be recording other kinds of "promotional" work for other parties that day (in other words, your game dialog got jammed somewhere into an already overly aggressive recording schedule) and you may only have access to them for 30 minutes or an hour despite the fact that you were told you would have two hours. Planning is critical. You must often revise and assess recording priorities in an instant.

Based on your story specifics, as suggested earlier, dialog must already have been written before it's time to record it for the game. From a content perspective, you know the game inside and out as well or better than anyone. You know when, why, and where the characters will be required to say things in the game. It's up to you to try to get the "right" game-relevant performance out of a very tired (and guaranteed to be cranky) actor who may not like games, may not understand why exactly they are doing this, and may have never even played a game.

It's not always the case, though. You might get lucky and get an excited actor, or an actor who has fantastic ideas about delivering the game lines. Always have a build of the game in the recording studio with you to show the "context" for the line or dialog you are asking for. Bring along with you as much visual reference material as is possible and available. You will refer to every bit of it.

Quite rapidly, under these conditions, you will get better at learning how to coax a performance out of the actors. Sometimes you'll have help from an audio director or from some other party working with the actor or studio. At other times, you won't get much help at all. I've found that voice actors from casting agencies are wonderful. They work very hard to give you the best that they can, based on everything you've shown them about the character and context for delivery of a line in your game.

SUMMARY OF DESIGNER'S WORK TOOLS

In the following summary list, I've assembled for you some of my suggestions on the important game design software tools we've discussed up to this point. These suggestions can be used across many game genres. Keep in mind that the application of these tools varies widely as you move around the industry from developer to developer, but in some form or another, everyone seems to use the following:

- A 3-D package (such as Maya, 3ds max, Lightwave, Mirai)

- Microsoft Visio (for flowcharting, screen logic, and topographic mapping)

- Photoshop (for basic texturing and various other applications)

- An HTML editor (for building your design and production documents)

- A BSP editor (stand-alone editors like the Unreal or Radiant series)

- Scripting language (Python, Visual Basic, proprietary)

CASE STUDY COMMENTS ON DESIGN FLUX

Since we have surveyed several design factors in this chapter, it seems appropriate to say something about the "design flux" process. Design flux refers to the shifting demands made on game developers for critical design changes (even complete changes in game genre direction) that are regularly based on the hot sales of recent successful titles or simple trend chasing.

Most commonly these days, when a publisher decides to pay for a game to be developed, they have a license for it in mind. Licenses for the publisher have the advantage of immediate perceived audience recognition. We all know about *SpongeBob SquarePants*. The thinking behind this is simple. If people already love *SpongeBob*, they'll probably buy a game based on *SpongeBob*. Of course, we know that this isn't always the case.

If people don't know anything about our great new title, and we can't spend the kind of money it would take to inform the public about our great new title via very expensive advertising, then, well, let's make more titles about *SpongeBob*.

Think about the number of original titles that come out now versus the number of licensed titles and you'll see which direction we're headed. Whether you're working on an original title or a licensed one, however, you won't be immune from design flux.

In the current game-publishing environment, your development studio will almost undoubtedly be asked to complete a rather sophisticated proof of concept (POC) to demonstrate what you would build if given a particular license (such as *SpongeBob SquarePants*) or, in the case of an original title, to show exactly how your original title works as a game. This requires plenty of costly exploratory work.

Typically, via the POC, a development team presents its ideas on what kind of game to make. This will regularly go through much iteration. At some point, maybe, a decision will be made about which game direction to pursue, and a development agreement between developer and publisher will be executed. Now it becomes the developer's responsibility to deliver the game discussed as promised.

Development begins on the game, but here's the catch: to stay competitive, game publishers respond to trends in game sales. What started out as a particular design direction (let's say a top-down action game) can easily become something else in response to a certain growing or peaking game sales trend. As a developer, this can require a complete redesign and it can require a whole new technology approach. The sands of game development shift quickly.

How does this process affect game developers? Well, game developers must always be prepared for sudden change. This is why a certain familiarity, understanding, and love for as many genres as possible is a requirement. Whereas you may have been working on an RPG yesterday, today you may be working on more of a third-person action game. Yet, even this scenario is changing, as developers are becoming more and more genre-focused. Part of this is due to game scope and complexity. Once you build technologies that support RTS creation, it's easier and more powerful to focus on RTS titles. Can you really do "everything" well in a fiercely competitive industry? Probably not.

Game titles are "grown" into life by developers and often change directions entirely along the way. Sometimes, after two or three directions, the title is ultimately cancelled and your 16 months of work is packaged up for delivery into storage.

Staying competitive in game development requires the ability to react quickly and remain available to constant change.

INTERVIEW WITH AARON ODLAND

Aaron Odland has produced game and web entertainment content based on many familiar licensed properties for Disney Channel and Disney Online. He earned a B.S. in radio, TV, film from Northwestern University and subsequently found work with Jellyvision, the Chicago-based creators of the "You Don't Know Jack" series of games. He is currently pursuing an interest in landscape architecture and swears that this isn't as disconnected from game development as it sounds.

TM: What is the primary difference between working on games you enjoy playing and building games for a wide web audience?

AO: I have found that when I play games on the PC, I have certain expectations about the quality of sound, graphics, controls, etc. based on the platform. The same is true for my expectations when playing a console game or when playing an old arcade game. The expectations are always different. The problem I have found with online content is that I'm usually playing on a PC platform where I have these high production-value expectations, and current data connections don't really allow for most server-delivered, web-based game content to meet those expectations. So, we're sent back to the days of 8-bit Nintendo on the same PC that is allowing us to play Unreal II.

TM: How do you orient game design for a wide audience made up primarily of younger players?

AO: You can't really clump all younger players into the same group when talking about game design. Preschoolers are quite different than preteens. I think you need to pick a specific age range when developing a game and focus on making the best piece of content for that group.

TM: What are some of the challenges you faced in working with licensed content?

AO: In some ways, I have found that working with licensed characters works very well for the short production timeframe that is characteristic of most online games that I have contributed to. You don't have to spend time on character design, and that certainly helps move things along. Of course, when working with third-party developers, there is time required to educate them about the property so they can understand it better. I have also found that working with licensed content involving real actors can present more challenges than working with animated characters.

Image approval is generally required, and the task of getting unique, new images for a piece of web content often seems out of the question due to budget and time concerns. So, the challenge becomes hunting down alternative sources of images, audio clips, etc. that might be able to suit your needs.

TM: How do you capture and grow an audience for delivery of games via the Web?

AO: I think that people constantly strive for recognition of their success or the success of things that they have created, and the online community really provides you with an opportunity to work this feedback into your games. High scoreboards certainly provide a basic form of this, but I am more intrigued by providing players with tools to build levels, create character texture maps, etc. The Internet provides a lot of collective time and energy, and if you can get it on the side of your product, I think that can be very powerful.

TM: What restrictions do you face in building games for a younger audience?

AO: Parents don't like their kids talking with strangers, but the Internet is a great tool for communication. So, how do you allow players to communicate without telling too much? This issue becomes particularly frustrating when you're dealing with preteens who are constantly using Instant Messenger and e-mailing, but then you often can't allow them to have the same interaction in your games.

As for this question in relation to games as a whole, I think a lot of the "restrictions" that people think of as necessary for games for kids are things that really should apply to all design. You shouldn't make the keyboard controls simple and intuitive just because the game is for kids who might have problems with the complexity; you should make them simple and intuitive because that will make for better gameplay for all groups.

TM: What do you like the most and the least about building web-oriented game content?

AO: One of the things that I like most about building web-oriented game content is that it's still something that can be done by creative individuals without the backing of some huge game publisher and distributor. Some of my favorite, small-scale games online have been completely crafted by a single person and provided to people around the world to play for free.

The short timeframe of online games also allows you to work on quite a variety of content without as much pressure based on time or budget. A downside of these short cycles is that you don't always have much time to invest in brainstorming new types of games, so a lot of what I have seen produced is very derivative.

TM: What would you say is the future of large-scale web gaming?

AO: I think that web gaming as a component of purchased CD-ROMs will continue to grow as you get mainstream examples like The Sims Online. As for server-delivered games, I think the future of that is harder to predict.

I'm not sure what the future of online entertainment in general holds. While completely online subscription services such as fantasy league sports teams have been successful, I don't know what new business models will arise to provide for outlet opportunities for more games.

TM: How does your background in radio, TV, film contribute to your work approach?

AO: One thing that was always stressed to me in my production classes was that the time you spend in preproduction will save you a great deal more time during actual production. So, I've tried to take that to heart and be sure to develop flow diagrams, use case studies and other guidelines that not only help me consider possible failure points but also make me think more in depth about the game experience as well as be able to better communicate to engineers and artists the creative and technical details of the game.

TM: What advice would you give to those interested in pursuing any form of game development?

AO: If you want to pursue game development, I would recommend that you spend some time analyzing your interest in the field and try and develop specific goals that you can work towards. This sort of focus will help you sell yourself to others as you look for a job, if that's the path you take.

TM: What three design features do you focus on as "critical" points of content evaluation?

AO: User interface, gameplay mechanics, and replay ability. I think basic user interface is often in danger of getting overlooked in game production. Thoughtful GUI design, menu designs, etc. can really help add to the depth of the game experience, as these are elements that the user is constantly interacting with.

Of course, if the game isn't fun to play, then you can have the best interface in the world and it doesn't matter.

And if your game doesn't provide something to bring players back to play again, then it's not going to have a long life.

TM: What near-future aspects of gaming excite you?

AO: I think the continued growth of online game communities is exciting. Even though AI keeps advancing, there's something cooler about playing a strat-sim game online against real people in different parts of the world.

TM: What advice do you have for others interested in game design?

AO: Find the specifics of what interests you in game design and pursue that. Study games you like and dislike, analyzing that specific area.

TM: What current games on any platform interest you?

AO: I'm excited about the community that's developing around the online version of Neverwinter Nights. Granted, you started here with a strong Dungeons & Dragons fan base, but I think it's great that Bioware created the tools to allow the fans to shape their own game experiences and create their own worlds.

TM: How do you measure whether a gameplay mechanic "works"?

AO: I guess the success of a gameplay mechanic is ultimately subjective. You could always improve everything, and as deadlines approach, sometimes you just have to ask "is it good enough?"

TM: What are your goals in gaming at this point?

AO: I've recently been pursuing an interest in landscape architecture, and this has got me thinking quite a bit about how this relates to creating game environments. I think there's a lot to learn from that design field as well as from architecture and urban planning.

Conversely, a lot of those fields have been using game tools to further their development of spaces and structures for the real world. It's an interesting relationship.

TM: What game industry trends disturb you?

AO: The consolidation of publishers and distributors in the game industry disturbs me, although this is certainly not a trend unique to the industry. I am also dismayed by the proliferation of game sequels.

There doesn't seem to be much support these days for independent, original games. I hope this will change in the future.

TM: What is the ultimate communal form of gaming in your opinion?

AO: I don't know that I have a single idea of this in mind. Watching groups of people play Sambe de Amigo and Dance Dance Revolution is fascinating and entertaining, and that's sort of communal and attracts nongamers as well.

A friend of mine had a virtual Labor Day barbeque with his playing group in Everquest, and that ranks pretty high up on the list of ultimate communal forms of gaming.

TM: What do good games accomplish?

AO: Good games tell a story, draw you into a world surrounding that story, and allow you to help shape that story and world.

TM: What three pieces of advice would you give to someone starting in games?

AO: Play lots of games. Hunt through bargain bins and play those cheap games as well as the new titles you would normally pick up. They'll all teach you something.

If you can, make lots of games.

Keep a sketchbook and try and draw everyday, even if you don't think you can draw.

Games are a visual design medium, and this will help you start interpreting the visual world around you as well as expressing the one trapped in your mind.

TM: What is your favorite memory working in games so far?

AO: My favorite memory working in games so far has been hearing crazy stories about the earlier days of console development, like when a Chuck E. Cheese repairman could get hired as a game engineer. I also have fond memories of after-hour network gaming.

TM: Aaron, thanks for your help!

MEGA TIPS

1. Focus your efforts on understanding a couple of genres deeply, while continuing to build your understanding of all the major genres.

2. Play genres you don't particularly like. Try to identify both why you don't like them and what would help make you like them more. Remember, there is a big difference between playing games for entertainment and being paid to build them.

3. Very important: As you play games, keep a design notes and interface journal with notes, examples, drawings, ideas, questions, and comparisons.

4. Once you've isolated some of your genre interests, study topics related to that genre. Pose questions to yourself. For sports, study player motion and sports history. Identify how fans respond to different physical sports. What are the most dramatic moments in each style of sport? How do these insights transfer into electronic sports games? How do you transfer sports excitement into gameplay? If you love RPGs, study character construction, character-based communities, and character hooks and details. Notice how people react in different ways to a character's visual construction. How do you try to operate these reactions? Can you predict them? Here's the point: no matter what the genre, it's often the related studies that bring force and dimension to your design ideas.

5. Utilize the game community. Interview players around you in every genre. Talk to all your friends. Try to determine why they like certain genres that you may not. Listen carefully to the feedback coming your way. Don't ask only to ignore the answers based on your own genre preferences. If you listen, you will start to hear common aggravations. When given the chance, try to fix these aggravating aspects in your own games.

6. Get way "outside" the game community to bring fresh design ideas back to it. Study widely and generally: archaeology, world history, industrial design, figure drawing, set design, lighting design, character design, vehicle design, landscape design, transportation design. Get away from gamers to bring something back to them. Remember, you are often asked to be a specialized generalist.

CHAPTER **6**

Scripting
Action
Events

SCRIPTING

SCRIPTING in games gives developers a pathway right into the control of many critical aspects of gameplay functionality, some of which are small and barely perceptible, while others are rather large and looming. At this point in the book, you're becoming familiar with the process of building up a polygonal game environment (for example, by using geometric primitives like planes, spheres, cones, and cylinders, and by "adding and subtracting" or merging these primitives together to form entirely new shapes) by introducing characters, props, and items. Now we're going to turn our attention to learning something about how to control each of these scripts for the purposes of building up gameplay.

Many kinds of behaviors can be controlled by a script system. Script systems in total are largely proprietary and currently vary greatly in approach among game developers. Many game engines provide scripting languages that let you program complex behaviors into your game. For instance, a monster might travel from the barn to the farmhouse to the silo and back over and over again, but walk toward the player if it sees him, run toward the player if the player is bleeding, and run away from the player and toward the silo if the player has a weapon. As today's games go, this is a moderately complex behavior, and it would be tedious to encode this behavior directly in C++. Scripting languages make it possible to "script" these actions so that you can focus on the behavior rather than the programming.

Here's a quick example of this behavior scenario:

```
behavior monster;
if (monster->idle) {
  monster->walk(barn);
  monster->walk(farmhouse);
  monster->walk(silo);
}elsif (monster->sees(player)) {
  if (player->bleeding) {
    monster->run(player);
  } elsif (player->has_weapon) {
    monster->run(silo);
  } else { monster->walk(player) }
}
```

In a nonprogrammatic scripting environment, sometimes the script system simply generates a file with values (velocity = 44.6) that you can edit for effect, and this file is then read into the game engine to control some behavioral aspects.

In many cases, the scripting system you use is built to interface with your game engine. It may have a full graphic user interface (GUI) like a standard familiar Windows program, or it may be some flavor of a simple text editor that allows you to edit values, rebuild, and then test the results of your changes and edits.

In this chapter, we're going to take a close look at how to use script systems to build a wide array of behavior types into a game. We'll also consider another powerful and primary scripting resource, the use of triggers!

SCRIPTING TECHNOLOGY CHOICES

As in many other areas of game development, today developers have several choices to make when choosing how they will handle scripting in their games. In the recent past, the practice of "scripting" game behaviors wasn't very common at all. Any direct change to gameplay, of any kind, had to be coded into the game directly by programmers. Scripting helps developers "dial in" and experiment with game behaviors (for example, a certain weapon's firing speed and range of effect, or vehicle and character traversal properties like friction, gravity, and pitch) more efficiently. Yet, we still have a very long way to go in being able to build complex behaviors quickly.

Nowadays, programmers face a considerable and constant challenge in keeping game engines fresh and powerful with technology and tools for a variety of ever-changing hardware platforms and devices. Programmers ultimately determine how much control and influence a scripting system will have on a game. Typically, game programmers collaborate with designers to build as much "power editing" as they can into a given script system. The goal is to have a scripting system that is so powerful and flexible that it can produce a wide array of possible gameplay results. This means that during development, game behaviors for your title can react to player feedback and focus dynamically. You can quickly answer "play-feel" questions like "What if we speed up the rocket boots, decrease gravity, and cut back the rate of fire?"

At the level of competition in the current game market, developers know that only the best-playing or best-performing content will probably succeed. It has become apparent to many developers that having team members focused exclusively on building and monitoring gameplay content via scripting tools can help shape a much stronger game title.

As the language of choice for scripting, some developers choose to use Visual Basic (http://msdn.microsoft.com/vbasic/), Python (www.python.org), or JavaScript/JScript (www.ngweb.biz/software/djsedit.shtml), while others build custom script systems into a complete stand-alone tool. In the latter case, right-clicking an actor in a scene might bring up a series of "property" editing tabs that can be used to specify a number of details for selected actors. Some examples of these properties include

❭ Actor's patrol speed (How fast does the actor move in protecting a boundary?)

❭ Actor's patrol shape (Does the actor walk a box perimeter, a semicircle, or a custom shape?)

❭ Actor's hostility towards other actor types (Friend or foe? Attack or defend?)

❭ Actor's default offensive weapon choice (Laser fire? Space baton?)

❭ Actor's default defense (Use shield, roll into a ball, or self-destruct?)

❭ Actor's default wait-state (Tap foot, sit down, or rub eyes?)

❭ Actor's inventory specifics (Order of item use? Weapon priority?)

❭ Actor's response to attack (Fight till death, fight till damage = 80 percent, or fight till out of ammo?)

❭ Actor's specialized orders (Seek another actor, seek map position, seek level midpoint, seek ammo cache, return to camp, band together with closest similar actor, play cards/dice [or other humor element], summon help, cloak or hide, shadow or follow another actor, chase distraction, search for something until the search condition is met?)

The properties listed here, as examples, as well as a vast number of other actor properties might be similarly editable in this fashion. You will often need tools programming support from a tools programmer to set up each of the properties you wish to edit, since ultimately your edits need to be reflected in the code when the game is recompiled or rebuilt.

To provide you with a sample of what different scripting languages look like, this section translates a simple monster behavior script into JavaScript, Visual Basic, Python, and Perl. Throughout this chapter, I'll show scripts in JavaScript most of the time, because it's a well-supported scripting language with editors freely available, but Visual Basic and Python are also gaining in popularity.

This script calls for the monster to attack the player if it sees the player, to pick up a weapon if it sees the weapon, and otherwise to simply patrol.

JavaScript Sample

```javascript
function moveMonster() {
    if(monster.canSeePlayer()) {
        monster.attack();
} else if(monster.canSeeWeapon()) {
        monster.pickupWeapon();
} else {
        monster.patrol();
}
}
```

Figure 6-1 shows what this script looks like inside an editor.

Visual Basic Sample

```vb
Sub moveMonster()
    If monster.canSeePlayer() Then
        monster.attack()
    ElseIf monster.canSeeWeapon() Then
        monster.pickupWeapon()
Else
        monster.patrol()
End If
End Sub
```

FIGURE 6-1

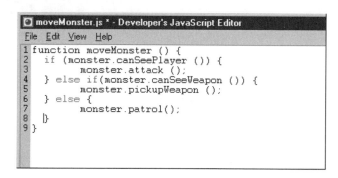

JavaScript sample view in editor

Python Sample

```python
def moveMonster():
    if monster.canSeePlayer():
        monster.attack()
    elif monster.canSeeWeapon():
        monster.pickupWeapon()
    else:
        monster.patrol()
```

Perl Sample

```perl
sub moveMonster {
    if( monster->canSeePlayer() ) {
        monster->attack();
    } elsif ( monster->canSeeWeapon() ) {
        monster->pickupWeapon();
    } else {
        monster->patrol();
    }
}
```

APPLIED SCRIPTING EXAMPLES

One of the best ways to demonstrate the power of scripting is to cover several common cases in which scripts are used in games to control behavior. Scripts can be used to control many kinds of custom events, so this is not by any means an exhaustive sampling of every possible script-based control. Script-based controls are custom- and user-defined. This is where collaboration with a tools or engine technology programmer or team is so very important. Both sides (programmer and scripter) need to agree on which behavior aspects make for the most powerful kinds of gameplay edits. The samples that follow should give you a solid idea of how you might use scripts to control different types of game behaviors.

NPC Conversation Templates

NPCs populate many game worlds and are used in a variety of ways. You might want to control how an NPC handles conversation with a player's character. Let's assume that actor_21 is a cave guard (a beast protecting the entrance to a cave). We want this cave guard actor to simply pass along three clues or pieces of information to the player about what's inside the cave. A script might look like this:

```
If (cave_guard.isDisturbed()) {
    playMessage(text1.txt);
    waitForUser();
    playMessage(text2.txt);
    waitForUser();
    playMessage(text3.txt);
    waitForUser();
}
```

In this example, the cave guard is disturbed and gives messages to the player, while waiting for the player to acknowledge receipt of the given messages. If the player came back to try to talk to the cave guard again after seeing the first three messages, you might want the cave guard to give random responses this time. You could do this by simply extending your script so that any contact after the first or initial contact would give random responses loaded into a file for playback to the player.

Shooter Flying Patterns

For arcade-style shooting games, enemies often attack in different formations, speeds, and flying patterns. These kinds of behaviors can be edited via a script system as well. Let's look at an example.

Suppose you're building a shooter. Enemies might simply attack from the far right and move toward the left of the screen. This is the formula for almost every classic side-scrolling shooter. Maybe we want to control the behaviors of those enemy attack formations. Here's where I hope we all paid attention in math class! D'oh! Games are pure math in motion. How does all of this amazing and brilliant 3-D manipulation happen? It's solid math, toes to top hats.

Scripting has become a very important part of the designer's role on a development team, so knowing (at the very least) some basic programming and math is extremely helpful here. If your basic programming skills are rusty or nonexistent, download a free version of a JavaScript editor at (www.ngweb.biz/software/djsedit.shtml) and start experimenting.

Here's a simple script for defining the attack behavior of an enemy actor (for example, a Martian horde or evil flying donut) called enemyactor:

```
function moveEnemy() {
    enemyactor.moveLeft();
    // Scale sine wave by 100 and add 240 to center
    // on a 640x480 screen
    var x = enemyactor.getX()%360;
    enemyactor.setY(100*sin(x*4)+240);
}
```

FIGURE 6-2

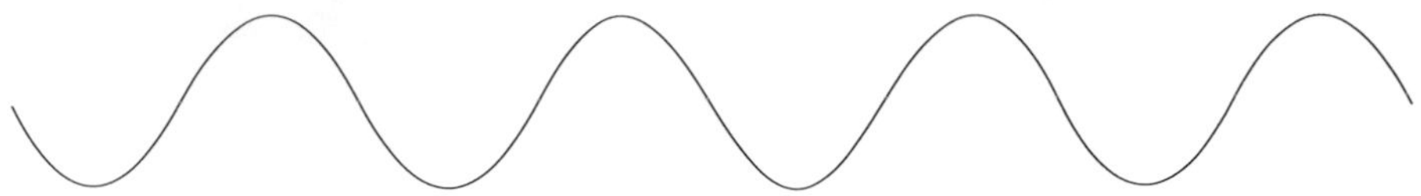

Simple sine wave attack

Figure 6-2 shows the shape of the resulting attack pattern for enemyactor as a standard sine wave.

All right, so enemyactor follows the sine wave path. Well that's okay for one attack pattern (I think we've seen it before), but we want to build many others. In a very simple shooter, we would probably want at least one unique attack pattern for each game level. Maybe we want a big lazy sloping attack pattern. We can start to build one by tweaking the sine wave values.

Here's a practical point: Plenty of scripting work involves just tweaking or editing variables, saving, and rebuilding. Sometimes you will spend days just working on many tweaked script versions for a range of behaviors. In some cases, you won't even be writing the scripts or "line commands" as we're looking at them here; you may just tweak values to get an intended effect.

Now, let's change the amplitude of the sine wave to create a different attack pattern. This example should help demonstrate the idea that shaping many behaviors, like this simple attack behavior, is often a matter of starting to tweak values:

```
// Alter sine wave attack for enemyactor by modulating amplitude
function moveEnemy() {
    enemyactor.moveLeft();
    // Modulate sine wave amplitude by another sine wave
    var x = enemyactor.getX()%360;
    enemyactor.setY((50*sin(x)+50) * sin(x*4) + 240);
}
```

Figure 6-3 shows the result of adjusting the attack pattern by modulating amplitude.

Now our enemyactor has a tweaked attack pattern. As you can see, we could make many other attack patterns by simply changing values and playing around with numbers. We might create even more types of attack patterns by altering the frequency of the sine wave.

FIGURE 6-3

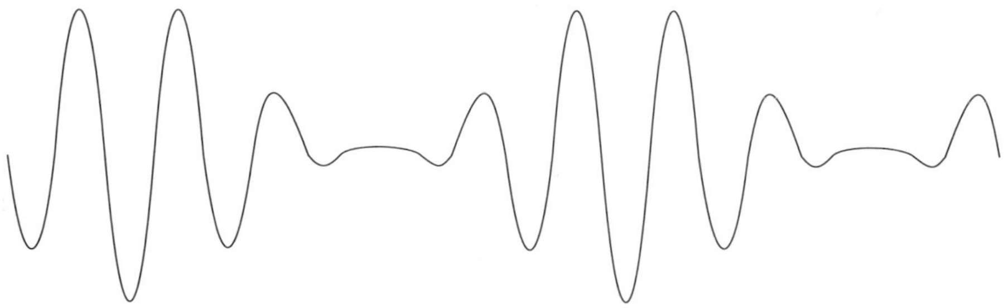

Amplitude-modulated sine attack

Here's an example of modulating the frequency to change the attack pattern:

```
// Alter sine wave attack for enemyactor by modulating frequency
function moveEnemy() {
    enemyactor.moveLeft();
    // Modulate sine wave frequency by another sine wave
    var x = enemyactor.getX%360;
    enemyactor.setY(100 * sin(x * (2*sin(x)+3) ) + 240);
}
```

Figure 6-4 shows the modified attack pattern with the frequency shifted or modulated.

FIGURE 6-4

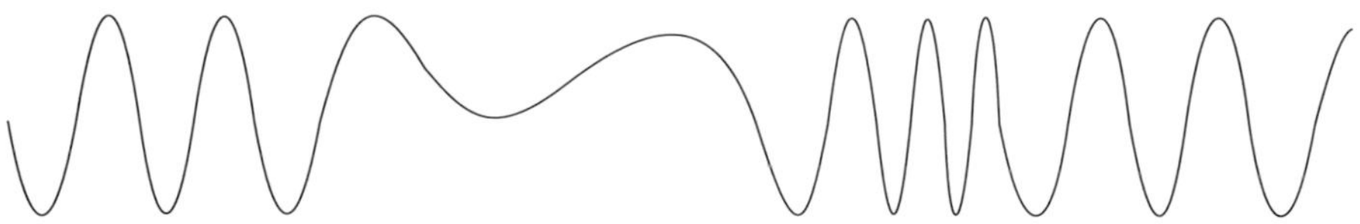

Frequency-modulated sine attack

USING TRIGGERS

As we've seen, some behaviors are handled with scripts built in JavaScript/JScript, Python, Visual Basic, or another proprietary language. Increasingly, however, to complement simple script systems, complex trigger systems are used. A *trigger* is simply a switch that can cause an event, or series of events, to occur when tripped. This is sometimes called *event handling*.

Building up and using complex trigger systems has a couple of practical advantages. First, value and parameter editors to control trigger properties can be built into Windows-based editors (GUI-based editors) quite easily. Second, designers and artists rarely have more than basic programming abilities (if any), so the property-editing nature and workflow of setting up trigger behavior is much easier for the nonprogrammer.

The most powerful world-editing systems combine trigger functionality with line-item scripting (like the shooter behaviors using a sine wave). Triggers are usually placed in a scene and represented by icons in a 3-D scene within an editor. They are completely invisible to the player. Triggers can be used in a number of interesting ways to build up game behaviors.

In most world-editing software, trigger properties can be set up to include several types of associated information. These include

- ❯ True and false modes (to set the logical state or condition of the trigger)

- ❯ Value fields (to enter radius, distance, strength, and offset information)

- ❯ Text fields (to print a message to the screen for a player, or for testing purposes)

- ❯ File pointers (to point to a file resource as part of a trigger event)

Let's look at a quick example from the very popular UnrealEd (version 3.0) showing the power of this kind of trigger-based editing. In many games, when an actor is shot by a weapon, we frequently want to launch a resulting behavior of some kind. For a *shoot* trigger, a trigger that trips when it has been shot by a projectile weapon, we want to launch a behavior—maybe a further scripted event—or maybe we want to display a simple text message.

Figure 6-5 shows that for an assigned shoot trigger type (TT_Shoot), when the trigger is tripped, a text message will be displayed: "Ouch, you shot me!"

This is a simple example to be sure, but it reveals the power of having a field-edited trigger system at your disposal for shaping actor-based behaviors. Many game developers create similar systems to enable trigger-based behavior editing.

It's important to remember that triggers can be edited in a field-edited GUI-type tool (like the UnrealEd example), edited directly in the script code, or edited in both.

FIGURE 6-5

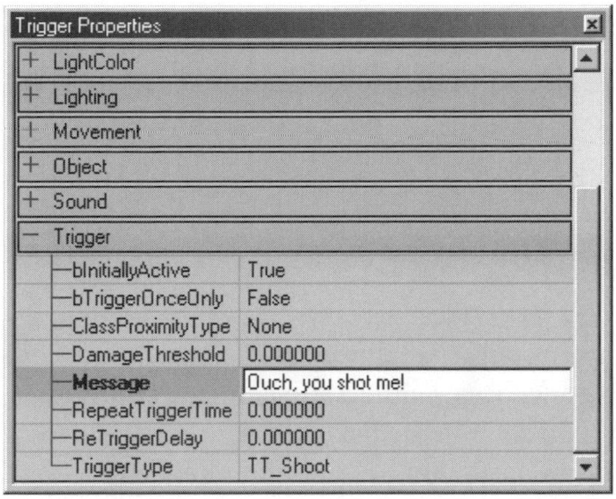

Trigger Properties	
+ LightColor	
+ Lighting	
+ Movement	
+ Object	
+ Sound	
− Trigger	
—bInitiallyActive	True
—bTriggerOnceOnly	False
—ClassProximityType	None
—DamageThreshold	0.000000
Message	Ouch, you shot me!
—RepeatTriggerTime	0.000000
—ReTriggerDelay	0.000000
—TriggerType	TT_Shoot

Display message using a trigger

Now, let's take a look at a selection of common trigger types. Again, trigger types can be built or custom-defined for your own gameplay purposes.

Fearthis

A "fearthis" trigger can be used to create "suction spots" where enemies fear to tread. You might use a "fearthis" trigger next to a large idol on your map—an idol of a hostile deity that causes fear in the heart of your enemy. This kind of trigger can be radius-driven so that enemies will not come any closer to the idol than defined by the "fearthis" radius properties (for example, within a 12-world-unit radius). For gameplay, these areas can be used as a safe spot or a recharge point for the player's character. Fighting might take place in spades outside the vicinity of such an idol with a "fearthis" trigger.

Players can take cover near the idol and use it as a free zone since some enemies (those set to respond to "fearthis") will not enter the "fearthis" radius. You might use this trigger with a command-line script (like the previous sine wave attack example) to play a "fear or cower" animation when enemies reach the "fearthis" trigger boundary or radius. The behavior result is that when these enemies encounter the trigger while chasing you, they begin to cower (cover their face with their arms, afraid to even see this idol) and flee (as one possible example).

Here's a script sample to make the enemies cower in fear and then flee once they have tripped the "fearthis" trigger:

```javascript
// JavaScript sample of "fearthis" trigger support
if(monster.inside(fearThisTrigger.getBoundary())) {
    monster.playAnimation(fearAnim);
    monster.reverseDirection();
}
```

Line of Sight

Line of sight has a couple of different uses and meanings in game terminology. Usually, it refers to what is visible to an actor. It could refer to what is visible to the particular actor representing the player in the game. Normally, it refers to whether or not an actor can see a particular object or another actor. Line of sight can be calculated in several ways, and doesn't always mean that something is physically viewable from a character's perspective. Enough semantics.

A line of sight trigger launches its event when a player breaks the line of sight radius; in other words, when the player gets physically close enough on the grid to the line of sight trigger. This can be used to start a giant boulder rolling perilously into motion (think of *Raiders of the Lost Ark/Indiana Jones*). When a character breaks the line of sight trigger, the boulder-rolling animation is launched on a motion path (in other words, where the boulder starts rolling from, what path it follows, and where it is destroyed or terminates).

Notice that many triggers rely on a radius. Much of tuning the right "feel" for the interaction between events comes down to tuning radii.

If the boulder is visible to a player, here's a script that starts the boulder rolling and focuses a camera on the action:

```javascript
// JavaScript sample of "line of sight" trigger support
if(objectVisible(player.currentPosition(), boulder)) {
    boulder.startRolling();
    playSound(boulderSound);
    camera.focus(boulder);
}
```

Crowd

A crowd trigger, when tripped, gives animation behavior information to a crowd of actors. For instance, you might have entered a tribal village with several warriors lined up at the village gateway to meet you. By picking up or attempting to steal something from the village, you might trip a crowd trigger. This might cause all of those warriors, who initially greeted you, to seek to your position on the map in a killing mood. The crowd trigger changes the warriors from a greeting state to a search-for-player attack state.

You can also use a crowd trigger less aggressively. A player might break a crowd trigger that causes warriors seated in a circle at their drums to start playing them. In this case, the crowd trigger simply tells the warrior actors to change from their seated-at-drum animation state to their playing-the-drums animation state. The crowd trigger also triggers an audio trigger (the warrior's drum sounds).

Many triggers "cascade" like this. A crowd trigger triggers an animation and audio trigger, which might trigger a particle event (for example, the fire starts to grow as the warrior drummers play their drum music).

Here's a sample script for controlling a given number of warriors, making them aware that the player has taken a sacred object from their village, and making them seek out the player in a killing mood:

```
// JavaScript sample of "crowd" trigger support
if(player.pickedUp(sacredObject)) {
    for(var n=0;n<numWarriors;n++) {
        warrior[n].seek(player);
        warrior[n].setState(HUNTING_STATE);
    }
}
```

Weather Effects

If your game doesn't have a dynamic weather system built in (a system to randomize and replicate weather patterns), then you might want to control the weather using a weather effects trigger. Maybe after a mission briefing, as the player sets out on a new quest, you would like to add some rain and/or fog. This can be accomplished with a weather effects trigger.

When this trigger is tripped, rain might begin to fall in easily editable regions of your map. Simple world position units can define any region on your map. You might even be able to determine the strength, size, and direction of the rain! You can set fog parameters in a similar way by region. However, these kinds of effects must be used sparingly, since they are computation-heavy like other particle system effects.

Here is a script sample for controlling, once the mission briefing is complete, two regions of rain at different strengths:

```
// JavaScript sample of "weather" trigger support
if(player.finishedBriefing()) {
    // Make "region1" rain lightly at level "20"
    weatherSystem.startRain(region1, 20);
```

```
        // Make "region2" rain more heavily at level "50"
        weatherSystem.startRain(region2, 50);
    }
```

Counter

A counter trigger simply counts down a number of time units and then launches its event. The amount of time the counter trigger waits to launch an event is set in its properties. This allows you to play with timing. How long should you give players to flee? How long until the next event? So, if a player trips a counter trigger, they might have a ten-second head start before a gigantic robotic spider is loosed into the level after them. You'll also want to tune the attack speed and attack properties of the spider to give the players a chance.

You might use a counter trigger on one side of the map to launch a counter trigger on the other side of the map. This allows for a "popcorn popping" effect as counter triggers launch their events across a map. These are very useful for action games and environmental shooters.

This script sample shows how you might warn the player that they have invaded the robotic spider's nesting point, give the player a chance to flee, and then set the spider hunting after the player:

```
// JavaScript sample of "counter" trigger support
if(player.intersects(spider.getBoundary())) {
    alertUser(spiderWarningText);
    waitSeconds(10);
    spider.startHunting();
}
```

Material

A material trigger, when tripped by a player location trigger (remember the "popcorn" effect), changes texture information in a scene. For instance, a player may have tripped a location trigger that causes an ice crystal formation to rise out of the ground covered by a dusty particle effect. As the ice crystals rise, light triggers are tripped and the light in the room intensifies (for dramatic and visual bang!).

Wouldn't it be nice to have the wall textures or wall materials somehow account for all the light bouncing off these cool ice crystals? Well, you could make an animated "light reflection" version of the wall texture and display it when the material trigger is tripped. Now, as the ice crystals rise, the animated light reflections on your custom wall texture or material are displayed! Very cool. If no new "material" information is given to the material trigger, it commonly does nothing. It doesn't know what to do if it doesn't have new material information.

This simple script replaces material information for the rising ice crystals:

```
// JavaScript sample of "material" trigger support
if(iceCrystal.rising()) {
    iceCrystal.setTexture(animatedLightTexture);
}
```

Audio

Audio triggers cover all audio events. If an audio trigger is tripped, it might cause the audio to change from ambient to "fight scene" music. It might simply start a new ambient audio event (like water-dripping echoes in a cave). It might cause some voice-over narration. It might cause a specialized "one off" sound, like a customized explosion with the last words of a dying character mumbled at a distance.

This script sample sets the background music to a fighting soundtrack when a fight breaks out:

```
// JavaScript sample of "audio" trigger support
if(player.startedFighting()) {
    audioSystem.setBackgroundMusic(fightingTrack);
}
```

Message

A message trigger can be used to print a message directly to the player, deliver a message to the player's interface system, or prompt an NPC event. Message triggers can also be used to print up messages for testing purposes to notify the player/tester about the state of something in the map.

Here's a sample message script for printing a bonus level message:

```
// JavaScript sample of "message" trigger support
if(player.hasEntered(bonusArea1)) {
messageSystem.prompt(bonusLevelMessage);
}
```

Light

Light triggers are used to create custom-lighting situations. Maybe we want to try to show visually an "end of time" scenario, as if day after day of sunlight is passing in the outside garden from our perspective inside a vast palace. We can do this with a light trigger that launches a repeating light-track animation simulating the position change of the sun in the sky.

Even simpler, we might just want to cause a couple of shafts of light to stream into a room onto a relic, a magical sword, or a hero helper character. We can also use a light trigger to build this behavior.

This sample shows how to create a spotlight on the hero helper when a player is near them:

```javascript
// JavaScript sample of "light" trigger support
if(player.nearHeroHelper()) {
    createSpotlight(heroHelper);
}
```

BUILDING BEHAVIORS

You've now seen some basic script examples and experienced some of the power in using triggers. Building behaviors often requires using a measure of both. It's important that you learn enough about scripting and triggers to combine their power together into building behaviors. Let's look at another example that demonstrates how you would use trigger information to control entire groups of creatures.

Creature Creator

Sometimes you will want to use triggers to control the behavior of prop creatures for pure visual effect. These might include insect swarms, flocks of birds, or schools of fish. Depending on your script system specifics, sometimes you will use command-line entries (like the sine wave attack pattern), and other times you will simply set properties in a tool—properties that define how your trigger is going to behave.

So, suppose we set down a trigger of the type creature_creator. The kinds of properties we might edit for its behavior include (but are not limited to) the following:

❱ The maximum number of creatures generated (let's say, 10)

❱ Which type of creature will spawn? (We might have 15 choices here, bug_1, bug_2, fish_1, fish_2, and so forth. Sometimes we can even spawn the same trigger with two or more types—like two different kinds of bugs coming from the same hive. We might "hide" the trigger inside a hive actor in the scene.)

❱ What is the spawn radius, in units? (How far around the trigger will these creatures spawn?)

❱ What is the spawning rate or speed? (How fast will these creatures spawn?)

❱ What is the spawn life? (How long do these creatures "live" on the screen before they die off or disappear?)

❭ What is the trigger radius? (How far from the trigger will the player be when the trigger begins to spawn these creatures?)

❭ What fields affect the spawns? (Are they repelled or attracted by the trigger? Do they dissipate away from the trigger randomly using a noise pattern? Do they disperse quickly as if searching for something and then return?)

❭ What is the spawn's motion path on birth? (Insects might fly, dart, and hover; birds could fly and flock together; fish might school together and cruise—here's where we might use a command line to point the spawn to a behavior path or curve that will define their behavior over time. Usually, at its heart, the motion path is a linear or trigonometric mathematical function.)

ENGINE SOLUTIONS AND THE UNREAL ENGINE

The Unreal game engine (www.epicgames.com) is a standout technology solution of choice for many game developers who build their own content based on Unreal technology. Choosing this development path has both advantages and disadvantages for developers. If a game developer uses a robust solution like the Unreal engine, which is constantly being enhanced and improved, the game developer can limit the amount of time and expense they would otherwise incur to develop their own game engine. This allows developers to take on game projects that might otherwise be impossible to complete, due to resource issues, if they had to create an original game engine from scratch.

Using a licensed engine, like Unreal, works best when the game project you wish to pursue is compatible content-wise with what the Unreal engine is designed to create. If you're building a first-person arena shooter, Unreal is a natural choice and a natural fit. If, on the other hand, you're building a combat racing game or a sports combat game, using the Unreal engine isn't such an easy choice. Game engines, by definition, are engineered to handle problems specific to certain genres. This is why having a complete and robust game engine brings obvious value to a developer. Which is a good reason, resources permitting, to build your own original engine. Tricky situation, eh?

Developers in it for the long haul want the value and flexibility that comes with creating their own game engine for their own game projects. Once they have taken the game engine through to completion on a title, and it has become stable and reliable, engine enhancements can be made to keep it current, and new titles can be built around it.

In terms of industry conformity, however, game engines are unique entities. As you move around from developer to developer, in essence, from engine to engine, you will find sizeable variations in the power, performance, support tools, and robustness among the game engines you encounter.

This environment helps make using a solid game engine to begin with a solid choice.

The Unreal engine is a good solution because it's a robust, multigenerational engine with strong game community support. Unreal technology offers a complete engine code base and toolset for game development. Publishers/developers license or pay for the use of the engine technology to build their games, which saves engine development costs and, in most cases, greatly shortens the time required to produce competitive game content.

Like I've said before, you can have a decent game engine with no tools pipeline, or no tools support, and end up with a very limited ability to build in great gameplay. The Unreal engine helps deliver in this area as well, with a detailed and powerful tools system that gets better with each new engine generation.

In the context of our look at using triggers in this chapter to build gameplay, let's take a quick look at how the Unreal engine handles these events. Figure 6-6 shows the power of the Unreal editor in setting up basic trigger properties in a clean and powerful way. In this case, we are setting the type of actor (pawn) that will trip a proximity trigger (TriggerType = TT_ClassProximity). So, any actor of type "pawn" will trip this trigger. Notice all the other property and configuration choices available to the content builder via this tool.

As you explore the various engines available for commercial game development, it becomes obvious that some have much more extensive abilities to accomplish gameplay construction available via their tools and scripting systems. This is perhaps one of the most important areas to consider when choosing a game engine technology.

FIGURE 6-6

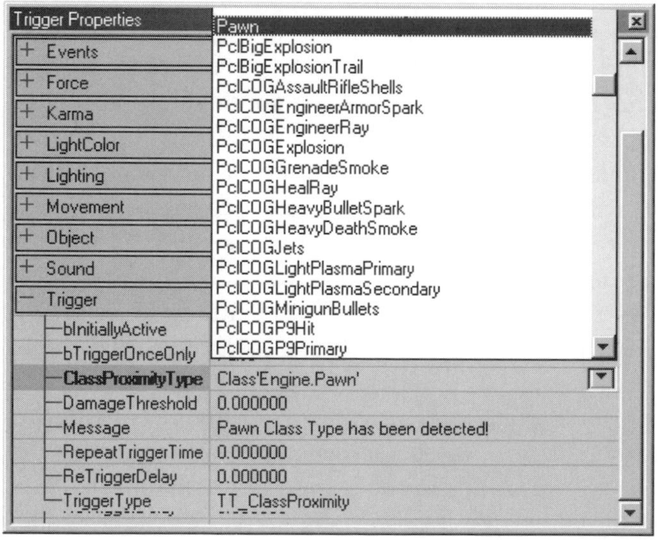

Setting trigger properties in UnrealEd

SCRIPT/EDITING SYSTEM CONSIDERATIONS

As you can see, there is plenty of room for growth among scripting and triggering systems in games. The practical considerations that constantly limit the growth of these tools are budgetary, schedule-sensitive, and resource-oriented (can you find exceptional programmers willing to devote themselves to tools creation—budget and schedule permitting?). Due to game complexity and scope for the current consoles and PCs, budgets are increasing slightly, while schedules for game content turn-around stay fixed.

Quite understandably, to the benefit of the industry as a whole, players want new titles coming out regularly in their favorite series or as original games. In addition, the demand for new game content grows rapidly with the wide success of consoles like the PlayStation 2, which has made it into a stunning number of homes around the world. These factors, combined with the burgeoning world of massively multiplayer online games (MMOGs) and their own demands for regular sequel packs and updates, create a scenario where developers begin to live or die based on their ability to turn around well crafted content quickly.

The grit and life-force of the game content itself is dependent on having robust scripting and construction tools in place. To date, a few developers have built very impressive scripting toolsets and abilities, but no one that I'm aware of has really offered up a unified solution. This solution would have to be part of an overall engine technology that is flexible enough to conform to the requirements of multiple developers and be widely used (licensed) throughout the industry.

To meet some of the demands I've mentioned here, developers and publishers in partnership will have to make a considerable investment. If they wish to remain competitive, and be able to respond in a timely and opportune way to the purchasing power of gamers, they will need construction systems that allow content to be built and tested with maximum efficiency. This is both a problem and a goal for many developers right now.

As discussed, a few of the summary features for a world-editing system include

❭ "Snap" geometry construction (the ability to use construction modules or pieces, reuse parts efficiently, and add accessories easily)

❭ Powerful animation blending (the ability to quickly generate *tweens*, in-between frames, for character, prop, and effects motions)

❭ Extensive built-in or engine-ready effects editing to include character effects, prop effects, and custom environmental effects (weather)

❭ Command-line editing (where useful) in actor and trigger definitions

❭ Audio tagging (the ability to attach audio events to actors)

How will a drag-and-drop construction system with immediate scripting power (right-clicking an actor in a scene not just to set but to "define" new behaviors) come together into one technology solution? It may very well end up being a per-genre solution. Remember that there is another sizeable problem to deal with: by definition, each genre game has its own unique construction and script facilitation requirements.

Some very nice efforts in this direction have been made by several developers to date. However, I'm not sure that very many in the industry would agree that any one of these systems approaches the kind of power and extensibility I've suggested here.

CASE STUDY COMMENTS ON SCRIPTING A BASEBALL GAME

If you're lucky, you will come into a game development situation during the planning phase. This is always a benefit since it's the best way to develop a real sense for the history of a given project in terms of the challenges and expectations for the game.

It's important to make sure that your team deliberates upon game tool considerations as early as possible in the development cycle, rather than as addendums to other forms of ongoing game development that have a way of charging forward with little or no consideration for game tools.

Unless your team plans carefully for a substantial script and trigger system, you probably won't get one. Programmers, facing constant time and functionality challenges already, will simply code game agent behavior functionality themselves deep within the actor code of the game engine. "Exposing" these variables (or making them available to a script system) adds complexity, planning, and execution requirements. There are cases in which a complete scripting system is unnecessary. In those cases, it might be easier to make edits directly in the game code itself. The determining factor should rely on whatever serves the needs of the game title the best.

However, most modern titles are both large in scope and potentially expandable (with add-on levels or mission packs, sequels, or subscription game delivery). Script systems regularly prove to be necessary and valuable undertakings to support the creation of current titles and should be flexible enough to account for future development needs. Keep in mind that it is often difficult to determine how to best manage and orient your scripting needs for future projects. Different game genres and styles require unique and particular scripting system support.

Once the design details for your title are established and basic design/feature lockdown has taken place (no new major elements can be added), your gameplay goals at the concept level should be very clear. You will need every bit of this clarity to build a script system. If you are still defining your game details, don't waste resources building up a script system yet. However, if your team is confident about the high-concept gameplay ideas, it's time to consider your scripting requirements.

Every genre has its own basic and unique requirements, and your own gameplay ideas will shape the needs as well. You'll probably want to start with a detailed list that describes exactly what kinds of parameters you would like to control. Sports games are always challenging and script-intensive. The tools behind them also go through rapid rounds of revisions. Let's take a look how you might begin the process of building up a scripting tool for a baseball game.

You might begin by breaking a baseball game up into field performance roles or field behaviors, and then building tool functionality around these categories. We start with five categories: General, Pitching, Fielding, Hitting, and Catching. What elements, under each of these categories, would we want to control for gameplay purposes? A breakdown begins to evolve, and you have a starting point for building your scripting tool.

General

The general category becomes our home or all-purpose category. This category can be expanded to include all of our general-purpose scripting and game control elements and might include

> **Crowd reactions**   Setting triggers for crowd audio and animation cues.

> **Play-by-play camera details**   Setting up camera routines. How will the camera follow each action from multiple views? Many games allow for user-configured game views, but these must be determined and crafted for the player.

> **Drama points or game highlights**   Setting up camera and playback details for homeruns, great catches, or clutch situations.

> **Instant replay tuning**   Configuring how plays are memory-cached and held for playback at the player's request.

> **Prop control**   Defining prop behaviors like mascot activities or overhead blimp passes.

> **AI controllers for each position type**   In player vs. CPU modes, configuring "best" actions for CPU players to take against human opponents.

> **Weather conditions**   Without a dynamic weather system, you must set up weather look and feel issues (for example, the wind's effect on ball carry and the amount of friction light rain adds to the ballpark grass).

Pitching

We want to use scripting and value tweaks to create fine control for different kinds of baseball pitches like breaking balls, curve balls, rising fastballs, sinking fastballs, and knuckle balls, among others. We can create entirely new pitches (some impossible for a human to throw!). What we really want to do is replicate for the player the feeling and presence of facing these various pitches as a batter. In the pitching category, we begin with some of the basics, including:

❯ **Velocity**   The ball speed coming at the player.

❯ **Ball spin**   Amount and direction of spin on the ball.

❯ **Rise over time**   How much the ball rises on its path coming into the catcher.

❯ **Drop over time**   How much the ball drops away on its path coming into the catcher.

❯ **Seek left plate edge**   How much "attraction" for the ball toward the left side of home plate.

❯ **Seek right plate edge**   How much "attraction" for the ball toward the right side of home plate.

❯ **Random**   Set all of these to a random number and see what happens!

❯ **Bad throw seed value**   Control the occurrence of bad pitches.

Most of these values can be tuned via a simple GUI tool that allows for value edits. No actual scripting is necessarily required. However, depending on your development configuration, you might not have a GUI tool available and may then find yourself editing these values either directly in the game code or in a script.

Fielding

Building behaviors for our fielders will be a complex undertaking, and never perfect, since baseball by its very nature demands a lighting-fast real-time analysis of any given situation in context. (Should I risk letting the ball roll foul? Should I try for a double play, or go for the easy out?) For fielding, we might start with the following:

❯ **Catch radius**   The radius within which a ball can be considered caught.

❯ **Throw speed**   The velocity a ball is thrown to a bag or another player.

❯ **Throw distance**   The distance in units that the ball is in the air.

❯ **Run speed**   How fast a fielder will run to make a catch, dive, or jump play.

❯ **Ball shadow scale**   How large the ball shadow is; useful for setting up a catch.

Again, you might use a GUI tool here to tweak values, or you might make edits directly into a script like this one:

```
// JavaScript sample for "fielding" edits
function processOutfielder(outFielder) {
    if(outFielder.neareastBall()) {
        outFielder.seekBall(20); // 20 is a "tweakable" range
    }
    if(outFielder.ballRadius(5)) { // Is outfielder within 5 units?
        outFielder.doCatch();
    }
    if(outFielder.hasBall()) { // caught ball
        // specify max range of this player as "60"
        outFielder.throwToNextPlayer(60);
    }
}
```

Hitting

Hitting in baseball games is a matter of determining a thin balance between several forces. You can't make hitting too easy, but you can't make it too hard. If you feel like you must err due to unavoidable circumstances, do it toward the player's favor. It's better to create a slugger than a frustrated player who throws your game away in disgust. This isn't just true of dialing in hitting behavior, either, as this kind of mental approach applies just as well to many other game genres. Believe me, I've known many who get some sort of thrill out of stupefying a player. I have never understood this kind of thinking. Here are some play factors to consider for building up hitting behavior:

> **Ball scale**   The size the ball should increase as it gets closer to you.

> **Swing speed**   How fast a hitter can swing, by body type. Larger players tend to swing slower, but with more force if contact is made.

> **Swing arc**   Hitter swings are not perfectly parallel with the ground. The swing arc can help set the frequency of ground balls versus flies.

> **Bunt speed**   How fast a player sets up for bunt contact.

> **Ball angle**   How much influence the angle of the ball leaving the bat has on hit outcomes.

> **Foul tip percentages**   How often foul tips into the catcher's mitt occur.

> **Foul factor**   Adjust to increase or decrease foul numbers.

❱ **Line factor**   Adjust to increase or decrease line-drive occurrences.

❱ **Fly factor**   Adjust to increase or decrease fly ball occurrences.

Here's what a hitting-oriented script might look like:

```
// JavaScript sample of "hitting" support
function hitBall() {
    // Let's determine what happens when the ball is hit.
    // This script only takes into account angle to bat, also
    // should use ball speed and angle of the bat to player,
    // bat speed, bat arc, etc.
    if(ball.getAngle()>75) {
        ball.popupFoul();
    } else if(ball.getAngle()>60 || ball.getAngle()<20) {
        ball.baseHit();
    } else if(ball.getAngle()>50 || ball.getAndle()<25) {
        ball.doubleBaseHit();
    } else if(ball.getAngle()>40 || ball.getAngle()<35) {
        ball.tripleBaseHit();
    } else {
        // angle is between 35 and 40 degrees
        ball.homeRun();
    }
}
```

Catching

In real baseball, the catcher is an information oasis about what's going on during the play of any game. Catchers help try to shape events and create situations that favor their team. This dynamic hasn't really come across in most baseball games made to the present; so much of the catcher behavior we see is still very basic. It begins with factors such as the following:

❱ **Catch radius**   The zone or range of catches a catcher can make successfully.

❱ **Passed ball percentage**   How frequently balls on the edge of the catch radius elude the catcher and become passed balls.

❱ **Throw speed**   How hard the catcher throws to defeat base stealing attempts.

❱ **Position defaults**   How the catcher "sets up" for different pitches.

Here's a sample script for tuning a catcher's catch zone:

```javascript
// JavaScript sample of "catching" support
function doCatcher() {
    // The "30" is an adjustable number to tweak based on
    // how accurate the game should be
    if(catcher.radiusFromBallToMit()<30) {
        catcher.catchBall();
    } else {
        catcher.runAfterBall();
    }
}
```

In this baseball example, each of these bulleted items becomes a starting point for building up your script system functionality. For other genres, you would want various and specific hero controls, enemy controls, NPC controls, prop controls, and so forth. The starting point of the process is the same. It starts with a concept breakdown of what behaviors and abilities you want to help shape in order to build up gameplay.

INTERVIEW WITH ANDREW FORSLUND

Andrew Forslund, a former lead engineer at Disney Online, created many hit games for Disney's Club Blast (a game content subscription service with hundreds of thousands of members) and Disney.com. While at Disney, he created dozens of Java games for the site, including single-player, peer-to-peer, and client/server games. These include Circuit Breaker, Bug Bot, Tarzan's Jungle Adventure, Pop-Up, Rat's Domino, Aladdin Experience *for WildTangent, and many more. Andrew earned a BSCS/EE degree from the University of California, Riverside. Andrew and I are founding partners of Magnet Island, Inc. (www.magnetisland.com), developers of game and entertainment content for multiple wireless devices. He also works as a consultant, focusing on distributed networked applications and web services.*

TM: Why the lack of standardization or focus in scripting language choices (JavaScript/JScript, Python, Visual Basic, C++-oriented, and others) for game developers?

AF: These kinds of choices often come down to programmer preference, what they're familiar with syntax-wise or from previous experience. It is also sometimes politically motivated within an organization where a certain scripting language may be mandated. Another factor is that many publicly available scripting languages are very mature, so a wide variety of choices are available when selecting a language. There isn't really a scripting language that has been specifically created for games, which is why some game companies go so far as to create their own proprietary languages.

TM: For general-purpose scripting of behaviors and prop actions, is there any preference for one language over the other?

AF: Most scripting languages that are used today, like Visual Basic, Python, and JavaScript, among others, are advanced and mature enough to do these tasks equally well; it again comes down to what a programmer is most familiar with and what language they can work fastest in.

TM: Basic programming familiarity or exposure is considered key for game scripters. Any advice for students?

AF: Probably the most important factor in getting familiar with programming is self-motivation and a willingness to learn new things and explore a language. Defining a specific task that you want to accomplish, like creating a simple shooter game, and going through with that to the end to finish up with an actual product is a great way to both learn programming and end up with something you can show to potential employers. Starting with something like WildTangent, which provides a complete scripting environment, and creating a complete game using the tutorials they provide in conjunction with programming resources on the web should give you a good foundation to build on.

TM: Many scripters simply edit command lines or tweak variables. How do you keep this straight for workflow purposes?

AF: One good approach is to keep all of the pieces of a script in some kind of source repository. A scripter may tweak a command line or tweak a single variable many times to get something just right, but these tweaks should be periodically checked in to the source repository and made available for others. Combining this with frequent builds and continuous testing will insure that all "tweaks" applied to the system will not affect it in a bad way.

TM: Tools are expensive and risky to develop. Are these the major reasons why most game tools are so limited?

AF: It's relatively simple to throw together a basic tool to accomplish a certain task. But it's much more difficult to develop that tool into something that would be considered good enough to be a product. Many times, developers that are already over-taxed with other responsibilities will take a short timeout to throw together enough of a tool to do basic editing. Most game budgets and schedules don't include enough time and resources for developing serious tools.

TM: How feasible is a drag-and-drop actor system attached to a drag-and-drop scripting system?

AF: It's definitely feasible, but requires a sophisticated and integrated environment. Many times, when highly sophisticated tools are attempted, they end up not being used because they don't provide that certain feature that an artist or designer may have access to in their favorite animator package. It could certainly be done, but to do it in such a way that it would feel natural and simple to use and integrate with existing tools would be very difficult.

TM: Do you see tool systems as one of the limiting factors in content development?

AF: Certainly having a smooth workflow is of paramount importance in developing content. It's not necessarily true that lack of mature tool systems has to limit development; if the artist-designer-developer loop can work efficiently, than advanced tools may be less necessary. Tools really become important when people with no previous experience with the game system and content being developed are asked to start producing something. At that point, a well-designed tool can mean the difference of several weeks for that person to ramp up.

TM: What do you do when there is no budget for script tools?

AF: Most scripting languages available today don't require tools, and are possible to develop and test using only a simple text editor. In addition, there are often many free or nearly free tools that will help scripters put together more complex scripts more easily.

TM: I try to learn more about scripting by "reversing" the behavior I see in a game back into simple script logic. Does this make sense to you?

AF: Absolutely. This goes back to the question about being driven enough to want to go the extra mile. Observing behavior and attempting to reproduce that behavior is a very good exercise, and will likely result in some hard-fought experience being won. Also, evaluating the behavior and trying to come up with several different ways that it could have been done will be helpful as well.

TM: Sports games are some of the hardest to script. What might be two considerations in scripting goalie behavior for a soccer game?

AF: Programming something that can evaluate a scene and look like it knows what it's doing can be very tricky, much more so than other kinds of scripting like triggers or puzzle sequences. Programming goalie behavior would have to take into account how close to the goal the ball is, who has it, where are the other players on the opposite team, what direction is the ball heading in, does it look like the ball will become dangerous in terms of scoring, etc.

TM: Where does scripting stop and programming begin?

AF: Programming, in the sense of programming a game engine, can be defined as developing all the individual components that can be reused by others, such as access to the screen, sound support, generic support for maintaining a 3-D scene, etc. Scripting would be the portion that interacts with this basic framework to control the gameplay aspects of it. Scripting will never have anything to do with complicated math and outputting the greatest number of polygons; it is for building on top of that framework to control what's being displayed.

TM: I consider setting flags (true/false), triggers, and conditions a part of the scripting process. Why do so few developers have adequate GUI scripting tools (UnrealEd 3 is an exception)?

AF: It comes back to lack of time and budget to follow through on the tools. Designing a tool also requires some pretty serious continuous brainstorming, as it's being developed, to try to maximize its usefulness and power. Unfortunately, the time to think about how to best develop a tool will probably not be available in the schedule.

TM: Do you agree that most modern content is entirely script-dependent now?

AF: Scripting has become a very important part of most current content, especially for big multimillion dollar projects, and it will continue to play a central role in development. The desirability and usefulness of scripting increases with the complexity of a project, since scripting is relatively safe compared to traditional programming with features like automatically managed memory, among others. Smaller projects, like mobile device games, or projects running on very limited platforms with smaller amounts of memory, will probably not use scripting to save on resources. So while scripting remains very important and will continue to increase in use, there will also continue to be content that's developed without it.

TM: What game behaviors (possibly scripted, possibly coded directly) have you seen that you find impressive?

AF: Path-finding and grouping algorithms in games like Age of Empires are very impressive. It's also impressive to see multiple agents interacting in an environment together, like a soccer team, when it works well. Getting these agents to work well together towards a common goal can be very complex and hard to have work well consistently.

TM: How would you try and script such a behavior? Do you mostly plan the logic of the behavior?

AF: It varies based on the context and goal of the behavior, but it generally starts with defining what the ultimate goal is and expanding from there. As many situations as possible should be thought of, and what the most optimal actions would be in those situations, until a fairly complete mapping can be constructed. Then these situations will be play-tested and the actions adjusted until the best solution is found. An example would be making a unit look at the position, direction, and velocity of all other units around it to take an action. It might cause a forward in a soccer game to make a move up the middle of the field, or cause a soldier unit to shift its position in line with the other units.

TM: What advice would you have for those with a technical fear of scripting?

AF: Scripting can be technically challenging, but the only way to overcome technical fear of scripting is to delve into it and try to get a handle on it. It requires motivation and self-discipline to be able to learn enough about scripting to get over the initial hump, but there's a lot of examples available online and many scripting engines available to work with.

TM: What games motivate and inspire you?

AF: I'm a fan of games that make the player think. One of my most favorite games has been the Zelda series, which is to me the perfect combination of action, exploration, adventure, and puzzle solving. I'm not that interested in first-person shooters, or mindless action games, but prefer a game that puts the player in control of their environment and lets them choose what kind of activity they want to do.

TM: Can scripting become more visual?

AF: Perhaps a tool could be constructed that would allow a scripter to drag and drop script elements and see how that affects the game in a visual way. It would be a challenging tool to create, as the seamless interaction between scripting and a visual display would be a hard problem to solve. Scripting can likely never become completely visual, since most games will require custom scripts, but default behaviors could be created that would be available in a visual library.

TM: Are you excited by wireless games?

AF: I've been working with wireless technology APIs for a couple of years now and it's been very exciting to finally see the phones come out that fully implement these APIs. The technology available today really only allows for limited games, but the sheer amount of cell phones that are out there and that will be sold in the coming years will make it one of the most prevalent platforms available for game development.

TM: Do smaller-scope games often require scripting?

AF: It depends on the type of game, but usually smaller games will not require scripting. Smaller games are usually written to run on more limited platforms, and since scripting languages generally consume a lot of memory, they are often inappropriate for smaller games. There are some situations where scripting may be appropriate for smaller games, especially if scripting means being able to load variables from external sources.

MEGA TIPS

1. Learn as much about basic programming, physics, and mathematics concepts as you possibly can. Python is a great language to start with (and it's free!), and a few game developers are building their script systems around it.

2. Reverse-engineer character and prop behaviors in your favorite games. For any behavior that you find intriguing, ask yourself how it might have been scripted. What factors are behind controlling such a behavior? What specific properties would you need to control in order to build such a behavior (for example, control over a character's inventory, gravity, weapon choice, and weapon range)?

3. Watch for the use of trigger systems (as described in this chapter) in your favorite games. Ask yourself what trigger properties would be required to execute such an event or behavior.

4. Using common triggers as a starting point, develop your own triggers to try out your own gameplay ideas. You might create a trigger that spawns an exploding "thorn" weapon only when a certain character is present. Another trigger might cause its spawns to search locally for a specific character and recharge that character's magical abilities. Try to think of new ways to use triggers.

5. With a game design idea in mind, think about breaking down unit behaviors into performance categories, such as in the baseball example. Make it a challenge to try to define the specific script controls you'll need.

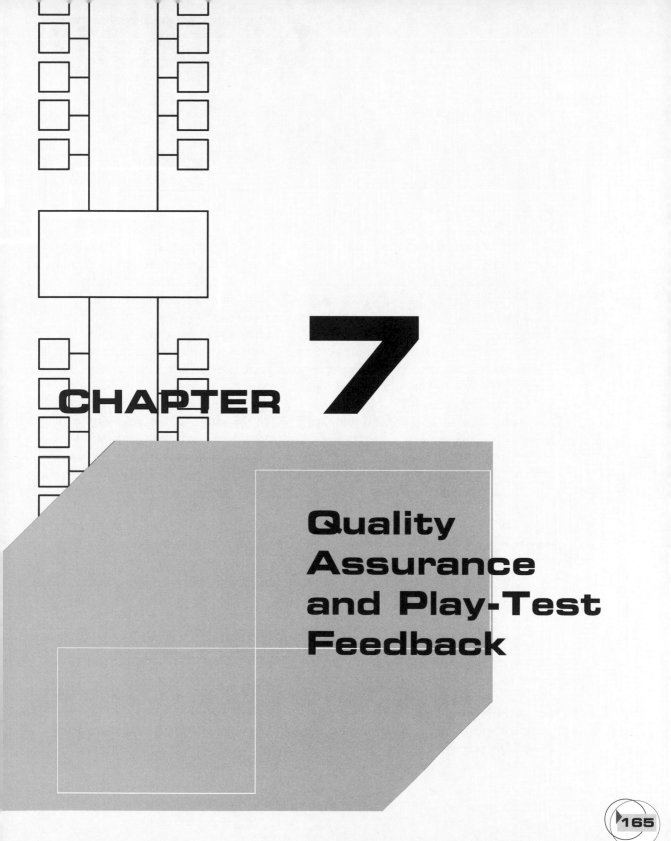

CHAPTER **7**

Quality Assurance and Play-Test Feedback

ONCE your game environment has come together into a cohesive whole with all basic actions, activities, and controlled behaviors built in via script, trigger, code, or any combination of these, you are ready to start getting some feedback from players. Developers have differing work styles and opinions about exactly when an entire game, level, mission, map, arena, or scenario is ready for delivery to the quality assurance (QA) or game-testing department.

As a general rule, the game content that you hand over to QA should be stable and functional enough to be considered playable (fundamentally navigable, functional, and operational—but not nearly perfectly so). Remember, there is an extended period of time during the early development of your game project when the game you're building is nowhere near playable. A "game" doesn't even exist yet. You have only primary art and technology objectives starting to mesh together. If your team handed off a game to QA at this point, it would clearly be way too early to obtain any meaningful feedback (nothing game-wise is happening yet). Before submission to any QA department, you need to wait until the game content is "playable enough" to be clearly representative of your game ideas as they unfold in execution.

In this chapter, we're going to look at the operation and influence of QA on game building. We'll look at the important role that QA plays in helping improve and refine game builds (game version iterations), and we'll stop to consider just how valuable play-test feedback can be in helping to create a game that is a satisfying and rewarding experience for players.

QUALITY ASSURANCE

The purpose of a QA or test department within a developer or publisher is to improve the quality of gameplay for a game title by testing it for bugs or errors and giving play feedback and content suggestions to developers. These folks, known as *game testers,* or simply *testers,* play games for endless hours, attempting to track down or shake out all the bugs or errors that have a negative impact on the play experience. They are your last line of defense before your game hits the public. If your development team thinks QA personnel are overly critical of their game (at least the testers are getting paid something to play it), just wait until the less-than-merciful public gets a shot at criticizing your title. They don't care at all about your team's particular technology hurdles, personality clashes, or budget woes, nor should they. They have paid to play your game. You must deliver a compelling gaming experience to succeed.

Some see life as a game tester as their definition of a dream job. Getting paid to play games all day long must be the life! Any tester will tell you that there is a huge difference between playing extensively for enjoyment (which helped get you the job in the first place) and testing a game title top to bottom by playing it for 14 hours straight through (many times). As a tester, you are asked to intensely monitor all kinds of game performance elements at once.

When considering game quality, you need to recognize the importance of the relationship between the QA department and a particular game title. In particular, the QA department will be giving your team volumes of valuable feedback on how your game is playing. It is extremely important to do everything possible to grow the relationship between your development team and the QA department. You must keep the communication loop between these two groups wide open in both directions at all times.

The goal is to have a seamless exchange of information traveling back and forth. The improvement of your game often depends on this very exchange. This is achieved by treating the test department with the fundamental respect they deserve, as collaborators with the same goal in mind: making great games. When they help solve significant problems, just like other developers, they should be rewarded immediately.

Not every developer has immediate access to a QA department. Building and maintaining a complete test department can be prohibitively expensive. The QA process itself varies in formality around the industry. Large game publishers (like Electronic Arts or Sony) have many testers onsite. An independent game developer, on the other hand, probably has no full-time testers whatsoever. They might have a few production assistants that help out with testing issues, but they usually rely on the publisher to provide detailed testing.

Sometimes even the publishers themselves do not want to build up expensive test departments, so they contract their testing needs out to an independent third-party testing facility or testing service. These services are starting to pop up all over the world. This can create workflow issues for game developers, since the game developers themselves might be halfway around the world from the testers. In this case, you can't simply walk over to the test department, see a particularly nasty bug in action, and walk back to your workspace to fix it. If your test department is on the other side of the globe, it might take several e-mails, intranet jumping, phone calls, time-zone considerations, and movie files to solve one of thousands of bugs. A developer sends *game builds* (working versions of the game) to the test facility, and then must manage and act on the testing feedback.

If your budget allows, it's best to hire your own team of full-time testers. That way, they'll be physically close to your programmers and designers, and you can give them new game builds to test regularly if you like. If you're on a shoestring budget, send e-mail to gaming newsgroups asking for volunteer testers. Keep in mind that someone will need to manage the feedback and coordination with the testers you choose. Many game players will work for nothing more than a free copy of the game once it's released.

QA Setups

How is a QA department physically configured to provide feedback to game developers? Generally, for console testing, large cubicles or open workspace areas support many consoles connected to VCRs. While testers are playing game builds, a VCR is recording the action. This is very useful in capturing bugs that are difficult to describe or difficult to repeat. The VCR tape position is recorded; a bug report is written and then passed to the appropriate developer for analysis. For PC testing, video cards with video outputs can be used in a similar fashion.

Bug Tracking

When a bug is discovered in a game build, it is written up as a bug report and given a bug ID number. The bug ID number attaches that bug to a description and associated details in a bug database. Testing departments use a wide variety of applications to create bug databases. The bug report attempts to fully describe the bug and provide as much information about its occurrence as possible, so that developers know how to approach fixing or solving the bug. In general, most bug reports contain information such as the following:

> ❭ Bug severity (minor, major, system crash)

> ❭ Bug type (text, graphics, audio, gameplay, AI, interface, peripheral)

> ❭ Bug description (a written description including the specific location of the bug observed)

> ❭ Repeatable or intermittent (whether the bug can be repeated or happens only occasionally or intermittently)

> ❭ Attached media displaying the bug as observed (VCR tape position, tape #, movie file, and so on)

Well, you might ask, what does all this have to do with game design? Plenty. At a minimum, your development and design team will get bug reports that detail a wide variety of problems.

Let's take a closer look at bug types:

》 **Text bugs**   Require fixes to misspellings, word omissions, rephrasing, or language localization (translation of game text into different languages).

》 **Graphics bugs**   Can be very serious low-level (deep in the support code) bugs. For example, characters might suddenly drop their texture information; textures may become distorted and appear to be scaled incorrectly; model geometry may display incorrectly; or an animation may fail (for example, a character floats up a ladder).

》 **Gameplay bugs**   Interfere with the play of the game. For example, a character's weapon doesn't fire when it should or fires the wrong projectile, the character freezes after firing it twice, or the player cannot exit the level.

》 **AI bugs**   Cause odd, unanticipated, and unexpected character behaviors (for example, a goalie who always moves to the wrong corner of the goal when a shot is taken by the opposing team's offense). Pathfinding problems (how actors move from point to point with obstacles in between) are always a good source of AI bugs. One common example might be monsters that are tricked into running toward an impassable fence or boundary with the player on the other side, instead of having the intelligence to walk around it.

》 **Interface bugs**   Often a subset of graphics bugs, these usually include failed functionality in the interface support for the game. Maybe items collected or picked up do not update or appear in the inventory, or perhaps the wrong items are displayed on the interface when selected.

》 **Peripheral bugs**   Related to the use and functioning of game peripherals like steering wheels, link cables, or maraca shakers.

》 **Installation bugs**   Involve errors in the installation process, ranging from the point of inserting a game CD to the successful and complete installation of the game onto your hard drive.

》 **Guidance bugs**   Related to interface or gameplay bugs, these often relate to a player successfully installing their game and not knowing how to proceed with playing it. For games targeted at newer players or young children, interface and prompts must be very clean and obvious (no extra-fancy embedded graphics with a game navigation message tucked somewhere imperceptibly inside).

It's important to understand that each of the bug types mentioned here can impede the formal playability of the game. These bugs must be fixed in any case. However, along with these formal bugs are the less formal bugs that often become "suggestions" in the gameplay bug category. Testers offer many suggestions. Quite regularly, they offer far more suggestions than any developer can address. Here's a critical point: it's very important for game designers to watch for patterns in these suggestions.

If testing feedback is starting to show that several testers are having problems with level difficulty, navigation, puzzle solving, item location, order of events, and so forth, it's time to take a closer look at the feedback from a design perspective. You must always pay attention to the fundamental problems players are reporting. This does not mean comments from testers such as "I wish his armor had more blue in it"; rather, look for comments like "Every time I reach the hydro facility section of the map, I can't find my way back out" or "I can't get 25 percent of the way into level 2 without dying several times." These are potential red flag issues.

Just like the game audience, testers vary in game skills. It's best to have a diverse test department staffed with extremely advanced players, semi-advanced players, as well as relative newcomers. Remember, as the gaming audience grows, the widening gap of game exposure and skill level grows accordingly. You want to give your title the chance to be enjoyed by the widest range of players possible.

You must build a good relationship with your testers and rely on them. Designers usually aren't good tester candidates, even if they came up through the test department and know how to test a game. They are too familiar with the idiosyncrasies of how their game plays, and often assume that others have a similar level of familiarity (but they don't). Also, their ego is often attached to the content and they will look over and play over parts of the game that others might find problematic or even bothersome.

Technical Support

Part of your design planning extends as far in scope as technical support issues. For console titles, the publisher will request information (for example, cheat codes, level walk-throughs, and so forth) from the developer to assist players that may call with gameplay-related questions. For PC titles, game patches and updates will require web support and release control. You may also be asked by the publisher to extend the title with expansion packs, including new characters or vehicles with new abilities, weapons, and environs.

Part of maintaining a good relationship with your player base involves providing useful and timely information to support your game titles (such as regularly updating 1-800 player counselors, and offering solid web support). If you plan to add features and functionality to a game post-release or predict that you may be asked to do so by the publisher, then don't forget about the impact that your design choices will have on technical support requirements.

Maintaining solid customer relations helps insure a future audience for your game titles. Many developers and publishers are known by their recognizable game titles, so players should not be left stranded for information once they have purchased a game.

Testing MMOGs

With the emergence of MMOGs comes a whole new set of testing requirements. Now that the consoles have moved online, these titles also provide new testing challenges. One- or two-player console titles can be tested with minimal hardware (TV, console, VCR, database). In the world of client/server games, entirely new testing requirements and challenges suddenly appear.

External testing labs are well equipped to test one- or two-player titles for consoles, PC, or handhelds. Very few are able to handle testing an MMOG title. This has led many developer/publisher MMOG builders to rely on the gaming audience itself as a testing force. Many popular titles allow beta testers (the beta phase in development immediately precedes the final release of a game) from the gaming community to take an active role in testing and shaping emerging game content. This method allows developers to get affordable (free) testing help and expose their game to a wide range of real-world PC systems featuring a multitude of hardware combinations (video cards, CPU speeds, memory configurations, and so forth).

This kind of collaboration is also intended to prove to beta testers that the game when complete is worth playing. It is no secret that MMOG makers would like beta testers to become game subscribers if the MMOG in question is part of a subscription model.

Testing MMOG titles thoroughly is a complex undertaking. You are testing not only game design factors, but also hardware requirements, bandwidth issues, latency problems, error checking and error correction, server timeouts, and dropped connections. For our purposes, we'll focus on some of the game design factors.

Since the MMOG genre is still so new and unexplored, many design issues become part-time sociology projects. It's both a fascinating and frustrating view of relatively anonymous human interaction. Those involved in building MMOGs are discovering the rules and/or guidelines for developing these kinds of gaming experiences at the very same time they're building them! Player-based powers and a player's individual ability to impact the world around them tend to take center stage when making design decisions.

We have simultaneous goals. We want to give players enough power to influence the environment in meaningful, fun, and interesting ways, but we also want to protect the play experience of other players. Some players, secure in relative anonymity, go ape inside MMOGs. They drop all inhibitions. They thrive on trying to ruin any positive experience another player might enjoy. As designers (and world cops), we have to acknowledge and account for this fact. Part of our job is to provide a fun, secure, reliable, addictive, and totally engaging gaming experience. The ability to run around an MMOG world as a joy-killer will shape and influence (some might even say dictate) our design decisions.

A Three-Stage Completion Process

As a game title or software product reaches completion, it passes through three critical development stages, commonly called alpha, beta, and final or "gold." The exact definition of each stage for any single game is somewhat nebulous. In general, the alpha stage is defined as a game that is essentially feature-complete, but remains extremely buggy with many fixes left to perform. The beta stage is reached when all of the considerable alpha bugs are fixed and only relatively minor bugs now remain. As each minor bug is fixed and settled, the game approaches its final or "gold" status. Gold refers to the final CD or cartridge burn of the game now ready for production mastering and replication. The amount of time between each of these stages often depends on your production schedule and how far your deliverable dates have slipped. It can be several months or a matter of weeks.

Writing a Test Plan

Each substantial new submission to the QA department should be accompanied by a test plan. The test plan should specify, in as much detail as possible, exactly which parts of game functionality testers should be watching for in the version of the game submitted for testing. In early submission to QA, the test plan can be somewhat open, since you're testing for any and every kind of problem imaginable. As the QA phase progresses and many bug fixes are made, you want to focus the test team on those areas of the game that have undergone considerable change. These are usually the areas where new bugs pop up as a result of the changes made. Your test plan should detail exactly which parts of the game to focus on (for example, specific multiplay features or client-server connection issues, inventory features, character ability changes, and so forth).

The more information you are able to provide about where potential new problems may arise, the more focused testers can be in providing valuable and time-saving functionality feedback.

Once a test plan has been followed (it's essential when games are really buggy), there are several more informal and ongoing kinds of testing that regularly take place:

> **"Just play!"** Testers play the game as normal players would, noting whether they find it difficult or easy, fun or boring. They record how long it takes them to complete each level or area, what they liked or disliked in the level or area, how the pacing and balancing of the game felt in play, and how long it took to play the entire game.

> **"See if you can break it!"** Testers try to play the game in ways that the designers never intended, to see if they can create a situation that impairs the game-playing experience, such as being trapped in a room or level section

Quality Assurance and Play-Test Feedback

with no chance of escape. They might also try firing multiple weapons at once, using crazy button combinations, and attempting other unusual moves in an attempt to break the game with an overload of input data.

> **"See if you can get out of this!"**   Testers are given a particularly unusual and often difficult saved-game position and are challenged to see if they can "get out of it."

PLAY-TEST FEEDBACK

Play-test feedback will be directed at your design team from a number of sources. It's important to begin to understand how this feedback is digested, relayed back to the design team, and used in game development. Among other possible sources, play-test feedback will come from the following:

> A licensor's representatives

> A publisher's producer and play-test team

> Marketing representatives conducting focus groups

> Development team members

> Art directors and other designers

> Magazine and web site previews

> Your own independent test team

Note that a licensor's representatives are those who are responsible for protecting the image and quality of a work owned by an intellectual property rights holder (IPRH); in other words, the owner of any content in your game. For example, if you're creating a game starring *The Simpsons*, expect Fox and Matt Groening to be very particular about how the characters are portrayed.

As you can see, play-test feedback comes from a number of sources. How do you manage all of this play-test data? Well, from a practical standpoint, it's important to be able to track each important issue and respond accordingly. Of course, ultimately the only kind of play-test feedback that is really valuable is the kind that actually improves the play of your game. You have to guard your game like a protective mother. If the feedback does not look likely to improve the game, it is often more harmful than helpful. This is why, at all times, you need to maintain that clear mental vision of your game's heartbeat (the shared team vision established at the onset of production, which should stay true to its origins as it evolves).

Keeping this in mind, there are also several commercial realities to consider. The licensor had better be satisfied with your game or they can choose to terminate the license, thus ending your ability to use their well-known characters or worlds. This can effectively kill your game. Your publisher may not want to pay for the development of a game without a well-known character universe attached. Sometimes licensors are not familiar with gaming, game genres, or player expectations at all, yet they have plenty of power over the game you're building (after all, it's using their well-protected characters or worlds!).

If you are a developer building a game that isn't somehow independently funded, you're probably building it for a publisher. The publisher covers the cost of development, so as an independent developer, the publisher is your valued client. In any business, you must strive to provide for the needs of your client. The publisher's vision for the game may be slightly or significantly different than your development team's vision. This "division in vision" is best reconciled early in development, but it often causes friction, factions, and egos to take center stage.

Marketing departments have considerable influence in modern game development. In fact, the marketing budgets to promote a game can far exceed the total game development costs. Marketers sometimes spend millions of dollars on TV and print ads to market a game. If they conduct formal or informal focus groups to get player feedback, and start to hear common complaints or frustrations, you can bet that these potential problems will find their way right back to the design and production team.

Development team members themselves usually have strong opinions about design direction. These recommendations are voiced passionately, and can cause "design factions" and team fracture if not addressed immediately by a producer capable of building bridges between people and ideas, and paying attention to their concerns.

Art directors and other designers, working on other simultaneous game titles, will often voice opinions while offering critiques and suggestions. These comments can be very helpful when a fresh perspective adds new insight into solving a problem. These comments can also be distracting and dividing remarks that start to build unnecessary tension between development teams.

Writers for gaming magazines and web sites, reviewers, and editors get many game previews to consider as a game gets close to its gold stage. Marketing is always trying to get magazine and web features for upcoming titles to create a buzz that will lead to sales. Negative reactions to these game previews will also rifle their way back to the design team.

Finally, you might have the luxury of having access to an internal test team. This team can be a reality check against your own individual testing and the comments coming at you from the various sources just considered.

Knowing that your design team will be receiving plenty of player feedback information from a number of sources, you need to be ready to handle it all. By necessity, it becomes a matter of priority ranking. You need to triage the information coming at you. Developers handle each of these feedback streams differently, some placing more or less emphasis on any one of the categories mentioned here.

As a developer, you must keep the licensor impressed with your handling of their characters and worlds. You must develop the best publisher relationship possible. They are your client, your partner in success or failure, and a source for future work building more games. If you don't deliver, they will find another developer. Feedback, requests, criticisms, directions, and demands from each of the remaining categories must be considered on a case-by-case basis. This is where ranking and priority based on the substance of the feedback (and what it suggests about the playability of your game) must be gauged and acted upon.

Managing Feedback

People seem to ask for the impossible on a regular basis. When this is clearly the case, it falls by definition to the bottom of your feedback list, or maybe it's not even entered into your notes. How do you handle all of this information? I use a template set up in Microsoft Excel to enter and track feedback from each of these disparate sources as it gets directed toward the design and production team. This feedback is kept separate from a bug database, unless the feedback given is itself an actual bug. In this case, a full bug report is written and entered into the bug database.

Hopefully by now you realize that an enormous physical amount of feedback will be coming at your design team. I've suggested a priority, ranking, and triage system for handling it at the top level. At the same time, during development, there is a parallel and more intimate feedback loop that exists. This loop focuses on the play feedback discussed amongst the actual development team.

Development Team Feedback Loop

The programmers, artists, designers, testers, audio engineers, producers, and writers all perform their craft, but they also test the game. They watch it come to life slowly, day after day, for a couple of years (in some cases!). They are trying to guide the game in the right direction—the direction established as the vision for the game. This process itself becomes an interior feedback loop or team loop, and is probably the most powerful one. If a team were to try to please everyone's random request, the game would never be completed—and wouldn't work cohesively if it could be completed.

You have to filter through all of the extraneous feedback and reconcile it with the team loop. This is rarely easy. The following are the kinds of issues that must be addressed at the team loop level:

❱ Item placement needs work

❱ Item powers are not working as intended

❯ Bad "built-in" resource balancing

❯ Various kinds of character speed and navigation issues

❯ A power, function, weapon, or ability is not working as intended

❯ Character, vehicle, or weapon physics are weak

❯ A clunky interface has emerged, making it hard to perform operations easily or quickly

❯ Bad animation elements, such as bad motion transitions from move to move

❯ Disconnected, awkward, or illogical map, arena, and level layouts

❯ Too few or too many enemies; enemy density is not balanced well

❯ Play is simply too hard or too easy

❯ Play is simply not fun or engaging

❯ Characters or units need a better balance of complementary powers and abilities

❯ Offense or defense is too high or low (for example, destroying opponents is too easy or too hard)

❯ Controller reaction "feels" too slow

❯ The camera moves are jilting, shaky, or prevent/obscure the play experience

❯ Character, effect, prop, or environmental features are visually unappealing

❯ Need better AI (actors are too stupid)

❯ Need more diversity in weapon type or kind and projectile abilities

❯ Performing moves using controller button combinations or mouse/keyboard is too confusing

❯ Audio support seems tacked-on, disconnected, or transparent

❯ Boss behaviors requiring impact and excitement for player are too simple

❯ Cinemas, segues, and intro and ending movies have grown way beyond the scope of available resources

❯ Game features and functions try to accomplish too much, rather than doing the simple things well (an all-too-common mistake; you can build a very solid game by doing the so-called "simple things" well—controller tuning, ease of operation, nicely "ramped" or ascending ease of objectives, solid player payoff points, and so on)

❱ The game is feature-complex but somewhat hollow in moment-to-moment content

❱ The design itself is too wide in scope or span and forces an out-of-balance play situation

The items mentioned here are just a survey of the kinds of considerations and feedback issues that a game development team commonly deals with. Many specific examples of these items are written up into formal bugs, while others are considered topically or conceptually. Many of these issues, despite several attempts to resolve them, continue to plague or gnaw at developers throughout the entire development cycle for any given game.

Listening to Feedback

Feedback isn't very useful if it doesn't make its way back into the game. Hard feedback, in the form of solid and obvious bug reports, takes priority. If you have a bug that is crashing the game, characters that are inexplicably stuck in the wall or floor, or an inventory update error, the reason to fix these problems is clear: it impairs basic gameplay.

It's the softer forms of feedback that often remain ignored, for many reasons. These softer forms include differing player reaction to game-wide difficulty, level-specific navigation issues and preferences, and a somewhat personal or subjective reaction to level layout, pacing, and continuity over many levels. Developers spend large amounts of time building up the play experience for a game, and many find it hard to take strongly voiced or constant waves of criticism. It's entirely understandable. You've just spent five weekends in a row at work, only to hear that the game still isn't testing well and still isn't getting favorable feedback from testers (or, even worse, from any number of other armchair critics). As I've tried to make clear, some criticism and feedback is useful, and some is not. You just have to learn to be a good feedback filter. Good producers always try to shield their team from unproductive or unsettling "mission-irrelevant" feedback.

To the extent that it's possible, developers shouldn't take pattern criticism (where "the many" comment on the same potential problem) personally. Pattern criticism should be evaluated quickly because it is a potential red flag. If several people are voicing similar concerns or frustrations with the play experience, you must work to reverse these negative patterns. It's okay if an idea you fell in love with for a level section isn't really panning out. It doesn't prove that you're a bad designer. Game design is fundamentally about experimentation, evolution, and risk. More likely, it means that you took a chance and can use what you've learned as a result to help inform your future ideas. In the observation of player feedback, you can learn to build your gaming intuition.

As far as I know, there is no set of rules that, when followed, is guaranteed to result in highly satisfying gameplay. Building a game is always a real-time experiment: as a project, as a technology hurdle, and as a form of content. You have to get your hands in the paint, move stuff around, and try out new ideas to get the play effect you're ultimately trying to define. This is never easy, and frequently requires much team support. In some cases, you may have an idea that might fundamentally improve gameplay in some way, but you may not be able to try out that idea due to technology barriers and resource issues.

Impact of Play-Test Feedback on Daily Design Tasks

Throughout the development cycle, a design team helps to shape details for the following:

❱ Character histories/backgrounds, abilities, behaviors, growth curves, and interplay

❱ Environmental details, features, and topography

❱ Gameplay ideas

❱ Challenges and definitions for actors, weapons, powers, and behaviors

❱ Storyboarding of cinemas, segues, intros, and endings

Each of these categories will regularly be altered by play-test feedback. Even before a game has grown up far enough to reach the testing department, designers are seeking to avoid bottlenecks by helping to get game definition information to the development team. If programmers are waiting on basic enemy behavior details, or artists have vague and incomplete descriptions of characters for modeling or animation, a design bottleneck is created. Design teams constantly work to avoid this scenario.

When the play-test feedback cycle roars into action, designers often have to shift into overdrive as well. New or improved functionality, often as a result of test feedback, may require further definition and tuning (for example, new interface elements or new character powers). The design team will be challenged to find timely solutions for such things as characters that aren't testing well or that offer unique challenges due to their physical construction; scenarios that are being identified as too easy, too cumbersome, too short, too long, or too hard; or the growing sense that the overall pacing of the game is becoming awkward.

The daily design tasks change momentum from helping to define gameplay functionality to avoid creating bottlenecks for your teammates, to helping manage and steer through changes within a frenzied revision process.

CASE STUDY COMMENTS ON THE IMPACT OF QA

It should be clear by now that QA performs a vital role in fixing errors in games, not only by reporting obvious bugs but also by providing much needed gameplay feedback. In this sense, QA also helps to shape and influence game design specifics by providing a player's reaction to game details that regularly require substantial tuning and tweaking. Again, QA will be the last chance and last line of defense before your game goes widely public. You know you have something solid when, despite the hundreds of hours spent in testing, testers are excited by the impending release of a game title, knowing that other players will enjoy the game experience that is just about to head their way.

There is another import impact consideration for the QA department. It is a breeding ground for future developers. Many game developers (programmers, artists, designers, producers, audio engineers, and so forth) have gotten their start in QA. In fact, some companies even require that everyone spend some amount of time in the QA department. It can be a great education.

Those with interest in game development as a career often wonder how they can find a job working on games. I don't think anyone working in the game industry would kid you or pull any punches—it's a very competitive business. This sounds like a cliché. After all, isn't all business by definition "very competitive"? Yes, indeed. But most other businesses function on a different kind of underlying economic model. They don't need a massive hit to pay for a whole slew of flops.

Games are built primarily by young, eager, and comparably affordable talent. It can be a brutal experience to watch all those around you sink a few years into a game that doesn't ship for a variety of reasons. This kind of experience can test your passion for games to the limit. One result is that many developers spend only a few years in the game industry and then make their transition right back out of it. It's a problem the game industry still struggles with, since this frequently results in experienced and talented developers lost to competing industries.

New developers may not be sure yet about which specific career track to pursue within game development. QA can be a great place to start. If you are growing your programming, art, audio, or design skills, experience in QA will give you direct access to the valuable experience of watching a game solidify. It will also help you understand more about exactly which role you might like to pursue.

Since modern game hardware has become so powerful and capable, the skills and abilities bar for each team member has been raised accordingly. Today, developers regularly look for programmers with a computer science or mathematics degree with an emphasis on 3-D graphics programming. Artists must demonstrate advanced traditional illustration and design skills and solid understanding of digital software tools.

Despite this preparation, many new developers are unable to secure jobs as programmers or artists directly without previous development experience. This is not to say that you shouldn't try to get a programming job right out of college. You might very well get one. Programmers are regularly in demand. Don't be afraid to take a job testing games along the way if you are still exploring your options. You will meet some very interesting, colorful, passionate, and exciting folks in most game-testing departments. Keep in mind that many companies promote developers directly from the test department into that ideal job making textures or models, scripting, or even programming. By taking a job testing games, the company will learn more about you. Be persistent, and they will see your dedication, desire, and ability.

As the development and design teams continue to work with the test department to finalize a game title, you may get to see firsthand the challenges and frustrations that accompany the game design and production process. Many new developers are simply overly idealistic. Those of us who have been around the game industry a little while were once that way too. Despite how it might seem, this is actually a healthy influence for the industry. We need some surprise ideas.

Working in the test department will make you a better game designer. In short, it will probably make you a better developer no matter what you ultimately choose to do. Even if you have incredible visual design skills and are well trained from a top-notch design school, if you have no exposure to the process of watching a game start to come together, there is a hole in your experience. Don't worry; one way or another, you'll fill that hole over the time you spend building games.

When you work in QA, you can literally spend all day taking mental and physical notes about what works, what doesn't work, and why. These are my mantra questions. As game builders, we always want to know what works, what doesn't, and why. This is very useful information for your future of building games.

Even with your best-planned production efforts, an airtight design plan, and an experienced development team, you have no guarantee that a hot-selling, award-winning game will pop out of the oven on the other side. Building great games is messy revision-laden experimental work. It is directly at odds with a "need it cheaper yesterday" mentality. It is always a sizeable risk. It is not for the faint of heart. Every developer knows it: to get it really right takes time and resources. What a concept. The vast majority of developers have little of either.

On the technological merry-go-round called game development, where you are literally inventing the ride while you ride it, how do you "time" a game's solid release date to hit an arbitrary marketing window date sequence attached to a movie? Whew. Are you dizzy yet? You will be.

Fortunately, to some extent, you can catch a glimpse of all of this going on around you in QA. If you find yourself working in QA, for whatever reason, use the time to your advantage. Use the time to hone and refine your understanding of game mechanics and to build your gaming intuition. If you choose to continue developing games, the time spent in QA should serve you well.

INTERVIEW WITH MELINDA WHITE

Melinda White is manager of US Recruiting, specializing in enterprise application integration technology, for SeeBeyond Technologies, Inc., a software developer located in Monrovia, CA. During her ten years of experience in recruiting, she has worked on the front lines of hiring technology personnel for many game developers, entertainment companies, and software companies. She holds a B.A. degree in psychology and French from Scripps College in Claremont, CA. We sat down to talk about how to pursue career opportunities in gaming and how companies perceive job candidates.

TM: How does the hiring process work for most game developers?

MW: Depending on their size, some have a very formal process, and some not very formal at all. A large company like Electronic Arts uses a web-based system to track résumé submissions. When a position becomes available, they can search the database for keyword matches and proceed to look at job candidates. Smaller game developers tend to work at a much more personal level, holding on to certain résumés and relying heavily on hiring friends and associates of the developers they already have on staff.

TM: As a new game developer, trying to get that first job, do you think it's best to start in the QA department or go straight for a development position?

MW: This really depends on your background. It used to be that you could start in the QA department and move anywhere in the company over time. This doesn't seem to be the case anymore. Developers are looking for individuals who can demonstrate highly specialized skill sets and hit the ground running from day one. Programmers need solid code samples, artists need compelling work on their reels, and designers need finished levels with attached design documentation. If you have this material already, then give yourself some time to find a position in your specialty area. If you're still trying to build these skills, you have a better shot at getting into QA, showing what you can do, and then making the move toward your dream job from there.

TM: Do you see demand for testers regularly?

MW: It seems to be seasonal and somewhat sporadic. Obviously, more testers get hired when a bunch of games are coming to completion. I concentrate more on placing software engineers, just because of demand.

TM: Do you know of many testers who have moved on to other jobs within the game industry?

MW: Sure. Many have moved on. It seems to have always been the "proving ground" for many. The difference now is the amount of specialized skill needed to break out of testing and into the other job categories.

TM: What about pay and salary issues for QA?

MW: Many testers are temporary; hence they are paid hourly ($10 to $14) with no benefits, although some have full-time regular positions with benefits. The pay isn't as competitive compared with QA test personnel in mainstream software, and the actual pay depends on your geographic location too. For most, it's just a position you take as a stepping-stone to somewhere else.

TM: How about programmers, artists, producers, and designers?

MW: I've known several developers that have worked in mainstream software companies, and taken pay cuts to work for game developers, and then returned fairly quickly to mainstream software. Working in games provides a grueling work schedule, but in all fairness that happens in mainstream software too. Game companies have always tended to value programmers the most. It's a wide range. They can make anywhere from $35K to $100K+, dependent on experience and expertise. Artists tend to make less, at about the $30K to $70K range. Keep in mind that there is wide variation in pay dependent on the size of the developer, developer/publisher, and so forth. Producers can make $30K to $90K and designers probably average about $30K to $60K, but again, there are many factors to consider. You can make less or more than each of these ranges would suggest.

TM: In today's market, how do you best prepare to work in games?

MW: There are the obvious requirements, like playing as many games as you can get your hands on. If you want to be a programmer, get a B.S. in computer science or mathematics. If you want to be an artist, finish your B.F.A. Same thing goes for designers. More and more developers are requiring degrees, simply because they can. The applicant pool is so large that they can pick and choose. You need to demonstrate that you can learn quickly in a challenging environment.

TM: Based on the numerous developers you've hired into companies, would you say they are happy working in the game industry?

MW: Some are happy and some are not. Some try it for a while and leave. Some last many years and have simply had enough. Some of the real pioneers leave. It's sad, because they are leaving an industry that they helped to establish. Despite its growth, the industry is still very young. For a long time, game companies haven't really known how to hire. It's been a very mixed-up process. Honestly, many of the hires I've seen defy any kind of logic but this is not entirely unusual in any industry. The seemingly best candidates, with the most relevant backgrounds, simply don't get the jobs for political, trivial, irrelevant, silly, or inexplicable reasons.

TM: What do you think about the growing trend of sending entire game development deals overseas for development?

MW: This is a serious issue. It has impact for everyone reading this book. It might very well be their job going away. However, it isn't shocking. Many industries, not just games, are taking a similar approach for fiscal reasons.

TM: As a person who hires developers every day, beyond a résumé and relevant and applicable experience, what do you look for in a candidate? What moves you to want to hire someone?

MW: A résumé is not an accurate representation of the person. There are factors that impact a person's success or lack thereof; for instance, layoffs, the economy, politics, or infrastructure of a company. A person's "soft skills" aren't evident in a résumé, and these are skills that you explore during an interview. Can this person communicate effectively? Can they express ideas succinctly? Can they write well? Can they collaborate with a team? Lead a team? Can they fit in culturally? Can they handle pressure? If a person has a formal college education, this generally indicates that they have the discipline to complete assignments and, depending on their area of study, the ability to think clearly and analytically.

TM: When you get out of school and are looking for that first game job, should you take one even if there is no pay involved?

MW: If you can afford to do so, yes, because it is experience. Then, of course, you can build upon this experience in your next games opportunity. There aren't too many internships in games, so these nonpaid experiences would probably be equity based or entirely without pay.

TM: How would you say you maintain a career in games over time?

MW: You must constantly update your skills; whether you are a programmer, artist, producer, or designer, companies don't always pay for education to keep your skills current, so you are often in a position where you must take the initiative. Along these lines, keep current with the upcoming platforms, tools, and industry trends, because these factors will affect your own "marketability"—as crass as that sounds, it's reality. Be open-minded and flexible with the volatility and deadline-driven nature of the games industry. It's extremely competitive out there! Anything you can do to try and set yourself apart will be helpful. It won't be easy. Just saying you're a member of Mensa is not what I'm talking about. You need quantifiable and unique aspects in your background to make it stand out. Even with proven experience, it may not be enough because it can be very subjective and specific. This is the reality of competition for only a select number of jobs.

TM: Do you see much overlap in artists, particularly from movie, TV, and comics, coming to games?

MW: I do. There is plenty of overlap. There is more overlap every day as the kind of art you can do for games starts to look like the art in movies and on TV. It's also a matter of perceived stability. TV and movie work gets cancelled or only lasts a couple of months. You know what, though, so do games. It's all unstable. If you're looking for stability, this probably isn't the industry for you.

TM: How about diversity in skills? Should aspiring game developers keep diversity in mind? I myself always preach diversity.

MW: Definitely. Ideally you want a whole wide range of abilities you can draw from at a moment's notice. If you need to get work fast, this will have to be the case. If you only do one thing in one way, you're going to be in trouble. This happened when many 2-D artists didn't or wouldn't make the leap to 3-D. It created opportunities for those willing to make the leap. We've seen, though, that once that area is saturated, the need diminishes and people become reasonable again with their rates and expectations. Same thing happened during the dot-bomb era.

TM: What is the best piece of advice you would offer to an aspiring developer these days?

MW: I would recommend completing a four-year college degree at an accredited college or university, because you will have a lifelong foundation and it will give you more earning potential as well as professional growth in the long run, and will set you apart with individual hiring managers who appreciate and/or require education. Play a lot of games, keep current on them, have opinions about them, and be unique in your passion for games.

TM: How do you survive a tough economy in an overly competitive industry?

MW: That goes back to having a diverse set of skills and a foundation built on education. While these factors alone may not save you from a layoff during a weak economy, you will stand out among the plethora of candidates that an employer considers. With a diverse skill set and an education, you can be resourceful in applying your background to a different angle of the games industry. Or, you may be able to transfer to mainstream software. Artists may not be able to do this as easily, but programmers can, while producers can become program or project managers.

TM: What are the best reasons to build a career in games?

MW: If you're a gamer, who I assume you are if you can persist in the games business, job satisfaction is one reason. Also, people in games bond because they tend to have common interests. It's a young and dynamic industry that offers someone a chance to learn tools and business practices that are niche-based and interesting. It's generally a casual environment with flexible hours.

TM: What do you like the least about the game industry?

MW: Two things—their hiring practices and the business itself. But this could apply to other businesses as well; nonetheless, the games business epitomizes politics and volatility. In terms of their hiring practices, game companies often have unrealistic requirements for tools and programming languages that have barely been on the market, or they require esoteric experience for particular kinds of games (for example, requiring a producer to have been a pro or semipro athlete to work on a sports game). While they have these lofty requirements, it's still just a buddy network. On many occasions in my experience, I don't believe developers have made good hiring choices. Regarding the business itself, it has a cycle of hiring a team for a game, then not necessarily being able to use the team when the game is done or is cancelled. It's not a smart way of using their resources, nor is it rational as a long-term business strategy. They may as well hire consultants, but this is a novel idea in games. Games are cancelled for arbitrary reasons, which ultimately hinders the careers of all involved. It is perceived that they [the game development team] are entirely accountable for failing to ship a game, when the real reason for cancellation is often far beyond the team's control. Your identity is established by the game you shipped, or didn't ship. You're only as good as your last shipped game, assuming it shipped. The industry has driven out the most passionate and legendary gamers and has become too glamour-oriented. Finally, it's not necessarily sensitive to the female market (Barbie and Lara Croft are not the healthiest role models to female game players) and females working in the industry.

TM: How important is reaching out to others or networking in finding a game job?

MW: It's essential. The games industry does not necessarily reward the most qualified, so they do overlook a lot of very talented and well educated people who are passionate about games and can contribute to great game development. It's definitely about who you know. A lot of positions are not advertised either.

TM: What's the best advice you would give a new game job candidate?

MW: Get ready for game reality to bite you! You will meet a lot of people that share your interests, and you will also work with people who have their own agendas, and who probably shouldn't be working in games. Keep current with games and your skills, remind yourself about why you're in the game industry, be flexible, and soak up as much information as possible.

MEGA TIPS

1. Practice writing thorough game reviews. Be sure to address the good with the bad. In particular, state how you would evolve the game title to address these issues.

2. Even if you're just building a small game among friends, always include test plan information when soliciting feedback from players. What are they looking for? Where would you like them to focus their attention? As a designer, you'll know which areas of your level or mission feel weak to you. See if test players agree or disagree.

3. This one seems obvious, but remember that play feedback must be managed and acted on if it is to retain its value toward building a better game. Passing off pattern feedback with arrogance will take its toll on your game.

4. Take advantage of open-beta tests announced by MMOG developers by offering to help. This can be a great way to gain early experience, and some careers have started this way.

5. When you find a bug in a game, write it up according to the bug report criteria discussed in this chapter. Demonstrating that you can write a clean bug report might help you land a local QA job.

6. When it comes to content specifics, try to open the mind and drop the ego. As a designer or design team, understand that QA feedback helps to shape solid content. Design ideas that are ultimately killed by feedback are not concrete proof of a designer's personal failings. Everyone suffers these moments, either as an individual or as a team. It's part of making games. I've found that these "failures" turn out to be valuable moments of learning and forward reflection.

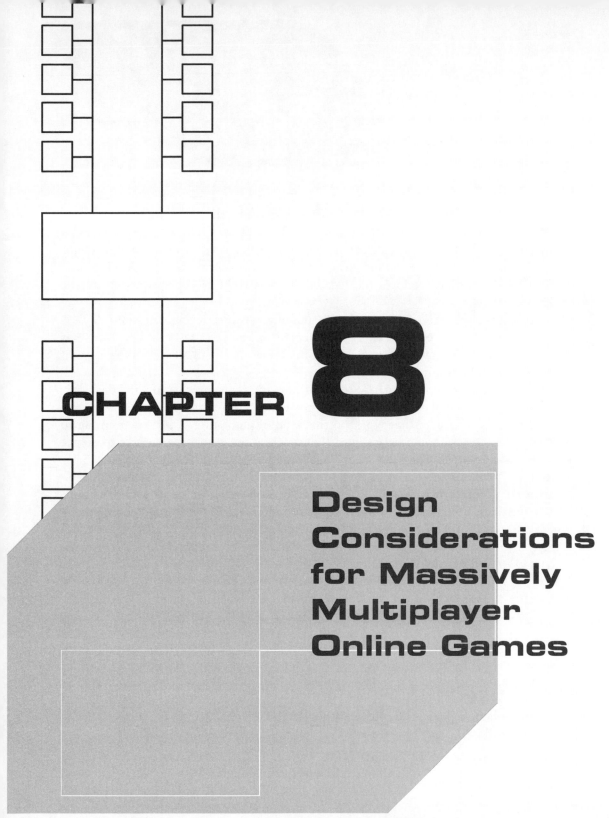

CHAPTER **8**

Design Considerations for Massively Multiplayer Online Games

A whole new avenue for games has arrived in the form of the massively multiplayer online game (MMOG). These games allow large numbers of players to collaborate and compete together in a persistent world. As you might imagine, developing this kind of game is among the most complex game development challenges any game developer has faced in the relatively short history of electronic gaming.

Up to this point, we've discussed game making in terms of single or multiplay experiences on the consoles or PC. The pure construction aspect of building MMOGs shares many of the same challenges, yet it offers entirely new challenges and points of learning for all developers.

In this chapter, we're going to take a look at many of the production and design issues and factors involved in building this particular kind of game. Right now, many game developers are hard at work on this kind of game title. They are learning to drive by driving. It should be assumed that much of the information and experience garnered from MMOG development is still fluid, ever-changing, and coming in daily from the "front lines." Let's not forget that MMOGs are in their infancy. For developers everywhere, there is still very much to be learned.

A massively multiplayer online role playing game (MMORPG) is a common game genre now and a popular form of MMOG. I use the general term "MMOG" because the challenges and design considerations of massively multiplayer games are not restricted to role-playing games alone.

MMOG PRODUCTION CHALLENGES

The sheer scope, scale, and complexity of MMOG titles helps to create a game development environment with a wide array of production challenges and issues. Since production details are the real-world implementation of design ideas, it will serve us well to stop and consider exactly what we're up against from a pure production perspective when we set out to create an MMOG title.

In the following sections, we will consider many of these issues in detail.

Defining Titles

In the short history of the MMOG, some of the defining titles include *Ultima Online* (www.uo.com), *Everquest* (http://everquest.station.sony.com/), and *Asheron's Call* (www.microsoft.com/games/zone/asheronscall/). These titles have been large experiments in attracting and keeping players excited about playing and unfolding their characters within these persistent worlds. To date, the most successful titles have been entirely character oriented. These games provide a social network or aspect that is unequalled by any other form of electronic gaming. For anyone unfamiliar with these game titles, they offer vast lands to explore as a lone player or in collaboration with other players, all the while focused on character growth, positioning, nuances in ability, efficacy, and social/power-oriented rankings.

How Is the MMOG Player Different from the Console Player?

Typically, it has been assumed that there is a sizeable divide between the console player and the PC/MMOG player. The rationale is that console players prefer fast action and sports games, while PC players prefer FPS, RPG, and strategy-oriented titles. There is significant sales evidence to back up this idea. The PC audience has made the MMOG successful. However, there is a bridge to the console world, as MMOG titles that have proven successful on the PC are becoming available on the consoles, primarily through the move of the Xbox and PlayStation 2 into the online universe.

In the recent past, players did tend to gravitate toward either console or PC play, while many of the die-hards played both with equal passion. These days, younger players have no fear of the PC, and therefore no reason to play exclusively on the easier-to-use consoles. The divide between the two kinds of players seems to be diminishing. Not entirely, however.

You still come across many players with strong platform preferences. Many players who prefer console gaming are not as eager to play PC titles, for a variety of reasons. The MMOG titles released to date have done a very good job of providing content that is pleasing and familiar to PC-oriented players. Whether these titles will make it over the bridge to the world of online console play remains to be determined.

From a design perspective, any title you envision as an MMOG may increasingly have to serve two masters. First will be the obvious need to connect with PC/MMOG players. This is your established audience. Second may be the need to understand more about exactly how the title will play for the online console audience.

Saturation Concerns for the MMOG

Most of the MMOG titles utilize a subscription service model. A player purchases the game at retail, installs the game, and must pay a monthly fee to continue to have access to the game. This has an obvious limit. How many game subscriptions will any one player maintain? Zero? One to three? You're not going to get very far by tacking on a subscription fee to every single MMOG experience that becomes available to players. This points to a saturation problem for MMOGs, since only the most dedicated players forming a much smaller audience may subscribe to a few subscription-based games.

One solution might be to "package" several MMOG subscriptions together and offer the player a choice of which particular titles they would like to play for a package price. Much thought has gone into several solutions along this line. In order to pay for MMOGs, publishers are eager to find ways to attach a subscription-oriented fee, yet this would seem to indicate that only a few titles could survive.

Despite this fact, many publishers are trying to capture an audience with an MMOG. The titles available vary in quality, for a number of reasons, and many are fighting just to stay afloat. One thing seems certain: no one really believes that game players will pay for large numbers of subscription-oriented games simultaneously.

Pure Production Risks for the MMOG

The cost of developing, deploying, and maintaining an MMOG can be astronomical. The risk level is very high. If a game publisher pours millions of dollars into an MMOG, only to have it fail to find an audience, that game publisher may not be around to make another game of any kind tomorrow. It seems that publishers regularly look at the success of *Everquest,* as an example, and hope to replicate the revenue stream created by having a successful subscription-based game. However, the risk and expense in building such a title are enormous. Only by taking that risk with a considerable budget and team composition in place were the developers of *Everquest* able to deliver. This did not happen overnight. It took time for subscribers to find and fall in love with the game, which is time other titles may not be able to pay for. If they don't find an immediate audience, they will die off quickly.

Everquest is now a good example of a soaring MMOG, but the competition to be "one" of the profitable MMOGs is intense. Consider *The Sims Online* by Electronic Arts (http://thesimsonline.ea.com/). This highly anticipated title, which was even featured on the cover of *Newsweek,* was developed at considerable expense to provide players with an MMOG version of the very popular *Sims* titles for the PC. It was a large risk, and has met with mixed results.

There is little room for mistakes when development costs are this high, yet mistakes will be made. Let's not mercilessly beat up the developers and publishers for trying to build an MMOG either. Don't forget that MMOG development is gaming evolution taking place before our eyes. Experimentation and progress do not deliver predictable results.

Many factors affect the success or failure of any game title, including MMOG titles based on subscription models. Some of these factors include the following:

> **Price**   How expensive is the title and the platform? Remember the saturation issue.

> **Availability**   How entrenched or available is the platform to players?

> **Content particulars**   Is it a great game? Does it find its audience? Does the game fill a need amongst competitors?

> **Familiarity**   How familiar are players with the type or style of game?

Many game publishers are being very cautious about overcommitting to MMOG development. They prefer to watch other publishers spend money and suffer the gains or losses. Based on this observation, they may or may not choose to enter the field and develop an MMOG title. Again, remember that the MMOG is a particularly risky and expensive proposition. Some publishers are simply more comfortable operating on more solid ground (like PlayStation 2 development).

Cost and Support Considerations for the MMOG

What are some of the risk areas and costs that make this form of game development so risky? There are many factors to consider carefully, a few of which are discussed in the following sections.

Server Installation and Redundancy

Since most MMOG titles are client/server oriented (where a game server hosts a game and clients/players connect to it), there is often substantial costs involved in setting up game server hardware (PCs) to host games. If your game is designed to host hundreds or thousands of simultaneous players, multiple servers will be required to host and accommodate the number of server-side game instances necessary to handle all of these potential players.

If you plan to roll out your game regionally, nationally, or internationally, you may need to scatter servers across the country or find a company with "regionalized" servers already in place to host your game serving needs. Companies like Akamai (www.akamai.com) offer server distribution and support services that can be utilized to place your game servers strategically around the United States, for instance, as you begin to roll out an MMOG for U.S.-based game players. For an Xbox Live game, Microsoft will provide all the hosting services. Microsoft has enormous provisioning right now to grow many Xbox Live game titles, running at a fraction of full capacity.

Bandwidth Support Issues

It can cost considerable amounts of money to keep large bandwidth pipes open for game data transfer between your game servers and your clients or players. This is a sizeable support expense that must be factored into the cost of maintaining the persistent game environment.

Hardware Support and Maintenance

Unlike client-based games, like a simple console title for instance, MMOG titles require significant server hardware support, updates, configuration, and maintenance. This includes not just the cost of hardware, of course, but also enough staff to keep it running with stability.

Database/Backend Construction and Maintenance

Where does all of that saved character and inventory item information go in an MMOG? It gets stored in a database or "backend" that interfaces with the game server. Popular database solutions include Oracle (www.oracle.com) on the high end, and MySQL (www.mysql.com) as a more affordable, yet very powerful choice, among many other options. The game server passes off character-based information regularly to the database. This helps to prevent cheating, maintain character integrity, and establish certain security features. Development and maintenance of this database backend is painstaking, deliberate, and expensive work.

QA Costs

It's very difficult to run an MMOG title through QA. You don't just show up with a game build on a fresh CD. You need a sophisticated test plan and a considerable staff to help test all of the game functionality checks you'll need to perform to get an MMOG to a point of stability. Player community beta testers are of great assistance, but in order for their feedback to be valuable, it has to be managed and prioritized.

The last thing you want to do is launch a bug-riddled MMOG, alienating your audience if players lose their hard-earned experience because the database chokes, drops game information, and crashes. All aspects of the client/server game application, database interface, connectivity issues, subscription functionality, and character or game data integrity must be thoroughly and systematically tested. It is quite simply a vast undertaking that very few game industry professionals have much experience with yet.

If you're going to deploy a professional testing team to complement free beta-test feedback from interested players, it's going to cost a considerable amount of money in staff support simply because MMOG titles are so difficult and time-consuming to test. It will take thousands of hours to complete the test phase and insure some measure of reliability for the title.

Worldwide Support Staff

Since MMOG titles are persistent and run in real time, we have entered the era of "game-masters," in which we need world support staff for our titles. Game-masters are like world referees. They try to resolve player issues and help to keep the peace, by acting as a police force in the live game world. Players will often get into bitter conflicts within the game. Some players will work to destroy the play experience of other players. They will work hard to cause problems. As a game publisher, you want to insure a solid and enjoyable play experience for your customer. In the world of MMOGs, this often necessitates the hiring of game-masters or world support staff to support the game title. This is obviously a new and unique staffing requirement.

Security and Attack Issues

Since the successful MMOG is reliant on a subscription model, there is an e-commerce element to your game. Players will need to manage their accounts and pay for game services. This involves the exchange of sensitive information, like credit card numbers. MMOGs require adequate and sometimes costly software security devices to insure that players can pay for their account details securely. And, of course, there is always the perennial problem of hackers trying to crash your game servers, crash your account information systems, and/or infiltrate player records or commerce information.

COPPA Issues

If your content is directed at a younger gaming audience, there are obvious safety concerns for younger players who may be vulnerable online. For games targeting players in the U.S., you should consult the COPPA (www.ftc.gov/bcp/conline/pubs/buspubs/coppa.htm) guidelines, effective since April 2001, for compliance.

MMOG CONSTRUCTION FACTORS AND SOLUTIONS

We've now seen some of the production challenges that accompany MMOGs. What further considerations and possible solutions arc there? In the following sections, we'll take a look at some of the specific considerations for building MMOGs. Each of these considerations is important for the design focus of an MMOG. In all of game development, but especially in MMOG creation, technical limitations play a large role in determining design orientation. If the technology support structure for game development were as wide open as our imaginations, there would be little need to consider these in any detail. However, this is clearly not the case. Technology parameters regularly forcefully shape design specifics.

General MMOG Structures

If we consider the structure of an MMOG, what do we find? We know that we want hundreds or maybe even thousands of players connected together inside each instance of our game world as it lives on each game server. We know that players will load the game on their PCs and become game clients, and then, via an ISP (Internet service provider) connection and a network cloud (what's between the ISP and the game server via the Internet), they can exchange data via a game server. Figure 8-1 represents this idea graphically.

You can see from Figure 8-1 that there are network cloud and ISP dependencies that the transfer or flow of the game data will encounter. As game data travels from the player's machine (the client) through its pathway to the game server, that data is acknowledged and acted on by the game server as input and sent back to the player's machine. Although this physical process is fairly rapid, for a real-time game, considerable amounts of time are being spent on data travel. This scenario creates one of the biggest problems for MMOG design, commonly called *latency*. Figure 8-2 illustrates how making router-to-router jumps within a network cloud as data travels back and forth to the player's client machine contributes to latency. We'll talk more about exactly why this is such a problem in the "Latency" section, later in this chapter.

If this is a typical MMOG structure, then, from a design standpoint, we know what we have to design around or consider in our design ideas. It's important to understand that for game event updating (like determining if a player's projectile "hits" an enemy and performing the resulting animation and damage updates), your messaging system has to traverse this somewhat slow and convoluted highway from point A to point B and then back to point A again.

Design Considerations for Massively Multiplayer Online Games

FIGURE 8-1

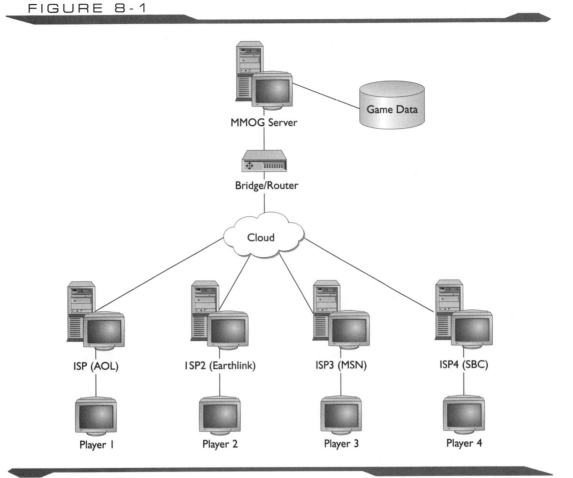

Basic MMOG structure

Many developers choose to write their own MMOG engine, database, and support tools. There are also a few boxed solutions becoming available to developers who may not have the time or resources to write an entire MMOG engine and all of the support code. One such solution is offered by LithTech (www.lithtech.com). The LithTech engine is a popular engine solution for standard PC and console development, but the folks at LithTech have gone a step further in providing an MMOG technology solution called the "LithTech Discovery System." This is a complete code base with support tools to allow game developers to build MMOG titles.

FIGURE 8-2

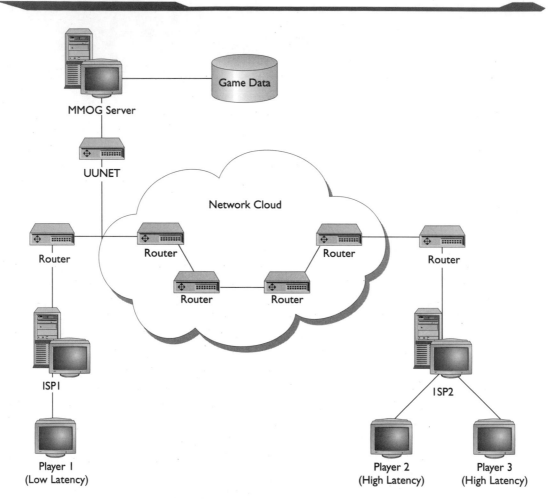

Latency from player's machine to game server

Another solution provider is Terra Zona (www.zona.net). Not surprisingly, developers routinely like to survey the experiences of other developers in using any one of these solutions. It's difficult for a prebuilt or boxed solution to anticipate the content needs and tools support requirements developers may need to create a wide variety of content. Vast amounts of technical refinement are normally required for any "out-of-the-box" solution, leading some developers to shy away from using boxed MMOG frameworks and toward taking the big plunge in developing all of their MMOG from scratch. This route, as we've said, can be devastating to timelines and budgets.

If you choose to write your own MMOG engine, the cost and time impact could be so steep that by the time the technology is stable, your content idea or game content direction may have lost some of its original appeal due to competitors. Preparing for the construction of an MMOG title requires serious preparation, market study, and technology evaluation. If there are no trade secret or disclosure issues applicable, it can be a serious advantage to have your MMOG construction plans subjected to a peer review by other developers with experience crafting MMOGs.

MMOG DESIGN FACTORS

We've seen how technical considerations shape design decisions. Now it's time to look at several of the design factors that play a part in building, enhancing, and maintaining MMOG content. Again, this is the newest and largest technology and design area to challenge game developers everywhere. If we're looking for comfortable MMOG design rules to lean on, they are still being written. Every developer is looking for answers to design issues (and not just for MMOGs!). Every developer is trying to understand how to best challenge and engage players in an MMOG setting using all the strengths (and none of the weaknesses) of the platform. No one really wants to simply repeat the same game ideas that worked well in non-MMOGs. Some of those ideas are an utter mismatch for the MMOG platform in any case.

In this section, we're going to focus on some of the critical design factors that affect the development of any kind of MMOG. These issues tend to apply across the board, and are not necessarily genre specific.

Latency

Latency, as mentioned earlier, is one of the biggest problems designers face in doing anything interesting (in a fast action sense) game-wise. This is why character-driven MMOG titles or MMORPGs work so well. Notice that the successful character-driven MMOG designs emphasize what the MMOG platform can do well, rather than what developers wish the platform would do well. This is smart design. There is combat in these titles, but it's not the kind of combat fast-action game players will probably appreciate. How about other genre extension into the MMOG? Why don't we see MMOG sports, racing, shooters, and so forth? Real-time operations, judgments, calculations, and latency don't mix very well at all.

Due to latency issues, the best MMOGs avoid trying to do "twitch" game features, because it's too difficult and the results are less than impressive. Remember also that your game players or clients are connected to your game server at different speeds and thus have different server-to-client update speeds. This means that player 1 could have performed an action and run around the corner before player 2 even knows what player 1 has done. Doesn't exactly make for a fair or playable game, does it? Often times latency issues can produce delays so distracting that a game becomes fundamentally unplayable. This is a critical point for our discussion in this chapter.

Modularity

Since most MMOGs are using a subscription model, game developers want to be able to update the world with new areas, regions, or entire sequel packs on a regular basis. This demands modular design. Your worlds and game environments by definition need to be extensible. Most importantly, your tool set must allow you to build in this fashion. If you have to undo prior world information details (in other words, geometry updates) to add on more world areas, you're in trouble. You want your environment to be entirely modular.

Monitoring

You need to plan for and build in a monitoring system in your game. You also need an offline test environment to try out your design changes and modular expansion that replicates real-world play conditions (including latency issues).

Tools Support

Tools support for MMOGs is not a luxury, it's a requirement. The power of your construction tools literally helps to make or break your title. If you have a monitored game environment, your game monitoring tools need to allow for player warnings and dismissals.

Special Events

One of the cool features of MMOG titles is the possibility of hosting special events within the game. Having this ability for a game-master or monitor also requires powerful tools support. Tournaments, special give-aways, or events related to holidays can all take place within the game world. These kinds of events are really new to gaming, and have only begun to grow inside some of the live MMOGs available.

Pace and Balance

Including proper pace and balance is a huge issue for MMOGs. Obviously, due to a subscription focus, developers want to keep you busy in the game world for extended periods of time. However, this can and does go overboard. There is a balance that must be found between keeping players active, happy, and subscribed, and building monotonous and tiresome gameplay tasks. Personally, I don't want to spend hundreds of hours achieving the simplest of tasks or climbing a never-ending ranking ladder with my character. As MMOGs continue to attract more mainstream players with busy and hurried lives, the demands for visible game progress in shorter time periods is bound to increase. If you are willing to commit 40–60 hours playing an MMOG per week, that's fine, but many players want the MMOG experience without the 40–60 hour weekly commitment. The MMOG design that caters to this reality will probably find a large audience.

Player Dropout/Lost Connections

Player dropout due to lost physical connections between a player's PC and the game server must be considered. Sudden exits from the game, caused perhaps by the player suddenly turning off the PC or a local power outage, affect character data and dependencies between players within the MMOG world. If you were playing a significant role in collaborating with other players performing some deed or action and suddenly drop out, play is obviously going to be affected adversely both for you and your peers. Your design and technical team will have to tackle the following questions:

❯ What will your game do if a packet is dropped?

❯ What will your game do if packets are received out of sequence?

❯ What will your game do if a player's computer suddenly loses power?

❯ What will your game do if one of the game servers goes down during play?

❯ How will your game verify that players are running the official game client, and not a hacked client that gives them perfect aim or some other unfair advantage?

Network protocols for MMOGs frequently use UDP rather than TCP. In short, your design must account for these potentialities with rapid and exhaustive saves of character information and careful analysis of in-game player-to-player dependencies. Notice that most successful MMOGs account for this fact by limiting extreme player-to-player dependencies. If a player drops out while banding together to kill a monster horde, it has some negative impact to be sure, but if a player drops out in an MMOG sports title, it can be devastating to the play experience (for example, the pitcher in a baseball game drops out mid-inning, mid-pitch).

MMOG Play Mechanics

When it comes down to building play mechanics for the MMOG, designers have to constantly weigh an intended play effect with "big" problems like latency. You can't really resolve latency, so you are forced to design around it. Again, this makes satisfying twitch game experiences in the MMOG basically impossible by definition. Play-wise, anything that you want to do in an MMOG must consider latency issues. Sometimes a team will overreach and try to build in ideas that, at first, seemed possible even with latency as a challenge.

Gameplay ideas that once seemed possible don't always pan out, and without a technology resolution in place for your idea, you end up spending valuable time and resources that would probably have been better spent working on what you know will work for the platform. *Everquest*, as an example, does a remarkable job of working around latency, even for players with lower-speed connections. As a point of design learning, notice that the play mechanics, actions, and abilities in *Everquest* are combined and geared well for the MMOG platform. The melee fight mechanics, for instance, are about as fast and fluid as can be currently conceived for an MMOG. These fight mechanics are nowhere near as fluid or dynamic as a console fighter, but you can't even begin to expect that kind of fluidity and response due to the very nature of the MMOG platform.

I like to say that game design is gaming technology's greatest partner, but also its prisoner. Design is always "handcuffed" by technology, and I don't mean this negatively. I mean that design limits are clearly a function of technology dependencies. In the early 1990s, as silly money and talent poured into the game industry, many seemed to believe that games could do "anything," limited only by imagination. Everyone seemed to forget the "handcuff" idea.

MMOGS AND DESIGN ORIENTATION

As we all know, MMOGs are relatively new on the game scene. Learning about how to design for (and capture) the MMOG audience is obviously important for the many MMOGs in production right now as well as for the future growth of this kind of gaming experience. Let's turn our attention for the moment to some of the design learning issues many in the industry are struggling with:

) MMOG genre growth

) NPCs and familiars

) Isolating MMOG strengths

) MMOG player categories

) Deep social factors

) Current challenges

MMOG Genre Growth

The most successful MMOGs to date are character development driven. There are several choices available for players looking to play these character-oriented titles. Some players complain that it seems like *only* character-oriented titles are available. I think titles like *PlanetSide* (www.planetside.com) from Sony Online Entertainment are attempting to change this dynamic. We haven't seen the successful spread of several popular console or PC platform genres into the MMOG world. Some of the reasons for the limit of genre availability for MMOGs are all of the inherent technology restrictions involved in making any MMOG title at all. Another, as we've said, is the huge financial risk. Despite these reasons, developers are constantly looking for ways to offer expansive gaming experiences. The question becomes: Which genres do you build around and why?

It seems that MMOGs will only grow out into new genre forms as developers begin to figure out how to offer other genres (or versions of other genres) built around many of the technology dependencies discussed in this chapter. These titles will survive only if the public receives them well and development, promotional, and support costs can be contained.

NPCs and Familiars

NPCs in many MMOGs are used functionally but often are somewhat sterile and hollow characters. Familiars or "pets" are used dynamically, and many players seem to like them. The game *Half-life* (a non-MMOG title) really raised the bar in the use of NPCs for first-person shooters. These are exactly the kind of incomplete or under-developed play areas that you want to try to address with your own games. Which MMOG title will do for MMOG familiars what *Half-life* did to raise the bar for NPC use and interaction in FPS titles? Don't forget that your design focus should consider what all the competitors have done well. When you understand why it works in play, you can try to evolve and refine your own play ideas into something exciting that we'll all enjoy playing.

Isolating MMOG Strengths

At this point, we know plenty about MMOG delivery weaknesses (like latency). We must also identify strengths for the MMOG. One strength, by definition, is that you have large numbers of players collected together in a game universe of some description. It should be no surprise that you'll probably want to tap *social forces* as inspiration points for play mechanics. Legendary game designer Chris Crawford wrote the game *Balance of Power* long before the advent of the MMOG, but he applied an under-standing of human conflict and human drama that helped to shape and inform gameplay. Ask yourself the question: How do you make the social forces we take for granted both exciting and interesting in play? How do you use social competition to create conflict?

MMOG Player Categories

The MMOG has also helped to annihilate rigid player categories. People of all ages and genders (from grandmothers to grade-schoolers) play the most popular MMOGs with passion. It's becoming harder in some gaming segments—MMOGs are probably a good example—for marketers to clearly identify "the gamer" or "the audience." I predict it will become harder every day. This fact alone opens up new vistas and venues for game makers.

Trying to build games for unknown, growing, or changing audiences (in other words, trying to be all things to all players) can also have a negative design effect. The idea of trying to please a wide and diverse audience can dilute a game to the extent that the kind of play that might have made the game successful simply gets lost in the dilution. You simply can't be the game of everything for everybody. Believe me, you'll get design input: don't make it too fast for the older players, don't make it too complicated for the younger players, don't make it too boring for the teens, don't make it too aggressive for the female players, and so on.

Deep Social Factors

The deep social factors involved in playing MMOGs are some of the most interesting informal sociology experiments to watch and build design orientations around. Players take tremendous psychological ownership of their characters. I suspect this will continue to be true for noncharacter items in MMOG worlds as well (earned vehicles, houses, riches, or status). The social aspect of MMOGs, missing in many other game forms, seems to attract more female players than similar content titles with very little or nonexistent social features. Guys like to chat, too, but taking on the role of a true character requires development, nurturing, and socialization.

Some MMOGs, like *The Sims Online* and *Everquest,* have created entire virtual economies. You've probably read news articles on the economics of Norrath (a land in *Everquest*), where players can actually earn $3.42/hour via bots that collect virtual goods that are then sold for real currency. This leads to the odd result that if Norrath were a real country, it would be the 77th richest. We've only just begun to see the impact of these kinds of virtual economies in MMOG gaming.

Appealing to the use and allotment of status items and status issues seems to work successfully in connecting emotions with play ideas. So does providing a means for players to "rise above" in game world rankings, as some players believe they will not or cannot rise above or transcend their own day-to-day lives. Remember when we talked about the importance of engaging emotions? MMOGs capture player emotions very well in some cases, often leading to emotional fervor for some.

The power of obtaining in-game status items should not be overlooked either. In a real-world society bent on never-ending status judgments, players often take great pleasure in the display of game-based status items. This propensity, from a content development standpoint, has only been explored on the surface. There are a large number of social-force phenomena that remain to be explored within the MMOG setting.

Current Challenges

The biggest design learning challenge for MMOGs today is trying to understand exactly how to best use the medium to entertain players while at the same time building commercial content. There is such an inordinate amount of risk involved that mistakes can be fatal. As we've seen, MMOGs demand huge resources. If huge resources are committed to a design idea that flops, the results for game publishers can be devastating.

Although there are similarities, game publishers do not yet operate under the exact same economic model as the movie business, where a monster hit can pay for many failures. Again, what makes an MMOG a "monster hit" is the subscription revenue combined with the game sales. However, as previously discussed, how many "monster hit" subscription models can survive together? What about saturation? You can see as many hit movies as you would like. You won't be paying for each of them on a month-to-month basis.

More than any other game type, the MMOG must reconcile huge financial risk with a perceived "sure thing" design idea. Perfect design ideas rarely equal perfect design implementations. Hence, the MMOG somewhat stands alone in forging out new content avenues for game players.

SPORTS FANS OR GROUPS AND MMOGS

If the past shapes the future, sports will most likely play a significant role in the growth of MMOGs if several technology hurdles can be overcome. Love them or hate them, sports titles have repeatedly driven console game hardware and software. Combine this force with every major console moving online with varying success so far, and you begin to create a very interesting scenario for sports game development. Sports game development for online consoles in an MMOG setting could quite certainly help innovate technology solutions that would help make other, even newer, genres available to players.

It's true that sports titles haven't had the same exact impact on the PC, for several reasons (like the controller difference between a game pad and a keyboard), but FPS titles that have continually pushed the PC forward don't typically do very well on the consoles.

Since the sports gaming community is so large on the consoles, many publishers are watching closely as the forces come together to make sports-oriented MMOGs a reality. I'm not going to downplay the large technology hurdles standing in the way. There are several. Yet for all the major sports games like baseball, football, basketball, hockey, golf, and soccer (among many others), game players are waiting to see where the next evolution in sports gaming will take them.

Recently, I've had the privilege of working on what appears to be the world's first baseball MMOG. For many of the reasons I've already given, this is a complex and difficult undertaking with sizeable technology hurdles at every corner. The game industry is often accused of simply cranking out safe, formula-based titles. There is some weight to this argument. If you *only* crank out safe formula titles, you will not create new opportunities to gain players. You simply cannot create entirely new markets without risk. Again, it's a matter of balance and execution. You can't just run out and create an MMOG as a wild risk, either, simply because it seems hot or trendy to do so.

Figure 8-3 is a screenshot from *Ultimate Baseball Online* (www.ultimatebase ballonline.com) that shows several players hooked up together via a game server playing each baseball field position together. As always, there are numerous design

FIGURE 8-3

Ultimate Baseball Online

challenges to consider. How do you keep the player engaged while waiting for action in right field? What do you do if the player currently pitching loses his or her connection to the game? How do you manage unruly players who want to run around blowing the game vibe? And there are a zillion other considerations besides.

This is the first attempt to try to build an MMOG sports title of any kind that I know about anywhere. Why aren't more of these titles in production? There are many reasons. First and foremost, publishers are hesitant to take on the extremely sizeable technology issues and potential large-scale costs of such an undertaking. There can be little doubt, however, that from a pure content perspective, this title attempts to innovate. That spirit to innovate against large odds, and a love for baseball itself, is what attracted me to the title initially. Whether the title ultimately succeeds or fails, it will certainly have tried something new. Either way, I was fortunate. How many titles these days are trying anything new?

I mention all of this simply because it suggests something about one possibility in the near future for MMOGs. Every kind of MMOG that succeeds (sports included!) helps make another one possible in some sense. With the large numbers of very dedicated sports players out there, always ready to get the next *Madden 2003* title for the next available platform, and with the consoles moving online, there is a sports-playing storm waiting to happen. More importantly, this storm will pass over into other genres as well.

Bringing traditional sports fans, fantasy fans, action/fighting fans, and science-fiction fans into the MMOG arena for PCs or online consoles is exactly what gaming needs in order to grow. As a designer, think about—and examine closely—each of these dedicated groups of fans. Remember, in MMOG design we're looking to create play scenarios for groups using social forces.

Each group's dynamics and particular affections bring dimension to the MMOG world. Consider how you might go about making MMOG content to bring one of these groups together in a persistent gaming environment. What are the social issues? What are the emotional hooks? Which "twitch" or thought behaviors are most compelling or exciting? Do they hold up over repetition? What behaviors best serve the fantasy socially, emotionally, and actively?

MMOG Opportunities

As MMOG titles mature, and technology becomes more stable, it will become easier for this type of title to be produced. The budgets will come back from orbit, and so might the timelines. MMOGs really are little immersive/persistent worlds. This idea is attractive to many at the pure concept level. The collision of concept worlds and game technology is one of the most exciting aspects of MMOG growth. The forthcoming *Star Wars Galaxies* is a perfect example to illustrate this idea; it uses much of the development experience gained in the creation and support of *Everquest* to create a gaming universe that utilizes one of the best known and loved fictional universes available.

Those entities/intellectual property rights holders (IPRHs) who have well-known and developed universes may decide to encapsulate players by creating the MMOG version of their worlds. These entities long ago offered their properties to console game makers. By doing so, they helped to drive console game engine development and innovation, despite the hesitance of some, and the preference of many, to work on all original titles. Access to reliable MMOG technology will create a number of new opportunities for game makers.

Advertising factions, heavy with promotional dollars and eager to have players "living in their ad worlds," will probably play a factor in the near future of MMOGs. These experiences won't require a subscription model at all. I know it sounds like heresy, but you can build a persistent *Star Trek* universe just as easily as one for McDonald's. Many developers cringe at this idea, and I can certainly understand why they might. Personally, my interest revolves around seeing technology solutions and opportunity come into gaming—whatever their source.

CASE STUDY COMMENTS ON CHALLENGES FOR UBO

Ultimate Baseball Online (*UBO*) is an innovation. The developers of this game chose to take on the great challenge of trying to build a complete MMOG baseball experience. In game development, as in many other related software development fields, any time real innovation is required, you can bet that production path stumbling blocks will become nearly impossible to avoid. It becomes very hard to predict the exact nature of the troubles you will face (and even harder to define the exact timelines and costs for a project-saving solution) as a development team when you are learning about failure while failing, and learning about success while succeeding. Rest assured, when you innovate, you can assume that even the best analysis and prediction techniques will be skewed and your time and budget resources will be affected considerably.

New area technology exploration, like the world of MMOG development, takes great time, money, and patience (each of these a particular kind of boon for the commercial game development world). These are just a few of the reasons why so many publishers have chosen to be very cautious about committing to MMOG projects. This leaves room for the small to medium-size developers and publishers to work hard at delivering a miracle, and gaining some of the MMOG audience for themselves.

Without committing to a full post-mortem (since the game is still in progress), I'd like to take a moment to evaluate some of the known challenges the developers of *UBO* faced in the building of this title.

First, this is not a licensed title. There is no Major League Baseball Player's Association (MLBPA) license attached to this game. As you might figure, these licenses are cost-prohibitive to say the very least. Several high-profile baseball titles by large game publishers pay for these licenses for their franchise baseball titles. The resultant effect is that *UBO* cannot use well-known players, teams, or stadiums in the title. Many players take access to these factors as a given for single- or two-player games. However, this is an MMOG title. Part of the fantasy in playing the game is to role-play up your own characters into the big leagues. In the recent past, if you made a solid game, titles could perform quite well without the "license factor." Today, for many reasons, this just doesn't seem to be the case.

Building a 3-D game engine with sophisticated client/server architecture capable of handling synchronized real-time baseball events proved, not surprisingly, to be a Herculean undertaking. Resolving latency under different player connection scenarios was the premiere issue. Of course, we also had to build in all of the game functionality recognized as the rules and play of baseball.

Pure engine development costs were sizeable, and the heavy support and maintenance costs put further pressure on budget details. Sony's *Everquest* and Microsoft's *Asheron's Call* have Sony and Microsoft behind them. This makes it extremely difficult for the independent developer to compete in this area, and extremely risky for everyone but the largest of publishers capable of taking multimillion dollar charges against their bottom lines.

For many reasons, including cost, development of the game engine was done in Korea. This created many production challenges, language barriers, and localization factors for a game destined to be deployed in the United States. Note that sending entire game titles overseas for development is a trend on the rise. This can be compared with sending animation projects around the world in an effort to save production costs.

Remote development is always a challenge, even with experienced teams, clear goals, and adequate resource support. It can be done successfully, but regularly involves significant challenges. However, when trying to innovate an entirely new title, it becomes a decent burden. I would not recommend remote development on such an innovative title, in a new content category, even for a team with solid MMOG creation experience.

Since the developers of *UBO* had enough challenge on their hands just implementing the basics for such an aggressive title, tools implementation tended to suffer. Without great tools, or great and constant programming resources, the play of your game will suffer. Plenty of necessary tool modifications were planned, but those plans were left on the backburner as more pressing mainline engine challenges would not relent.

In terms of resources, MMOG development is not for the faint of heart. After all, the MMOG is the most complex and sophisticated kind of gaming experience available today. It's going to cost plenty of money to meet the technology challenges. But let's face it, very few small to medium-size developers/publishers have pockets deep enough to weather the storm of MMOG development. Tight resources will take their toll on a title as much as any other factor. Tight resources definitely took their toll on *UBO*.

Preferring to incur all of the risk, and most of the potential gain, many of the publishing details for *UBO* were left open ended. The developer wanted to self-publish the title in a way similar to titles like *Anarchy Online*. Self-publishing allows for great risk and innovation (let's not forget that id Software started this way …), but has an obvious downside insofar as getting your game out there in front of potential players quickly and effectively is much more difficult. With *UBO*, the decision of exactly which publishing relationship would work best for all parties involved remained unresolved for some time.

There was tremendous benefit to participating in the development of *UBO*. If you work around game development long enough, you will often reflect on how a project could have been improved, and every project remains a chance for learning. The spirit of innovation that surrounded this game title attracted me to it. Everyone was focused on a best-faith effort to make this game a reality.

Creating new content of any kind, especially for new or unfamiliar platforms, is often a painful experience for developers. *UBO* was no different. I suspect that every MMOG that has entered the gaming market since *Everquest* or *Asheron's Call* has gone through its share of pain. Over time, as platform familiarities arise and team learning occurs, the pain can be quelled somewhat.

UBO partnered with MLB great Darrell Evans to help build in the feel of a major league experience. This kind of content collaboration has been done before, but as MMOGs require unheard-of levels of authenticity for sports experiences, this may form an exciting new partnership.

I'm always interested in trying to bring new details to a game design that helps make a game more fun to play, and helps to set it apart from competitors. We should always be looking for a way to turn around a play idea, but we also want to bring new edges to our games. No matter what genre, if every developer keeps putting the same details into their games, then the industry really isn't heading anywhere. We're only getting sharper or prettier versions of the same old picture.

Throughout the course of *UBO* development, it has been very helpful to have access to baseball experts (former all-star players on hitting and pitching for instance). They help reveal subtle nuances of the game that can help influence and shape game design details to provide the best gaming experience possible. They won't necessarily understand why a development team makes the trade-offs and choices it does to preserve game action, but their insight will help transfer experience to the enthusiastic player.

Another outstanding element to *UBO* is that it tries to extend the genre categories for the MMOG. If MMOG-based gaming experiences are going to survive, they have to move beyond an RPG core. There is nothing wrong with the MMOG titles out there—I think they are brilliant game feats—but much work remains to be done in scattering around the kind of content they offer to the player.

Again, success or failure for *UBO* will not change the fact that the development team tried to extend the genre offerings for MMOGs. Innovation is painful. Bumpy development histories are okay. Some developers believe that if you haven't shipped every title you've ever touched, you must not be very good at what you do professionally. Nothing could be further from the truth. Talk to the creators of many of the best-made and best-selling game titles available and you'll hear another story. If you catch them in the right mood, they'll tell you all about the games that got away and didn't ship. It's part of the growth process.

Plenty of the technology developed in the course of building *UBO* can be used in a number of other ways. This is true for other developers of MMOG titles as well. They can reuse their technologies to offer other types of game or game-related content.

Probably most important in the development curve of an MMOG is the experience gained that can be directly applied to your next venture. This is true, of course, for non-MMOG titles as well, but it's particularly true of MMOGs because they are so wide in scope.

If you are developing an MMOG title or are planning one in your mind, take some comfort; remember we're all in this together. At the end of the day, what we're really looking for are new opportunities to grow gaming. MMOGs will continue to be a very important part of that plan into the future.

usiness courses, computer courses, all excellent ways to prepare. Nothing makes a hiring manager feel better than hiring the right qualified person for the job and

INTERVIEW WITH MICHAEL WEINER

Michael Weiner has been in the game industry since 1989 when he joined what was then Buena Vista Software (now Disney Interactive) to start both its Customer Support and Quality Assurance departments. After a couple of years with Disney, Michael moved on to Sierra Online (then still in Oakhurst, CA) and took his first formal QA manager position with Sierra's daughter company, The Sierra Network. From there he went through a series of positions with Sega of America, Acclaim Entertainment, Disney Online, 3DO, and Hasbro. Michael has also worked as an executive recruiter for Studio Search in Las Vegas, NV and is currently doing consulting for the Ultimate Baseball Online team. His work with them centers around helping ensure proper QA practices and procedures are followed as well as running their remote testing teams. Michael has twice been a selected speaker at the industry's Game Developers Conference (2000 and 2002).

TM: What do companies look for in game design candidates?

MW: Mostly, companies look for experience and passion. There's a lot of "wannabes" out there trying to get into the industry, and while that's great—it keeps our industry fresh—the hiring managers are looking for the people that will give them the most bang for their buck … and that is someone who's already got a proven track record of success. And that success means they've worked on a title that's shipped, they've worked on a hit title, they've got proof of the quality of the work they can do, they've shown they can work on a team, under pressure, through long hours, and still come back for more.

TM: How do recruiters assist game developers?

MW: We provide developers with a new resource for finding the best talent out there. Most companies simply can't spend all day hunting for talented people. They have to depend on traditional channels like job listings, shows, job fairs, or word of mouth. As recruiters, we spend all day looking for people with experience to show to the developers.

TM: What are some do's and don'ts when approaching recruiters, and how much experience should you have before contacting a recruiter?

MW: One thing you definitely don't want to do is hound a recruiter. Most recruiters don't get paid unless they place you. So they don't need you calling or writing each day saying "Anything yet?", "Anything yet?", "Anything yet?". Asking once a week is enough. But believe me, when a recruiter has a job for you, they will let you know!

As for how much experience should you have, the more you have the better. If you have less than two years' experience, even if you worked on a big kick-ass title, a recruiter won't be able to place you. Why? Because two years in this industry is a minimum! There's lots of people who have been in it far longer who may also be looking for something new, and when a company looks for experience … well, you can do the math.

TM: How volatile does the gaming market appear to be with respect to hiring and layoffs?

MW: This is one of the most volatile businesses I could imagine. I talk almost every week to people who have just been laid off. I've been in it close to 15 years and I've been laid off twice myself! This industry is very much a "who's hot now" kind of business and companies must constantly evaluate and adjust their positions to stay either on top or at least solvent. There's nothing guaranteed here, even with the "big boys." We are at the whim of fickle consumers, changing economic conditions, changing technologies, and attempts to run sound business plans against it all. Make no mistake … its the toughest industry I've ever seen.

TM: What advice would you offer to a new game designer in finding work in this area?

MW: First, be prepared to "pay your dues." Many, many people who are now designers started in QA as testers. Not everyone, some got lucky, but starting in QA is the surest way. It also has the benefit of letting you see how things operate first hand. Who knows, in the end a would-be designer may find it's a lot more work than they thought and explore something else. Once you're on the inside, make friends with people. And not just in QA. Without causing a disruption, talk to the people on the development teams, ask them what they're doing. If you have some samples you've done, take them to lunch and ask them to critique your work. But do not impose yourself on anyone who is busy, under a deadline, or working like mad. This industry is too small to make any enemies. But take your time, pay your dues, have patience, have confidence, and you'll make it.

TM: What materials do most companies require from game design candidates?

MW: Depending on the type of designer position, it will vary slightly. For level designers, they mostly ask for screenshots of levels you've created. For game designers, those who design the look, feel, plot, characters, action, and everything else in the game, they will sometimes ask for writing samples. This may mean they give you a one-sentence idea and look for how you grow it into a game. It's all about being sure you can do the work, not just want to do the work.

TM: What kind of backgrounds (education and experience) do most successful design candidates have?

MW: First and foremost, game companies want gamers. That may sound like it should go without saying, but you'd be surprised how many people I met, even as interviewees for game testing jobs, who never played a game or didn't know even the most popular game titles. If you aren't passionate about gaming, how can you be passionate about the work they're going to have you do? And even more to the point, how can they expect you to know what makes a game good? When companies sink millions of dollars into a title, they need to know that you are going to deliver a hit. As for education, a lot of colleges and universities are starting to offer courses in game design. Always a good thing to be able to say you've studied. And business courses, computer courses, all excellent ways to prepare. Nothing makes a hiring manager feel better than hiring the right qualified person for the job and knowing that they can be grown into a higher-level position because they already learned the technical or business side of things in school.

TM: How should one prepare to work in game design?

MW: Play, play, play! And read every single game review you can. Pay close attention to what is being critiqued in each case. No one worth their salt writes a game review saying "Yeah, umm … it was good! It was fun. I liked it." That's no review … it's barely an opinion! But a real review will give you insight as to what it is that is making the game good! And that's what you're after … and that's what you want to bring to a company. Then write some reviews of your own and send them out to publishers and various web sites. This could get your name out there and most certainly is a good thing to put on your resume when you are starting out. It shows the managers that you take the business seriously and are becoming more and more involved. Finally, and most importantly … listen! When you hear someone talking about what they are looking for in the job … listen! If you have strengths that match it, talk about them! But don't just tell them what you want them to know, tell them what they want to know about you! You can't do that if you don't listen. Then, after you get that first job (tester, designer, whatever), keep listening. Most of the time, those who are doing the talking are the ones who can best move you along.

TM: What are your thoughts on the near-future demand for game designers?

MW: I'd like to see demand growing, and I think it's a natural thing for it to happen. While it's possible to make a long living as a game designer, it's also important to have fresh ideas constantly flowing into the business. In the near future, demand will follow the economy. The better the economy does, the more money people have to spend on games, the more demand grows, the more game designers are needed to make games to meet the demand. We're what economists would call a "disposable income" business. We depend on people spending their "extra" cash on what we've created … and that requires a good economy.

TM: In your own experience, what are the positives and negatives to working in game development?

MW: Positives … getting paid to make games … what can be better than that? I've worked a number of different jobs both in and out of our industry and I've never had more fun than when I was working for game companies. The people are great, the atmospheres are always creative, alive, electric, and fun. And it's a big rush to then be in a store and see something you helped create sitting there waiting to be taken home and enjoyed. Likewise when you see a commercial or an ad for your game, or you read a review. Its just always a blast!

Negatives … lots of those too. This is still a very immature industry. And by that I mean that we are still learning how to run our businesses year in and year out, and through the constantly evolving technologies. Game companies have to always be looking and planning years in advance and making commitments of millions of dollars to gaming consoles, or broadband connections, or PC systems that are sometimes still in the planning stages. That's a crazy way to run a business! It can be done, however, as the success stories of our industry show, but it sometimes takes huge sacrifices from everyone involved and sometimes leaves even the best people behind.

MEGA TIPS

1. Do a thorough peer review (utilize a consultant's experience if necessary) of your technology foundation before committing to any kind of MMOG development.

2. Consider in as much detail as possible the exact scope, scale, and complexity your MMOG design will require. A fundamental miscalculation at the design stage will plague your development team throughout the development sequence should you choose to proceed with your design.

3. Be an MMOG analyst. Watch all of your competitors very closely. Troll through the newsgroups and fan sites listening carefully for patterns in player reaction to existing titles.

4. It seems kind of obvious, but it's probably not a great idea to try to make your first project as a newly formed developer an MMOG title. Build some solid client-networked games to test your production pipeline first.

5. Examine very carefully all of the cost and support considerations for MMOG titles mentioned in this chapter. Failure to meet these demands helps insure a bad play experience, and greatly harms your chances for success.

6. Before assuming a certain kind of MMOG play mechanic is possible, investigate with your team the effects of latency and dropout (among many others) to determine feasibility for your game ideas.

7. Remember that MMOGs are fundamentally another way to grow gaming, and that innovation is frequently painful, but ultimately worthwhile.

CHAPTER **9**

Cell Phones and Wireless Gaming

ANOTHER

new content horizon for gaming comes in the form of wireless devices and cell phones. This is a very new arena for gaming, where many of the most important economic factors remain unsettled. Yet, if the progress in building and delivering games made so far is to be believed, there is a very exciting future looming for wireless gaming. In my opinion, each and every possible gaming platform should always be viewed as an opportunity to grow gaming further, and wireless or mobile phone devices are no exception.

Adults who wouldn't be caught dead in public playing on a colorful chunk of plastic like a Gameboy Advance (GBA) will happily plunk away at a game on a mobile phone. Whereas a Gameboy Advance looks like a toy, mobile phones look like phones, so adults don't mind being seen using them.

Games built for these devices offer an obvious portability factor and an exciting new way to grow the gaming player base. Up to this point in the book, we've talked about the design process for game console and PC development. These platforms continue to be the "bread and butter" content areas for the largest number of game developers. However, to grow and prosper, independent game developers are constantly searching for sources of development revenue. The career of many developers and the ability to continue making games depend on it.

New opportunities to grow gaming should never be considered a blight on the game industry. Do not forget that, despite the highest-horsepower hardware on the hottest new game machine, if you can't deliver a compelling game experience that speaks to human players in some fundamental way, you have only a pricey technology demonstration on your hands. It's a similar story for many other forms of entertainment media.

Chess doesn't inspire our predictive abilities, grow us, or challenge us by the measure of polygons blasted to a screen. In other words, technology doesn't determine play value. Many have said it before me, and I couldn't agree more: if you want to know how to connect your particular game design with an audience, you must try to understand how to tap, needle, and play around with basic human desires within the context of your game—even if you're hamstrung by technology.

Players all have wants and desires. Your game designs have to satisfy these wants and desires in some way. Players project these wants into your suspended game worlds, whether the vehicle is total 3-D immersion or slow 2-D sprites.

In this chapter, we are going to explore wireless and mobile phone gaming, focusing on several practical issues, technology points, and design factors for this new gaming venue.

THE IMPENDING BOOM

Based on the estimates of large numbers of wireless subscribers in the future (which vary depending on who you ask or whose statistics you believe to be the most reliable), the future of wireless game development looks promising. I think I can safely say that the wireless revolution in communication undoubtedly will bring a revolution of sorts to gaming. How big will the revolution be? Time will tell. I don't like to quote statistics or point to bar graphs and pie charts, but many millions of potential players are out there waiting for great content.

Some believe that the wireless and cell phone hardware itself is too flawed to be attractive to gamers. This criticism seems short-sighted, because device hardware continues to improve rapidly and, over the next few years, will most likely cease to be an issue even worth considering.

In this discussion, references to wireless devices mean hardware like the Palm system (www.palm.com) or the new Nokia N-Gage game deck (www.n-gage.com), a game deck/mobile phone hybrid. N-Gage is an interesting experiment, with a high projected price point and a group of established publishers signed on in the early stages at least to support it. Figure 9-1 shows what the Nokia N-Gage game deck looks like.

FIGURE 9-1

Nokia N-Gage

References to cell phones mean any of the phones built by multiple manufacturers that are compliant with BREW (Binary Runtime Environment for Wireless, www.qualcomm.com/brew2001/) or J2ME (www.sun.com).

BREW is an operating system that allows you to download games to a BREW-enabled wireless phone. If the downloaded application does not require network access, you can use it anywhere without consuming your airtime. BREW allows developers to build applications in C, C++, or Java and has a speed performance edge over J2ME. BREW is starting to gain momentum as carriers go looking for BREW- based applications. Getting set up to develop for BREW, however, can be cost prohibitive for many small developers.

Java and J2ME are programming languages invented by Sun Microsystems, and J2ME is a version of Java specifically designed to work on small devices such as mobile phones. J2ME allows you to download games to a J2ME-enabled phone. Figure 9-2 is an example of a puzzle game application being coded or constructed within a J2ME development environment.

Other development choices include developing applications for the Symbian mobile operating system (www.symbian.com) and for Smartphones, which run a mobile

FIGURE 9-2

Game construction in J2ME development environment

version of Microsoft Windows. Figure 9-3 shows a Smartphone now available in the United Kingdom.

It is also worth mentioning the Mobile Information Device Profile (MIDP) specification, which can be used to tell your application about the kind of device on which it's running. MIDP can provide the basic application functionality required by mobile applications—like games; functionality like user interface configuration, network connectivity, local data storage, and application lifecycle management. All of this control is wrapped up in a standardized Java run-time environment with a set of Java APIs.

It's exciting to see that even as these devices are starting to have games built for them by developers, some forward-thinking companies are already preparing for the 3-D invasion on wireless units. Fathammer is currently a leader in this area (www.fathammer.com). Current-generation phones are not strong enough in processing power to handle 3-D applications, so it will take time for the hardware to catch up with the software.

Global Competition

Different parts of the world currently have varying levels of wireless networking ability. Companies that provide wireless networking services are commonly called "carriers," like Sprint PCS (www.sprintpcs.com) in the United States. You can't have millions of

FIGURE 9-3

Smartphone

you have the processing speed to take advantage of button simultaneity. Some game developers, in an effort to use the single button available, use the single key press, the hold, and the release to determine things such as momentum in a golf swing, for instance.

These are only a few of the factors, but each poses limitations that play a role in determining exactly which kinds of games you can build. It's an interesting time for cell phone game development, because to many developers who have been around for awhile, today feels much like the early days in game development when game devices like the early consoles (Intellivision, Atari 2600) had very limited processing power and memory to work with.

DESIGN ISSUES FOR CELL PHONES

It's time to dust off that 1970s material and sit down to review it for a moment. I'm not kidding. The newer phones have small color screens. Hey, at least we can use some color. They still have limited processing and memory power. Also, the programming APIs (Application Programming Interface (API) is a method given by an operating system or application program that allows a programmer writing a game to make requests of the operating system or some other application) for developing on the phones are limited. They do not currently include much of the functionality game programmers have access to on every other platform, like scaling, image flipping, and complex mathematical functions.

What does this mean? It means that the kind of games you build cannot be processor-intensive, cannot be memory hogs, and must be visible on tiny color screens. Ouch! You must always remember, however, that these are the early days, and these days will pass. Much more sophisticated gaming applications will be available shortly. Until then, you need to try to satisfy gamers and create new gamers in the best way possible given your limitations.

Figures 9-4 and 9-5 demonstrate two sample games built for J2ME-compatible phones. Figure 9-4 shows a puzzle game built for an I-Mode phone (F503i) for the Asian wireless market. Figure 9-5 is an example of a platform-style game. This type of game pushes the phone handset hardware to its limits, since most cell phone handsets require that an application fit within a 64K–100K file size or impression. Newer models hitting the market are making slightly more memory available for applications like games.

Even with a slight increase in memory availability, most games we're familiar with require processing ability, so building a platform game with satisfying speed performance on a cell phone handset is no easy task.

Keep in mind that developers of content for cell phones need access to the airwaves (to the carrier providing service to a phone) to build and update games easily. What if

FIGURE 9-4

SlideNmatch puzzle game by Magnet Island, Inc.

a developer located in the United States is building games for cell phones only available in Asia? You have no access to the carriers while sitting with the phone in the United States, so the phone hardware must be shipped back and forth to make changes to game content. This is not a very effective development route.

It's important to consider which kinds of games work well so far for the cell phone handset. This is by no means an exhaustive list, but games that tend to work well include the following:

❭ **Low-intensity shooters**   Performance-related issues determine the speed or intensity of a shooter game. Don't expect the same kind of experience available on a Gameboy Advance just yet. Remember that the Gameboy Advance is a portable platform with custom-engineered hardware built specifically for running games. Cell phone handsets simply can't blast sprites on the screen and move them around with great speed (like a Gameboy Advance). In short,

FIGURE 9-5

Kanga Kaos platform game by Magnet Island, Inc.

it's very difficult to get a shooter to behave even as well as an old shooter game for the 8-bit Nintendo.

❱ **Simple arcade games**   These work well if they don't require great speed. A good example is any game where your lead game character doesn't have to move across the screen at lightning speed, yet engages the player with simple challenges or collection goals. You will want to design around this consideration.

❱ **Sports "instance" games**   These games typically take an instance or action event from a sport and build a game around it. Examples include a "shot on goal" game using hockey or basketball. Currently, these games simply have to use sports "instances" since it would be extremely difficult to put a whole baseball or football game onto a cell phone handset and have the game be visible to the eye and perform well enough to offer satisfying game play.

❱ **Simple sports games**   These are sports games that can be represented well enough without being graphically intense. Shuffleboard and bowling are good examples. Sports that are engaging and graphics-light make a good fit for the handsets.

▶ Puzzle games or simple matching games These games are a more natural fit for handsets, as long as they don't require intense calculations or blazing speed. These restrictions, as always, factor directly into your design of a puzzle game. Figure 9-6 shows another example of a puzzle game. These games have the advantage of being graphically "light" and can be configured for simple control using the odd key arrangements available on different cell phone handset models.

▶ Themed quiz games These trivia games (about sports, movies, pop culture, and so on) work well if questions and answers are kept short and responses can be made easily by pressing a number key. These kinds of games can be popular and informative when matched with the right source content to create the questions and answers.

FIGURE 9-6

Puzzle/match game by Magnet Island, Inc.

Which games don't work well on cell phone handsets? Well, just about everything else most gamers are used to playing on one portable platform or another. Again, 3-D development is very early, and current physical screen size issues offer some large hurdles. These hurdles will be overcome in time, but for now most developers concentrate on providing content that will perform well and provide for some satisfying play. The goal is to build game content that finds its way to people on their handsets while standing in line at the DMV or sitting in an airport terminal waiting for a flight.

Any experience building small games for modest hardware will come in handy in developing these games. I'm even seeing a resurgence of veteran game programmers from the early Atari days coming out of hiding to build cell phone games or update some of their classic libraries for a new era.

Multiplay Cell Phone Gaming

Several wireless carriers, having experienced some success with single-player stand-alone games, are pushing developers toward building multiplay cell phone gaming titles. Currently, these are turn-based games that allow players to be matched up to compete. Most turn-based games work well as test subjects in order to start creating this kind of content. Most of these game titles are very early in execution, so there is no way to determine how popular this form of gaming might be, but it seems like the right kind of game could capture a sizeable audience.

Mobiles are starting to use Bluetooth (www.bluetooth.com) to enable players to discover other players. For instance, if a player is on a train and wants to play a game, but isn't close to other players or doesn't know who or where they are, the player's phone can broadcast an "Anyone want to play *Mortal Kombat*?" message to potential players.

You can bet that multiple carriers will be looking for the right kind of content to keep their subscribers happy in game offerings. Plenty of content will be focused on capturing and entertaining teenage wireless subscribers.

Having a large audience already extremely familiar with gaming is fortunate for game developers, since part of adding value to a wireless subscription service will depend on game content, among other content offerings, to keep subscribers satisfied with the value of their services.

Wireless Toy Networks

This is an expansion area for some game developers, especially for those that have built game content based on toy licenses. Toy manufacturers appear to be collaborating more frequently with game developers to provide local wireless toy and game entertainment. Some toys feature specific game elements built into the toys in a number of ways, and others offer game interaction among toys as part of a local wireless toy network.

Think for a moment about the variety of game experiences available to next-generation toys with local wireless command centers. These command centers can be connected easily via USB to the PC for online updates, and will broadcast simple game commands to "recognized" toy units. The possibilities are endless for action figures, vehicle armadas of many kinds, and so forth.

Another offering in this area are dedicated wireless gaming units like the Cybiko Xtreme (www.cybikoxtreme.com/). These units deliver portable gaming and local networking capability for chatting with friends and playing games. Figure 9-7 shows the portable Cybiko Xtreme device.

Common drawbacks to these devices are their retail cost after manufacture, their expandability and upgrade issues, and their inability to draw developers and compelling content due to a lack of a large, sustainable player base. Again, developers rarely want to develop for platforms that have not already reached a sizeable audience or shown every indication of reaching a mass audience rapidly. Many toy and game companies have explored portable gaming by offering various kinds of hardware. The results have varied widely. The reason Cybiko has lasted and has evolved its offerings is that it makes an attractive product.

Other offerings, including the electronic Pikachu toys from the *Pokemon* games, are popular but remain fairly limited in game and wireless functionality. Toy manufacturers face significant risk in recovering research and manufacturing costs for elaborate wireless toys—despite the projected fun factor! Some developers are working on solutions to help minimize these costs while maximizing the potency of the offerings with simple yet fun interaction and game elements.

FIGURE 9-7

Cybiko Xtreme

Building the Cell Phone Gaming Market

Just like in the console world, many popular licensed titles are being offered on a great number of cell phone handsets. Game publishers specializing in mobile game development have grown up with large-scale plans to deliver various kinds of content to wireless carriers around the world. These publishers include JAMDAT (www.jamdatgames.com), Digital Bridges (www.digitalbridges.com), and Unplugged, Inc. (www.unplugged-inc.com).

High-profile licenses have appeared on cell phone handsets, including JAMDAT's *The Lord of the Rings: The Two Towers* (see Figure 9-8), JAMDAT/Activision's *Tony Hawk Pro Skater 4*, and EA Sports' *Tiger Woods PGA Tour Wireless Golf* (see Figure 9-9).

As millions of new subscribers sign up for wireless service packages, mobile game publishers hope their well-known licensed offerings will provide an incentive for players to purchase these titles and download them into their phones. The younger population of cell phone users and players, entirely unintimidated by wireless technology, is an attractive potential audience for each of these titles and many more. Yet, as I've previously mentioned, the economic model for determining pricing that affords the best possible results for all parties involved and provides this content to the greatest number of users possible remains an ongoing experiment.

Just as other platforms are somewhat segmented by player preferences and age boundaries, look for a similar dynamic in the wireless world, where certain kinds of game and entertainment applications find their way to their natural audience. There is plenty of room for a wide array of content designed to satisfy a wide and growing player base. In the months and years to come, it will be very interesting to see how many people are enticed to become new game players through cell phone games, and where their content preferences will reside on the game genre spectrum.

FIGURE 9-8

The Lord of the Rings: The Two Towers

FIGURE 9-9

Tiger Woods PGA Tour Wireless Golf

The growth of the cell phone gaming market is just one reason why it's so exciting to see how many new game players will come to experience the excitement of gaming over time in new ways on very new platforms. This aspect of the game industry provides for constant excitement and challenge for game developers, but it requires an equal amount of patience and staying power as new content areas develop around us. For those who love gaming, there are always new and interesting ways to bring games to game players. Since game playing itself is central to the human experience, it's always inspiring to think about the variety of possibilities for providing new kinds of gaming to help nurture entirely new kinds of gamers. This area is somewhat less dependent on hard-edged demographic data, since the wireless audience is so wide.

Opportunities in Wireless

As you've seen in this chapter, there is a wide and growing number of opportunities to marry up wireless technologies of several types (local versus carrier-based) with game and entertainment content. Not confined even to cell phone handsets, or any other specific platform, there are expansion opportunities in wireless where the talents of game developers can be applied to whole new gaming experiences. In fact, entirely new content areas are waiting to be defined.

It's hard to predict exactly where game content will go among all the divergent aspects of wireless, but one idea is becoming more clear to me every day: wireless games offer a unique pathway to break out into a much bigger gaming world than ever before realized. This is a gaming world for developers in which game content is destined for previously unheard-of numbers of potential gamers. Just as game design learning among game developers in the industry's short history has largely been a matter of comparison, evolution, and refinement, wireless game feedback from players will continue to challenge game designers to respond quickly in providing content to match the wishes and desires of the players. What an opportunity to take gaming past everyone's wildest speculations!

The best games on wireless probably won't come first. This is no surprise. The best games on any new platform tend to be the second- or third-generation games. Developers are always learning feverishly how to do more with less, and how to erode every limit. Some industry commentators don't even seem to believe that wireless can or will deliver at all. On this score, only patience and time will tell.

Personally, I believe that every opportunity to build game content should be pursued to the fullest. Let's not back down or give up on wireless simply because of weak processors and small, nonstandardized screen sizes. Patience is required.

In my mind, every opportunity to grow new gaming venues needs to be explored fully in order to bring much needed new blood and the attendant new forms of content inspiration into a sometimes stagnant industry—despite the constant challenges. If we continue to make games in three genres for a "handful of hard-cores" on two platforms, we will never grow as an industry or as developers, and opportunity for everyone will diminish in kind.

CASE STUDY COMMENTS ON DEVELOPMENT FACTORS IN THE INFANCY OF WIRELESS

"Infancy" almost implies too much maturity when it comes to mobile game development. Right now, it's a crazy world out there in wireless game development. If you've looked around at many of the available games, I'm sure you've seen games built for cell phones and delivered by a wireless carrier that barely perform at all.

As mentioned earlier, international development on any game title is difficult due to region-based carrier access for any given handset. You might find yourself working on a handset from another country with no way to test your game or download successive game builds into it. To test your game, you need to ship the handset back to the country in which wireless service is available for it, and then have someone download and test your game on the handset. As you can see, this is far from an optimal development process, and is a reason why developers located within the region where the game ultimately is to be deployed continue to get the important work contracts for their geographic areas.

It would seem logical for phone handset manufacturers to offer a docking device for application development on their handsets that would enable developers to transfer application information to phones that are out of their service area, but I haven't seen anything like this yet (which doesn't mean that a solution isn't out there!). When it comes to games, the wireless carriers themselves are entering uncharted territory. They are not set up, nor do they intend to function, as QA clearing houses for phone applications like games or other kinds of content.

Testing phone handsets loaded with your game content provides several unique challenges. If you are building content for a series of handset models (as seems to be commonly required by many mobile game publishers), as a developer, you probably don't have access in any easy way to each of these handset models. Technical specifications vary from model to model, and games seem to perform differently from model to model as well. What runs seamlessly, even perfectly, on one model phone will suspiciously crash another.

What about the economics? Since mobile game publishers aren't sure what they can expect to earn for any given title, they are understandably not necessarily willing to risk much money in development. Many developers, eager to enter this market, must work with these "experimental" budgets carefully. Mobile publishers and developers alike are eager to understand just how mobile games translate into sales, and what this means for the future of mobile development.

Obviously, only if a strong and clear market for these titles emerges will publishers of any kind continue to put games or other applications on this platform. As in any other area of game development, those developers with strong titles and proven sales become attractive partners for any publisher involved. Publishers always seek to place content with proven developers, which can be a sizeable hurdle for new developers.

Many mobile publishers are betting that the future demand for mobile content far exceeds the present and have committed relatively small amounts of funding to current projects, betting that this will be enough to grow the market at a reasonable rate until risking larger funding is warranted by newly created demand for game content.

Many games that seem to fit perfectly on the low-horsepower cell phone handsets are becoming available and will help to test out the market for similar titles. In short, it's a large experiment right now as many competing technologies start to settle into place.

A fairly even-handed analysis of the potential, however, should prove that initial investments into this gaming arena are well worthwhile. Very little will probably stand in the way of more people taking out wireless service plans every day as a one-time luxury device becomes absolutely commonplace. As a delivery mechanism, the game industry has never seen such a wide potential audience looming. Will it turn everyone into gamers? No. But you really can't ignore the idea that, given the right kind of content, many new players will be created simply by increased access.

And now for some good news! Earlier in this chapter, we looked at some of the specific development challenges related to building wireless games. While these definitely hold true in the present, there is every reason to believe that the future for this content will evolve quickly. Here are some of the positive aspects related to the state of wireless gaming:

> **Impending graphics solutions**   Graphics chip manufacturers like ATI (www.ati.com) and NVIDIA (www.nvidia.com) are watching the mobile market very carefully and will no doubt offer graphics chip solutions to phone handset manufacturers, making much more robust graphic content possible. This will allow developers to do much more in the visual presentation of their games.

> **Larger, clearer view screens**   With clever designs, cell phone handset manufacturers are finding ways to build in larger physical view screens, without substantially increasing the weight or size of their phones. This factor, along with technological improvements in the physical view screens, allows for much better visibility and fairly sharp detail display.

> **Engaging multiplay applications**   Even with the popularity of stand-alone game offerings growing, some publishers are looking for a way to get players hooked up together via multiplay titles. Some titles are being developed to meet these needs in an effort to try to grow the multiplay gaming base on the cell phone handsets. This allows a new range of opportunities for developers.

> **New gaming audiences and culture related to wireless games**   Potentially, entire subcultures could sprout up around the right kind of wireless game applications that succeed in grabbing hold of an audience. In recent gaming history, the same phenomenon happened on the PC with several genre-defining titles that grew into large communities and subcultures.

INTERVIEW WITH DAVE WARHOL

Dave Warhol is an industry pioneer and a member of the Blue Sky Rangers (original Intellivison developers). He is the founder and president of Realtime Associates, which under his direction has created over 80 games for a wide range of game publishers, including Bug!, a launch title for the Sega Saturn. I wanted to get Dave's thoughts on several industry-wide issues.

TM: What are your best memories from the days of Intellivision?

DW: We were in an environment where everyone felt extraordinarily lucky. We had been given the chance to make games at a time when there wasn't a game industry. The "old-timers" had a year of experience. This created a situation where everyone was excited, learning, and experimenting with fundamental game design issues and technology constructs. It was a time of discovery. It wasn't a very big envelope by today's standards, but there was a lot of envelope pushing going on! My fondest general memories are learning from other programmers; my fondest specific memory was walking down a hall and hearing a group of people playing my project—for fun!

TM: What are some of the biggest changes you've seen in the industry?

DW: The biggest change over the years has been technology and what that means to product scope and team size. In 1980, a complete game could be done in three to four months with just one person plus an artist for a couple weeks and a sound guy for a few days. This means that probably 5 to 10 percent of the effort was connecting assets, and the other 90 to 95 percent was game design, coding, and tuning. We would constantly play the games with/against one another during development. They were small enough that integrated technical designs weren't created, which is now essential; the design evolved as a natural consequence of playing. Think about that in terms of today's projects, where a much more significant amount of time is spent just "making things work" or "hooking assets up" or "adding effects." Sure, these are all part of a competitive contemporary game experience, but from a gameplay aspect, the percentage of overall time dedicated to that discipline has dropped relative to the overall effort.

TM: How has the climate for game development changed over time?

DW: There used to be a certain novelty to it that no longer exists. It used to have lots of late nights, but now because of the interdependence of the contributors, that's no longer effective. So the climate has become one of planning, teamwork, and communication, where it used to be "jump in and start swimming."

TM: These days how much influence does the "business" of making games have on design choices?

DW: As a businessman, I respect that the business of game production should have 100 percent influence over everything. Bottom line, a game needs to make money, or nobody will get to make games. And, the best games always tend to be commercial successes.

We have outlets for people who are not interested in making money; they're called "the arts." If someone wants to complain about financial pressures in the game industry, then they should stop taking money from the game industry, get a loft in Venice, stop bathing, get a favorite seat in their local coffee shop, and start creating pure artistic endeavors like all of the other poor musicians, painters, and poets in the world.

Seriously, business pressures require that designs remain fairly homogenous. To the same degree that TV and film has become all of the same form, so have games. It's unfortunate on the one hand, but it also creates a sustainable, predictable marketplace. Perhaps there are only a certain number of categories of interactive, and they're all being well exploited; or perhaps the categorization is all based on "safe market choices," which only allow those choices. Either way, the consumers are still buying, so it's good. A great game that doesn't fit into preexisting categories will always break through; it just has to be pretty darn great.

TM: How do you approach game design today, compared with the early cartridge days?

DW: One thing that's much better nowadays is that you can start at a much more theoretical foundation—start with the "second derivative"—of what you want to accomplish in game design. There's a much wider palette of techniques, a much more descriptive language, available to contemporary game designers. Before, there were fewer, smaller molds: did you want to make a sports game, a maze game, or another kind of game? Now, you can talk about how you want the player to "feel," whereas before your task was simply to make an engaging game.

In the past, due to smaller budgets, you could "afford" to be more iterative in your design. Get the whole thing up in a week or two, play it, decide what was working and what was not, and make changes.

TM: What game ideas still excite you?

DW: Massively multiplayer games are interesting; they are now completing their first generation and are where console games were in the mid-'80s. Open-ended and nondirected games still have a lot to offer; the typical game in five years will probably be self-directed. I like designs that take risks.

TM: What positive or negative industry trends alarm you?

DW: The main negative trend is the "more of the same" syndrome. (There are more first-person shooters than there are Phil Collins ballads—and that's a lot—and they are pretty much just as indistinguishable from one another!) Publishers want to minimize risks by coming up with games in established genres, so they can turn to market data and be assured that a game will sell enough copies to pay for itself. At the same time, they want something different; so just make something that is both different from, and the same as, another success.

Another disturbing trend is that games need to be massive to sell. To make a Hollywood movie, you need to spend anywhere from $20 million to $200 million—it's quite a wide range. But it seems that in games, publishers are only interested in producing fewer, larger games.

I like the trend of continuing to capture non-hardcore gamers, like the Sims has.

TM: What are you watching for in the near future of gaming?

DW: The day that TV network executives are grousing when their ratings for a particular night are down because some Internet-supplied content was released at a certain time and took a significant dent out of their viewer base that week.

TM: Where do games go from here?

DW: Open-ended games. Dynamically updated content. Multiplayer and massively multiplayer.

TM: How do you prepare for the game industry today?

DW: Play, play, play, play, play!

In addition to enjoying it, tear the game apart in your mind. Figure out what its components are, what design decisions and trade-offs were made. Deconstruct it; don't just play it. Write reviews for your own benefit.

As far as career opportunities, test, test, test, test, test. Getting a job as a tester is a great way into the industry.

MEGA TIPS

1. Simple designs, like those forced by cell phone handsets, are good design exercises. Remember to try to deliver on the notion of feeding a player's desires, despite the gaming platform or location.

2. Among many of your own ideas for games, be mindful of which ideas might be best suited for portable handsets.

3. Portable limitations present good design challenges. These force designers to concentrate on making a game both simple and addictive. This is easy to say and very hard to do.

4. Watch and be responsive to global game design trends on wireless.

5. Refer to your own game library and favorite games. Experiment with "adapting" your favorite games into less-robust portable versions. Does a game still hold up without the supporting technology? You may be surprised.

CHAPTER **10**

Getting Started in Game Development

THERE is a wide and growing range of opportunities available for those passionate about game design elements. The more you can learn about scripting, staging, lighting, programming, modeling, layout, and "play-feel," the better. It's already assumed that you play every kind of game available to study and compare them!

As you diversify your specific skill base, you open up new possibilities. I won't pull any punches here: working professionally in game or entertainment design is extremely competitive. Typically, many developers compete for a single game development position. Employers know that there are many people who want a job working in games. In general, people who work in game development can't really see themselves doing anything else. A severe love for games is a job requirement. Why else would you subject yourself to the long hours, constantly looming deadlines, and dwindling budgets? You will need plenty of love in reserve for what you are trying to accomplish in your game.

Part of finding a way to succeed as a commercial game designer involves selling the particular skills you have acquired. Many of the designers that I know did plenty of work for free along the way. I started by writing simple text adventure games and either giving them or trading them to friends. Once you begin building games and growing your experience and capabilities further, you may want to make sure that your skills have "crossover" value for industries related in some fashion to gaming. I don't say this to direct you away from the game industry at all—quite the opposite. This recommendation is meant to genuinely prepare you for the nature of project-based game work in a commercial setting.

The game industry can be volatile. Projects get cancelled at a moment's notice, and when projects go away, often times, so does your job. This is why I bother with mentioning the "crossover" factor at all. I've known many game developers who have made successful career crossovers into film and TV/CGI effects, character design, storyboarding, web entertainment, production, comics, toy design, product design, and other disciplines as well. These days, people tend to move back and forth. Each of these areas has unique production requirements and workflows and offers new kinds of project learning for the designer at large.

The reality is that only a fixed number of game titles are in production at any one time. If you're not working on one of them, you'll want to be continuing to grow your abilities on a project. One of the great elements, and one of the steepest challenges, to working in games is being disciplined about constantly growing and updating your skills.

Also, don't forget that opening yourself up to a wide range of gaming projects on many platforms gives you critical insight into project problem solving that can cut across genres, budgets, and platform specifics.

In this chapter, as we finish up our conversation about building game content, I'm going to talk about several diverse kinds of opportunities in gaming available to the modern game designer, and the importance of keeping your own set of skills diversified.

WHY DIVERSIFY?

There are many great practical and growth-oriented reasons to diversify your skill set and even your method of approach to the game industry. It's tough out there! It can be very difficult to get your first game development job. I have shoeboxes full of rejection letters at home to prove it. Talk to other developers and you'll hear the same thing … getting that first job wasn't easy, but the good news is that you can afford to be optimistic.

Even game developers with many years of experience on well-known titles face rejection along the way. It's hard not to take it personally at times, but you simply can't afford to let it weigh on you. Here's my advice: keep an eye on *your* target goals in gaming (these you'll have to define for yourself), and then keep your head and heart behind your skills pursuit at all times. To the best of your ability, practice your craft regularly. Try not to let any one industry get you down, and if it's any comfort at all, try to remember that many people before you have felt the same kinds of anxieties in their own pursuits.

If you have a strong love for game programming, pursue it with all of your might. Good game programmers are always in demand. In my experience, it's a different kind of employment picture for artists and designers. The only artists and designers I've known who have been able to work constantly for extended periods of time are those who have significantly diversified their skills. When they're not working on game projects, they are storyboarding; illustrating magazine, CD, or book covers; doing stop-motion animation for music videos; doing web work; doing concept and character designs; and so forth. In short, they never entirely "rely" on the game industry, or any one industry for work, and they try not to get pegged down as *only* a texture artist or *only* a modeler. Even if they are currently hard at work on the perfect game title and times are good, they keep their skills tuned and ready to change direction at a moment's notice.

Gaming is clearly a growth industry. It's had shakes and bumps from the beginning. It is somewhat recession-proof, as people are *always* going to want to play games, and the number of gamers grows every year. The best game developers will always have opportunity of some kind open to them. It really is essential to try to become the best at something. You might get lucky! Smaller subsets of the game artists and designers I've known have experienced relatively constant work. In trying to help point you in the right direction, it's best to be prepared for either case.

One thing is sure: artists and game designers are always looking for opportunities. First and foremost, you want to build games. Day and night, you want to build games, but stay open to new kinds of game entertainment by type and by kind. Don't limit yourself to a single genre or necessarily to a single platform. The more kinds of game production experiences you participate in, the more you will learn about the process of building games. This is not to say that you shouldn't try to get core experience on specific platforms; you should always try to do this as opportunity allows.

If you're not geographically located near the offices of some local game developers, you may have to relocate. Try to build a relationship with a "somewhat" local developer before making any moves. Don't be overly aggressive, just follow the web postings and be consistent. You probably won't be able to start in a design capacity until you can prove that you've had a hand in building commercially successful games at some level. Don't be too impatient. Like I've said, if you're just starting out you'll have to find your way into a game developer and then show them what you can do. Check out Appendix A as a starting point.

Role Definition for Game Designers

Your contribution to a game developer as a game designer is largely dependent on your own skills, goals, background, aptitudes, and interests. Different game development studios (from the largest to the smallest) have dramatically different ideas about which kinds of skills are required to be a game design team member or a lead designer. Some choose to focus on art skills like traditional design, while others focus on scripting language ability. Still others focus on having art and scripting skills in abundance, while also being able to double as a character rigger or technical director (setting up character or prop models for animation).

In terms of job descriptions, you have three common classifications: lead designer, game designer, and level designer. There is often plenty of overlap in these classifications. A lead designer is a senior position, although game and level designers can have senior positions as well. Seniority, no surprise, is based on experience and exposure.

A lead designer is responsible for defining, creating, and supporting any and all overarching gameplay functionality details. They help to keep focus on building a game title that plays with fundamental fluidity and excitement. They make sure that a title is competitive from a gameplay and visual design standpoint.

A game designer can also be the lead designer, and vice versa. Game designers are focused on defining and developing the big picture gameplay details for a game developed often from scratch using a variety of means. Many have sufficient art and scripting skills. They will write a complete game design document specifying all relevant design details and production considerations for any given game title.

A level designer focuses on creating levels as opposed to creating support structures for entire games. This is not to say that they can't create complete support structures. Typically, they are plenty busy creating and managing the multiple details associated with building great playing levels.

Some game designers come from a hardcore programming background and prefer scripting and design detailing. Others come from a more arts-oriented background and prefer environmental modeling, character design, and writing.

A few things are fairly certain these days: You'll need basic drawing and design skills. You'll need solid writing skills. You'll need a thorough understanding of "play" and "feel" dynamics. You'll need to understand prop, character, and item staging in a layout. Knowing some scripting will be of huge benefit as well.

How do you build up some of these skills? It doesn't happen overnight, and no one ever stops learning or trying to improve their skills. I'm always trying to build my game skills further, and I always feel behind. Every game developer, designers included, is constantly hard at work building their skills. It never ends. I want to pass on to you some of the areas of study and focus that I've found useful in trying to build game-oriented design skills:

❭ Industrial design

❭ Writing and presentation

❭ Scripting

❭ 3-D modeling

❭ Leading teams

Industrial design emphasizes the development of visual concepts that optimize function, value, and appearance. Coincidentally, this is exactly what you're trying to do when building game props or objects to populate your game scenes. I tend to try to collect books with industrial design components. There is more information on this area of study available at the web site for the Industrial Designers Society of America (www.idsa.org).

The now classic *Star Wars Sketchbook*, by Joe Johnston (Ballantine, 1977), is one of my own favorite titles relating to industrial and vehicle design. Fortunately, there are many more reference books of this kind available today, and most of them are extremely useful.

For the working game designer, writing and verbal presentation skills are very important tools. As discussed earlier, part of being an effective game designer requires the ability to synthesize large amounts of verbal and visual design information into a cohesive and easily digestible game design document. Some designers make the mistake of writing huge, densely worded design documents that seem to fixate on nonessential details, therefore making them very hard for anyone to read. Trust me on this one—a busy programmer or artist is not going to spend whatever limited time he or she has remaining in a cramped day poring over a badly written design document. No one will bother.

Over time and exposure to development cycles, you begin to understand better exactly which design details are useful and essential. These are the design details you formalize into your design document and make available to your team on an intranet.

However, the writing, presentation, and communication skills don't end with the assembly of a design document. You will often find yourself presenting game design ideas to a wide variety of audiences in person. You may be presenting development team ideas to management teams hoping to secure a budget for development. You may be presenting the results of your design synthesis efforts to your own team or to other on-site developers. You may be "selling" your game development ideas to many departments within a single company. Each of these endeavors requires the best writing and verbal presentation skills you can muster. In some form or another, your job is dependent on successfully selling your game design ideas.

We certainly know by now how critical and valuable scripting skills can be in game development. It is well worth the effort and expense to get books like *Python in a Nutshell,* by Alex Martelli (O'Reilly & Associates, 2003) or *VBScript in a Nutshell,* by Paul Lomax, Matt Childs, and Ron Petrusha (O'Reilly & Associates, 2003) and learn how to work with scripts. The more you can learn about scripting and demonstrate in your scripting skills, the better.

Learning how to model precise and useable low-polygon models takes serious time and effort. I'm always trying to get better at it, and sometimes I succeed. I've spent many hours talking with a wide array of 3-D artists, and let's face it: sitting in front of some 3-D packages makes you feel like you're trying to land the space shuttle. 3-D application interfaces have gotten better, but there's still a long way to go in making these applications easier to use.

If you're brand new to 3-D, I suggest starting with a free program like Wings 3D (www.wings3d.com). I find this application to be intuitive and surprisingly powerful as a starting point in 3-D. It tends to focus on a more sculptural approach to model building, as opposed to a never-ending series of face extrusions and scales, although there is obvious power in that method too. I'm a big fan of Bay Raitt, whose work in 3-D applications like Nendo and Mirai predate Wings 3D. Figure 10-1 is an example of a model Bay built to demonstrate his sculptural approach to modeling.

As you progress in your game design career, you may find yourself leading a design team. I suggest that you get some pure production experience along the way. Learning how to task and track assets, work effectively with a variety of developers,

FIGURE 10-1

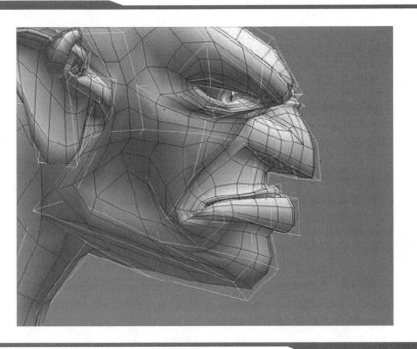

Bay Raitt's sculptural modeling technique

and manage timely content delivery is very useful experience in a lead design role. Try to remember that other designers have the same goals you do. They want to grow and work on diverse aspects of a game's overall design requirements. As a team lead, you will walk a fine line between trying your best to support the growth and development of your peers, while maintaining commercial product goals and budgets.

Each of the suggestions that I've mentioned here is aimed at helping you start or continue to define yourself as a game designer. As a practical point, don't forget that for every developer engaged in making a game, you have a potentially different definition of exactly what a designer's role is on the development team. It's best to be prepared for any opportunity that might come your way by having as diverse a skill set as you possibly can. This doesn't mean that you have to be able to do everything game building requires. You need to focus your efforts on defining core abilities. Unless you're building a very small game, you'll be working with a team of highly specialized contributors.

GROWTH AREAS AND NEW OPPORTUNITIES

Keeping your skills diverse should help you grow toward being a game designer who can create content independent, yet mindful of, any platform specifics. You should be able to work with paper, cards, small pieces of plastic, toy networks, action figures, key fobs, wireless devices, *and* the hottest gaming hardware consoles available. Ideally, this offers quite a range of applications for your game skills. You won't need advanced scripting techniques and a deep understanding of forces on particle dynamics to develop a card game, but you should always be trying to understand what makes any game—using any means of delivering a gaming experience possible—a successful gaming experience. Your specific knowledge in this area is part of your stock and trade.

With this in mind, let's take a look at some growth areas and new opportunities.

Microsoft, Mattel, Intel, and LeapFrog

You might not have envisioned working on a Microsoft toy like *Barney* or *Teletubbies* as the apex of you game design career when you began working in gaming, but as a professional commercial designer, you become interested in every chance to use your abilities and to grow opportunities. If these projects require game building elements or direction, you are a game builder: Sony PlayStation 2, Microsoft Xbox, PC, Nintendo GameCube, portable, theme park kiosk, location-based entertainment (LBE), Web, cards, toys, smart cards, slinkys—it doesn't matter. Always remember, there is a vast difference between being a game aficionado and being a commercial game developer. Odds are, you may not find yourself, especially in the early days of your career, working on your favorite kind of game for pay. You have to love more than a genre or two to last in the games business.

As we've seen, the marriage of toys and gaming is providing new opportunities. Toy makers understand the power of gaming and always have. They are constantly looking for ways to add game elements to toys. Microsoft's ActiMates series of toys, including *Barney*, *Teletubbies*, and *Arthur* (from the PBS program *Arthur*), are just a few examples of extremely simple game elements mixing in with toy development. These toys, developed for younger children, offer the ability to play peek-a-boo and to play simple games. To be sure, these are extremely simple game offerings, but the next-generation interactive toys are starting to look much more sophisticated with complete game offerings of several kinds included for older children.

Mattel has used games to bolster recognition and support entire communities of fans for brands like *Hot Wheels* and *Barbie*. It has licensed these properties for standard game development, as well, but it also has built large web-based game communities around these brands. Web games of this kind are typically built as Java applets, or as Flash/Shockwave applications.

Despite the fact that Intel has discontinued its Intel Play (www.intel.com/intelplay/) series of chip-based toys that includes a microscope connected via USB to a computer, a virtual game system, a sound morpher, and a digital movie creator, these kinds of PC toys have offered promise at several stages to game makers. It is a market that has some serious challenges and stability issues, but many manufacturers of PC toys continue to try to bring game and educational material into the home this way.

One standout success story in this general category would be LeapFrog (www.leapfrog.com). LeapFrog offers simple game-based educational content for young children available on its LeapPad Learning System. LeapFrog has shown solid success in building up a sizeable library of available content for young kids. The educational side of the gaming market has always had the benefit of added educational value, which many parents and purchasers find attractive, although, for many reasons, it has been a bumpy ride for many developers who have crossed over into educational content, or supplemented their revenues by working on education-based content.

Each of these opportunity areas is mentioned to make the simple point that the world of independent game development requires a constant search for new revenue. Whether you are working on a state-of-the-art console title or not (remember that development funding for these can be cut in an instant at a publisher's discretion), as an independent game developer, you often must find several revenue streams to keep your development studio afloat. Many development studios simply do not find adequate revenue streams. It is not uncommon for a development studio to fail within its first two years. This is why many in the game industry are concerned with finding new ways to apply game technology to a wide variety of industries that might benefit from gaming technologies.

Challenges for PC Toys

There are some considerable challenges limiting the ability of game developers engaged in such work to contribute game content to PC toy manufacturers. First of all, PC toys are very expensive to design in research and development. Once designed, they are expensive to manufacture. This means that it's hard to keep the retail price point low enough to sell large numbers of toys. This fact alone discourages many toy manufacturers from even taking the plunge into trying to develop successful PC/Game toys.

There are other limitations as well. Since these toys are regularly more expensive than many other kinds of toys, you can't serialize them easily and sell several characters or toys in a series. Very few purchasers will pay for one of each kind of toy, especially at the cost or price point of most PC toys.

Another interesting physical limitation and perception issue is the idea that mom and dad don't necessarily want Interactive Barney hooked up to their PC on their desk at home for extended periods of time. The main household PC doesn't tend to be in the youngest child's bedroom either. You can see that when you add up each of these factors, there are some significant problems to overcome in getting large numbers of PC toys out there successfully. This doesn't mean that toy manufacturers won't try to crack this market with future products; they no doubt will, and it's just this kind of work that most independent developers don't mind taking on to offset their own costs in building more traditional electronic games.

ADVERGAMES

This is a sore spot for many developers, and I can sympathize entirely. You probably don't or didn't want to get into the game business to make ads right? You fell in love with *Metroid* and you said to yourself: "That's it! That's what I want to do!" Right? Those are the perfect reasons to want to pursue gaming. Everyone wants to be a part of building the next revolutionary game title. In fact, it's why you suffer the multiple trials of being a game developer in the first place.

Many (some would say "most") of the games that get built today are based on licenses. You can build an excellent game based on a license, but for the license holder the game "is" essentially a commercial. At the least, it's a form of commercial for the brand based on the license.

Companies of every description that create products or services for specific demographics by age and gender are eager to promote their offerings using games. If this idea is a shock, it really shouldn't be since this idea has been with gaming from the beginning. Because of the increased risk and cost of making games for every next generation of consoles, publishers are always looking for ways to offset their own costs and limit risks. Getting corporations to buy in on the risk of a game is an attractive idea to most publishers, and probably indicates a strong pattern for things to come.

Honda, for instance, spends more money on TV commercials in a single day than it would cost to make a rock-solid PlayStation 2 game based on a series of its current and forthcoming street bikes. A solid game has huge replay value. Many in the industry hate to think this way, but you experience the commercial every time you play the game. Remember *Cool Spot* for the Sega Genesis? A great game; plenty of fun. Based on a state-of-the-art 16-bit engine for the Genesis at the time, it was ultimately an ad for the soft drink 7-Up. If you spend $2 million on TV network ads for two days, that's it. You had an expensive impression, and it has passed. In the near future, next time you go to the Honda dealer to check out some motorcycles, you might take a game home with you to experience the ride as often as you'd like.

The success of *America's Army*, a collaboration between military advertisers and game developers, is exactly what I'm talking about when I mention "advergames." Considering the U.S. Army's advertising budget, the cost of developing a game to excite recruiting efforts isn't even worth mentioning. It's an insignificant expense for the Army. It's a serious source of much-needed revenue for an independent game developer. It's also further proof that you can make a good game while working within the context of a license.

Look for plenty of game development in the near future to borrow on the success of titles like *America's Army,* especially as games become more mainstream and more traditional companies begin to embrace the power of gaming. In the coming years, publishers and developers alike will be looking to collaborate in a number of ways with large company efforts to support brands and capture audiences by building game content. Think about *The Sims Online* deal with Intel and McDonald's to include "Intel Inside" PCs, Big Macs, and entire McDonald's franchises within the world of *The Sims Online.*

There's no reason to fight it … at this point it's inevitable. The offbeat game industry building those pleasant little time wasters for the local pizza palace crowd has grown up into a corporate behemoth. It is big business when the Super Bowl telecast starts with professional football players challenging each other to a game of *Madden Football* with "EA Sports" logos conveniently scattered everywhere amidst scads of the latest consoles.

So what do we do about it? How do we build games in this climate? We focus on what's still important and what will always be most important as developers—making great games. They might not be our own original characters in our own unique worlds anymore (some of them probably will), but we can all still work our hardest at coming up with entirely new kinds of games to play and finding new play mechanics for character to world interaction. The actors and environments are important, but ultimately arbitrary when compared to the kinds of actions and play they participate in. Refining the game design process itself, in my opinion, is one of the next great areas of revolution in the game business. Even given the conditions I've tried to describe for you, there is always a need for executable gameplay ideas that capture a player's emotions.

Interesting Trends for the Near Future

I think we'll begin to see even more kinds of crazy partnerships between several factions in the near future for gaming. Some of these partnerships will probably surprise all of us. Just as in every other area of modern commerce, corporate influence will continue to grow and most independent developers will simply have to ally themselves with a diminishing number of *uber-publishers.* We've already seen this happening all over town.

Most independent game developers, when given the chance, make quick and deep alliances with the biggest-name game publishers. When viewed from the perspective of an independent game developer, you can't blame them. There are numerous advantages to participating in this kind of alliance and even exposing yourself to potential acquisition by a publisher. This can be of great benefit for game studio owners or game studio partners, but isn't always a great situation for developers at large in terms of creating opportunity. But creating opportunity is not the ultimate goal of the independent game developer: having a big payday on acquisition is. In today's market, if you're not working on a game connected back to a "big five" publisher, uh oh.

The ability to take chances with game content may continue to decrease, while the search for risk-sharing capital from the companies looking to bring their brands to gaming will no doubt accelerate.

If the industry is going to continue its growth and expand its opportunities, gaming will need to make even more inroads with travel providers, hotel chains, promotional settings, education, even government and will need to continue growing its relationships with other kinds of more traditional entertainment media providers.

WEB GAME ENTERTAINMENT WITH PHYSICAL COUNTERPARTS

Before the bust of everything remotely related to web entertainment, several entertainment companies with a gaming focus were pursuing ideas related to gaming on the Web with "physical counterparts." These physical counterparts might include, but are not limited to, customized game-feature-dependent action figures, toys, game pieces, tokens, gems, cards, and so forth.

Web-oriented game entertainment also experimented with ideas like providing payoff for players that could be redeemed physically. As an example, suppose you are encouraged to play some multiplayer web games of a certain kind (many kinds of games fit the bill). A tournament environment is created around a player community. Players can earn points for play, as well as prizes and give-aways based on points accumulated and their own tournament standings. This creates several security problems, but that's another issue.

These earned player points might be redeemed as prizes or might convert into a limited kind of purchasing power in participating retail stores. The idea is to try to create extra value for the player engaged in the experience. Who doesn't enjoy winning cool stuff for having fun? It's almost too good to be true and that might be the problem.

This kind of experiment is still in progress with sites like pogo (www.pogo.com), which cater to the so-called casual gamer. I'm always fascinated to see 32,655 players hard at work playing solitaire. You really need to understand your audience. How would *Extreme Solitaire* perform on the PlayStation 2?

No matter which gaming audience you build content for, the idea is always to grow your player base. Can physical counterparts grow the gaming universe? They are probably only attractive to certain segments. This is the question many are still trying to answer, and I'm not just talking about offering *Everquest* action figures to set on top of your monitor while you play either. I'm talking about physical game elements that are directly connected to a gaming experience, and that help to grow, augment, and expand that experience.

Toys and Card Games Go Online

Toys are using games as online components, and so are card games. Some of these games grew in popularity as card games among card game players, and others are card and web games built on well-known properties like *Harry Potter* or *Dungeons and Dragons*. It's important to understand that games these days are often part of an entire licensing package. If you have a hit show like *SpongeBob SquarePants,* the majority of the revenues generated by the show will come from product licensing. You will license the manufacture of everything from night-lights and picture frames to video games.

For your most successful card games, you will want to support and grow your player base by offering an online version. A good example would be *Magic The Gathering*. The online setting offers all kinds of new opportunities to build play for card game players. This tends to be a slightly smaller audience, so you don't necessarily see tons of online card games available.

There are many novel and unique challenges to "porting" a physical game like *Magic The Gathering* online. It's unclear whether games that are perceived by players as being physical and portable will have much success in an online format. Efforts will continue to be made in these areas only if significant player numbers support this kind of development with their purchases. There is no guarantee that they will succeed, and maybe are best left alone.

Keep in mind, too, that many successful game designers helping to build content in the digital age can trace their roots right back to paper and card gaming. Other modern game designers have little or no experience in paper or card gaming.

Many popular toy franchises have had plans that incorporate games and online elements at one point or another in the recent past. As of late, much of this work has been slowed down or entirely cancelled by our current economic conditions as companies set their focus on known and repeatable results with much less tolerance for experimentation.

Toy franchises like Lego, which experienced success with its *Mindstorms* series (http://mindstorms.lego.com/) before the economic downturn, were able to create and support new fans with their online offerings.

There will be new opportunities in the coming years for game developers to participate in the creation of game elements that support various toy and card games. Undoubtedly, there will also be growth in the numbers and types of successful toy and card games that will require support from game developers.

The Importance of New Opportunities for Developers

Console, PC, and MMOG game development is always challenging and exciting. These are the "blue chip" game staples. The competition to gain development contracts on these platforms is fierce, and many developers are starting to notice a dwindling number of opportunities for their development services.

It's a simple fact for publishers. Committing to the huge risks that accompany the development and promotion of a $3.5 million game force fewer titles to go into production, and the titles that do make it into production are becoming larger in scope, profile, and scale. Rather than do three high-profile games and seven to ten titles with a lower profile, publishers are choosing to do four high-profile titles and experiment much less with the more "questionable" titles—for whatever reasons, they view the other titles to be questionable.

It is extremely important for the growth and future of the game industry to find new opportunities for game developers. I'm sure you can sense my take on this. Finding "lighter" kinds of revenue-generating game work mixed in with a couple of console titles allows your development staff time to decompress on a smaller project after finishing up a mammoth title.

Make no mistake about it, building games is hard work. If you finish a 26-month game development cycle with no vacations, many worked weekends, extremely stressed personal relationships, your physical health intact, and some kind of lingering mental stability, you should take a week in Fiji to sing your own praises.

Without the expansion of game development into new areas and venues for gaming, there simply won't be enough opportunities to support the numbers of dedicated game enthusiasts looking to make a career out of building games.

ANECDOTES FROM THE GAME DEVELOPMENT FRONTLINES

One thing is certain: hang around game development long enough and you are destined to see some truly wacky behavior. Let me be clear on this. I don't mean off-base or silly behavior from those "crazy creative guys" that ride unicycles in the halls or storm marketing with Nerf toys on their 30th birthday before going out for sushi in their BMW. I'm talking truly wacky—you know, like mind bent, canine-frothing, penny whistle "goofy goes goo-goo" kind of stuff.

I couldn't possibly tell you half the really good stories. I just can't do it. I would love to do it at some point, but that point isn't now. They involve topics far too colorful and unseemly to be discussed in such a public forum. I could be black balled. No joke. ("Sonny, you'll be lucky to find work tying a cape on a batman action figure.") I'm afraid that most of these anecdotes you'll simply have to live through for yourself.

It's fair to say that the pressure of building games alone is enough to drive any normal person loopy. Jump around from development fire to fire for long enough and you will start taking crystal healing and weird ancient religions very seriously. You'll wonder why you never built puppets as a hobby. You'll find yourself going to your dentist just to sit in front of the fish tank. You will get angered when people leave your office before you've finished your lecture on what a certain episode of *Felix the Cat* is really trying to communicate about capitalism, Dostoyevsky, and the social fabric. You won't question drinking strange pieces of chemistry shoved in front of you by those around you. Part of it all results from a pure state of sleep deprivation paralysis.

Here are couple simple stories I *can* share with you. Being a game developer sometimes feels like trying to find an electrical outlet in the dark using only your wet fingers to guide you.

Think Fish

Our team was working on a fishing game during the height of the 1994 Malibu, California firestorms. One day I was burning EPROMs for a Sega Genesis game in my office when I heard a muffled wailing coming from somewhere down the hall. I investigated. As I got closer the sound changed to a tortured kind of shouting now coming out in bursts of whining and garbled profanities. Our offices were in the hills, so some kind of animal making these noises wasn't out of the question ... although I decided pretty quickly for myself that this raccoon can cuss like my Uncle Burt. As I arrived at the sound source, I realized that it wasn't a trapped animal at all; it was a collapsed programmer. I would soon learn that collapsed programmers are just as snarly and frothy as trapped animals. If we were in a pool at the YMCA, he would have tried to drown me. "Holy cripe, what's the matter?" I asked him. "I'm dying" he lipped and muttered to me from his green puffy face as he flopped into a fetal position.

Well, shoot. I calmly panicked. I rushed to find the office manager—too many Ding Dongs eaten to prop myself up at 3 A.M. while wrapping up a game build had somewhat diminished my "rushing" ability. I try to go to the gym more now. We called 911. The 911 dispatcher said, "All emergency personnel are busy fighting the firestorms, sir." I took a quick breath and said something like: "Look, if our programmer dies we can't finish our game and we're already late on several milestones. I don't think he commented the code very well either. At some point someone mentioned spaghetti and it wasn't dinner time. Please get someone out here! He's getting more green while I speak with you." The dispatcher assured me that emergency personnel would respond as soon as they could pull back from the firestorm lines.

I gathered a couple of team members and we ran around the office to see if anyone had dropped out of medical school to become a texture artist. Maybe someone had studied the symptomology of turning green. Not one. Surprised?

ULTIMATE GAME DESIGN

While we waited for help, the collapsed programmer never stopped crying and moaning, which proves that he'd probably never make it as a producer. In about 40 minutes, the doors to our office blasted open and some big, yellow, ash-laden, tarred-up firemen sporting bright-red oxygen tanks burst in and we directed them immediately to our green friend.

They loaded our green associate onto a stretcher and attached an IV and monitors. As he was being wheeled out the front doors of our offices, the VP of product development returned from lunch, and quite possibly from a round of golf or two. He looked at our green programmer on the gurney, and then he looked at me (the producer type) with his eyebrows raised into a "We're not slipping the milestone, are we?" posture. He looked back at the green programmer now mounted and ready for stuffing and he simply said, "Think fish" while he patted a fireman on the oxygen tank, the Morse code for "take him away, boys."

End result: You may be dying, but that's no excuse to stop thinking about the code for the fishing game. My mouth dropped. Are we savages? We could have avoided the whole mess if somebody had time to throw away old orange juice. Bad orange stuff is what apparently turned him green.

Sacking Sanka

Around the offices of a game development studio, you regularly hear noises of all kinds. You might hear sound effects or music loops being edited or composed. You might hear artists having interesting conversations with their significant others. You will hear many Coke cans opening. Anyone, at any moment, could be stuffed in a corner or sleeping under a desk. Hygiene will be uniformly suspicious. You might even begin to hear air leaking from the valve stem at the back of your head. Don't worry. You are not a beach toy, you just really need a vacation with one. When I reach this point, I normally leave for the batting cages. Every game developer needs to know what to do when the pressure gauge needle gets stuck in the little red quadrant. Watch your team members carefully. If you see someone starting to melt, guide them to the refrigerator to congeal them back together.

On one particular day there had been heated shouting matches going off all day long between a certain programmer and another producer. Programmers have the unenviable task of creating all the code assets to support a game. Producers have the unenviable task of dealing with almost every single aspect of game development that a programmer or artist doesn't care to be bothered with. These collective "aspects" will often fall and make for a messy floor, unless a good producer regularly mops up. There is some friction between all developers by definition. Programmers can get into an "I am the controller of code, my little minions, behold my deeds" mindset. Producers can get into an "I understand this, and I want you to have time to make the *Star Trek* convention this year, but we still have commercial obligations" mindset.

As these two parties proceeded to slug it out all day long, by the end of the day there seemed to be some resolution and it had quieted down for a little bit. Soon after the calming passage, we suddenly heard some tires screeching. It didn't sound like someone playing *Twisted Metal Black* in the game room down the hall. Before we knew it, we heard an explosion of glass and timber and ceramics and we wondered why the walls were shaking. It sounded like a missile hit the front of the building. I ran out of my work area, down the hallway, and around the corner. I saw a coffee pot rolling around on the floor. It wasn't even full. I didn't have my *Underdog* cup. I thought: "C'mon guys, that's just wasteful. You'll get carpet hair in the coffee!—and we'll want coffee later because I have to finish another proof of concept before leaving tonight. You knuckleheads."

A missile had hit the front of the building. It turned out to be a missile driven by a Brillo-haired programmer in a Dodge. Apparently, he had popped his cork and the stereo circus music was now playing full blast inside his disgruntled noodle. He'd had enough of this game development life, so he had decided to drive his Jeep through the reception area and into the coffee bar. God help us. I mean, we didn't really care about the reception area, insurance would pay for it, but couldn't he have swerved to avoid the coffee bar? That's just malicious.

He wasn't injured much, and after some mental adjusting he went on to work again for many companies. But future developers take note: this is probably not the kind of workflow you should be striving for.

CASE STUDY COMMENTS ON FINAL THOUGHTS FOR DESIGNERS

If you stick around the game industry long enough, you will go through several booms and busts. It's been the same for everyone that has gone before you. In the industry's earlier days, nobody assumed you could earn "a living" off of making games anyway. By day, you programmed databases for some city's weed abatement program, and by night you made games.

To last over the long run in games, you have only one ally: a diversified approach. Your own skill set must be game ready (some pun intended), but at the same time you need to stay flexible and able to apply your abilities to a few parallel endeavors. The booms and busts are always relative, and you may feel either one of these extremes deeply or only marginally. When you read the nonstop news articles about the billions upon billions of dollars being hefted away by each and every local game developer on your block, don't be deceived. These numbers are humorous, amusing, even suspicious, and that's about all. Developers do not share the biggest portion of the game industry's revenue.

Don't get me wrong; a handful of developers have made quite a bit of money. This too is relative. I know plenty of developers hard at work on a wide range of games for every platform you can name who don't stumble over large piles of cash in the garage while strolling to the Ferrari to play golf on a summer's day. Game development is hard work. If one of the "handful" owns a Ferrari, they often drive it to the office to work for 14 hours straight on a tighter BSP parser or some such thing. If you want to stay competitive in the game industry as a developer, you can't be neglectful.

Keep in mind that as a game designer or in any other game development role, you are offering your skills, services, and abilities to a game development studio (whether they are affiliated directly with a game publisher or not). Your fate is largely connected to their own. If a game studio loses a development contract for whatever reason (and there are many possible reasons), the funding covering your position flies away with that contract. In an industry as volatile as gaming, this can happen in rapid succession.

I've known developers who have worked on three cancelled games in a row. If this happens to you, it can be problematic, since other developers who now become your potential employers begin to wonder what went wrong (if anything) on the titles you worked on that were cancelled. Oddly enough, they begin to transfer some of that blame to you, even though you may have had absolutely nothing to do with any of the reasons, motivations, ego-clashes, or simple business decisions that led to your title's cancellation.

At some point, despite your own best efforts, you may find that your ability to deliver the best quality work possible is negatively affected, even ended, by any number of decisions made around you. Again, this is where you must strive to remain flexible to survive. I've known a few game designers who are now quite happy in other fields. Others will ride the game industry out wherever it might lead. For them, a day came when the minuses simply outweighed the pluses. It's hard to be 40 and living like you're 22. Even if you can handle it, no one around you can. This should not imply that you can't be way over 40 *and* a successful game developer. You can be, but there will be sacrifice involved.

Here's another factor to consider. It's no secret that independent developers working with tight budgets have little left over to spend on training. In many cases, if you're going to keep your skills current and competitive—and you had better if you'd like to stay working—it's going to cost you personally. Hold off on the sports car, and put that cash from the garage into a T-bill. You better set something aside for training and evolving your own skills.

What's it like to work as a game designer? It means different things in different places. Some teams run smoothly, with confidence that their designers will provide all mission-critical design details in a timely matter. Other teams run by having team members "own" more of the design details individually, and the designer becomes more of a design facilitator between having other responsibilities. Development teams establish trust with their fellow team members over time. This is why teams that gel together and know how to work well together are so highly sought after.

The team-specific design mix is a serious piece of chemistry in action. Remember that as a commercial game designer, you are working to support and help define the design intentions for a game title. It is usually an extremely collaborative process. You do not work on an island. You might be asked to lead something up, and begin to feel like you're on an island for a particular project or miniproject, but normally you work in heavy collaboration with everyone around you. You are not creating your own personal piece of art. There is no shortage of ego inside the war rooms of many game developers, and one of your most important skills as a designer will be to navigate the ego minefields.

You will have to find quick resolutions and approaches to design ideas headed in seemingly opposite directions. (For example, for a given license, Herb may want to do an action-oriented RPG, because that's his personal favorite game style, whereas Virgil may want to mix puzzle-based operations into the world's first FPS puzzle/shooter.) You need to be able to quickly recognize design factions segmenting your team into neat little pie pieces, and do your best to eliminate the choosing of sides. There are no sides. You have to manage the situation with a sports team mindset. You have to build propaganda, and reinforce the idea that divided you will fall—and you will. I can't tell you how many teams I've seen spin out on the game development highway due to ridiculous divisions among "team" members.

Why the ridiculous divisions? Well, you wouldn't believe how many professional game developers seem to think that game titles are their personal canvas of expression and their own unique little chance for some weird and meaningless gaming immortality (great work needs no introduction—it speaks for itself). The "personal canvas" idea couldn't be more opposite the commercial confines and realities of modern game development.

On the other hand, some developers really get it. They know what the stakes are, and they show up ready to play hard for the team. They never trot to first base. They never fail to slide into a base headfirst. As game studio management, these are the folks you want to keep. I'll take a hard-working, talented individual with a team ethic any day over a so-called "superstar" talent with a galaxy of ego to match. One misplaced "superstar" can kill your game project in time for lunch. Five talented team-ethic players can help build five successful games in a row, and still be fun to play foosball with at 3:30 in the morning.

Your physical working conditions will probably vary by the size of the developer you join. Smaller developers, say 15 to 30 people, may work under fairly cramped quarters, and may be in the early phase of their growth as a development studio. They can run out of money by dinnertime. You won't even want to ask where the payroll is coming from. It's best not to know. That way you might avoid being subpoenaed.

Larger developers or developers associated with big publishers may have more spacious physical surroundings. Although, just like large companies in any other industry, it can get very difficult to make snap decisions in a changing market and react quickly enough to set a new steering course. Large companies probably insure multiple lengthy meetings, duplicitous layers of approval, and plenty of machine grinding to get even the simplest of tasks done. It's always about the trade-offs, and that's okay.

Small developers usually offer the benefit of a close-knit, family-like atmosphere. You will miss this at some point. In many cases, small developers struggle desperately just to get by. You probably won't get extended benefits of any kind and your paycheck might even bounce. You might not even get a paycheck; they might just tell you to take your computer home and call it square. Most likely, you will have more freedom and leisure to explore your interests.

Larger companies might offer extensive benefits, and your paycheck will never bounce, but you will give up some autonomy. Odds are, in larger companies, you will be asked to make a certain kind of contribution to a project and your application to other projects will be closely guarded and monitored since project budgets are not normally shared, although they can be. Whichever team is using you on a project internally is paying for you out of their own budget. If you work for a smaller developer, you might work in a couple areas (staging, character rigging), even on a couple of titles simultaneously.

Your geographic location will influence your salary, just like many other industries. You may or may not be able to get the kind of cost of living adjustments necessary to maintain a constant lifestyle level as you wander the globe making games. You may experience feast followed by famine, or its opposite. You will meet plenty of great people who passionately share your interests.

Is it worth it? Of course it is. We could be selling insurance. (There's absolutely nothing wrong with selling insurance, as long as I don't have to do it.)

Concentrate on your skills, stay diversified, and stay flexible. If you enjoy character rigging, become the best darn character rigger in your state, keeping in mind while you do it that the world is not yet clamoring for character riggers. If you're a good programmer, congratulations are in order. You will probably be less familiar with your state's unemployment development department than the rest of us. Be persistent, but not annoying. I know it's a fine balance, but most things are. In order to support your game design career, law school at night is not a bad option. Solid cabinetry experience is not a bad thing either, nor is having a significant other a heartbeat away from finishing their medical degree.

If you're in seventh grade, love games, and are dealing with "being in seventh grade," hang in there. Stay focused on turning your interests and passions into skills to support your gaming ambitions. I was busy with games in seventh grade, and I still am. You will be able to make games for consoles and devices that baffle my comprehension. They will probably start your car and warm your coffee in between game sessions. If you're 70, the game industry needs you. Maybe no one is making the kind of games that you would enjoy, and console games are not the only kind of games worth making. Some of the best games ever made didn't start with poorly constructed design documents. They started with an idea about what kind of action might be fun to manipulate. They started with a feeling and someone saying "I'd like to make a game that ..."

You don't stop being able to contribute to gaming at 24 years old, and you don't need to be 24 to contribute—regardless of what they tell you in job interviews.

Seventh grade, 70, or anywhere in between, I applaud your interest in trying to learn more about game design. I can't wait to play the games that you'll make for all of us.

Creating Your Perspective and Maintaining Your Passion

If you are beginning your foray into the game industry, it is extremely important that you define certain goals for yourself. "Get a job in games" is not the kind of goal I'm talking about, but it is an obvious part of the process. If you are persistent, flexible, and passionate, you will find a way into the game industry if you haven't already. When I speak of goals, I'm not talking about deciding on a choice between becoming a programmer versus becoming a texture artist either. I'm referring to your own individual goals about what you want to accomplish in games, how you define yourself, and about what you expect from your time in the game industry.

You'll have to decide for yourself what you would like to accomplish in games, but remember to enjoy the journey. It will be the journey that makes you look back and smile more than any single ship date. It will be the barbecues and the road trips between the milestones. If your game doesn't ship after 19 long months of development, if it gets cancelled, your team will experience a mini-grieving period, but believe me, you will last and move beyond. I've seen developers have nervous breakdowns trying to ship games. It isn't possibly worth it in any way, and it is a tragic ending to a story that began with great hope and excitement.

I can tell you that many developers start out in the game industry wanting to build their own version of the greatest game ever made. Some have been thinking about this particular game for much of their gaming life. This is a perfectly natural beginning. Other new developers may dream of having their own game development studio some day. This is another perfectly natural aspiration. Make sure that what you want to accomplish in games stays true to something deeply grounded within you.

Some developers "define" themselves by their affiliation or work in the game industry. If they couldn't mention the fact that they work at such and such a game company at a cocktail party, they just might shrivel up and die. You should absolutely take pride in your work, but don't make the mistake of defining yourself by it. When you get your first game job at 19 or 22, it's an exciting feeling to start living out your dreams. By the time you're working for your tenth or twelfth gaming company, saying that your building textures for *The New Adventures of Bozo* might not sound so musical anymore.

Remember that, whether you're a programmer, artist, designer, producer, studio management, audio engineer, or tester, you should not define yourself exclusively in terms of your relationship to games. You will be a better developer if you don't. At times, you must live outside of the game industry to bring anything useful back to it. Many developers make the mistake of living only in and around games and the game industry. This does not help grow games.

Be mindful of your expectations. You should definitely dream and aspire, but remember that even as a dedicated and passionate game developer, you are more than that besides. You are not *only* a game developer. I've seen too many developers sacrifice too much in the mythic quest to ship a game. It isn't worth sacrificing your marriage for a game that gets cancelled four days after your divorce is finalized. The best game developers making very successful games (not coincidentally) know that balance is critical—balance in development goals, timelines, expectations, relationships, and so forth. If balance is the essence of a well-paced game, it is also the essence of a game developer that can endure.

If you expect too much, you will probably be disappointed. Another reason why I like to reinforce the idea of staying "diversified" in your skills, and in your approach to the industry, is that it gives you the ability to make quick changes to correct your balance.

Once you've worked in gaming for a while, you may be challenged to maintain your level of passion. You may know the old saying: "If you really want to kill your passion, do it for a living." There's some truth in it. If you have been working on a game all day long every day (weekends too), you may not want to play games in whatever "spare" time you can hobble together. You might want to get outside and go hiking.

The great thing about the game industry is that even after working on many games, as platforms come and go, there is one constant: you can always learn more about areas related to game construction. You can bring a wide range of subjects together for your own gaming purposes. I find that the best way to keep the passion up for games is to challenge myself, and those around me, with assignments to explore a new topic. I'll choose three, four, or more per year depending on my schedule. You'll soon find yourself dating years by the game you were working on.

Sometimes these explorations, which began with game development, lead away from game development. That's okay; remember that we're always looking to bring something back. I'll take a character design class. I'll take a head modeling class. I'll try to learn more scripting. I'll take a drawing or lighting class. I'll use my rare vacation time to visit a Scottish castle. I like game research that involves travel. I've always envied the Disney animators who are sent all over the globe to sketch and study and prepare for movie productions.

I find connections to games in many places, and you will too if you don't already. I think about games at sporting events, concerts, and museum visits. I like to visit museum bookstores and purchase books like *Pieter Saenredam: The Utrecht Work* by the 17th century master of beautifully rendered perspectives on church chapel interiors. I consider all of this "field work" for game development. I might need a good-looking chapel soon. I'm always aware that I have a long way to go in my learning.

You may find that some of the most exciting work you eventually complete is inspired by the work you were doing in order to grow your game skills. I encourage you to find entirely new ways to explore each of your gaming interests. I know you'll be excited by what you will find.

The best developers I've ever worked with are slightly mad by definition, interested in everything around them, and some of the best people you'll ever get a chance to meet. I remember one artist, absolutely brilliant at modeling and texturing; I told him flat out that he was an amazing digital artist. He paused a moment, looked up at me from his stylus, Wacom tablet, and mouse after making his next move and said, "I'm not a digital artist. I'm a painter." And I'd forgotten he was—classically trained. "Beautiful" I thought to myself. He didn't define himself by games alone, but brought everything he knew outside of games to their construction.

INTERVIEW WITH BILL ROPER

Bill Roper is the vice president of Blizzard Entertainment North. Blizzard Entertainment needs little introduction as the creators of the best selling Warcraft, Starcraft, and Diablo series of games, as well as the forthcoming Worlds of Warcraft. I had the opportunity to interview Bill about how to approach game design.

TM: How do you start to develop a game design idea?

BR: Did you ever get stuck on the freeway and daydream about blasting through traffic, sailing off the side of the road, and skidding to a halt in the local 7-11 parking lot so you could grab a soda while waiting for traffic to break? Welcome to Grand Theft Auto III. Anything and everything that touches your life is a potential launching point for a game. Music, art, literature, television, comic books, movies, sports, food, basic social interaction—these are all things that can spark ideas for a game designer. The key is to find something that is a personal interest, enjoyment, or passion and make that into your game. Whether it is certain subject matter, a particular game mechanic, or even an artistic expression, you need a guiding vision. Within that vision, however, must reside a true focus on fun.

Too many designers get caught up in the need to make a game that has cutting-edge technology, or the best-looking artwork, or the smartest AI ever created, or a wholly bizarre and innovative twist while losing sight of the need for the game to be fun. Stay true to that vision of creating something that you want to play over and over and over, and never forget that the design of the game needs to be something that people can understand, easily access, and get emotionally involved in. Even a "low-technology" game like Tetris makes you sweat and panic and squirm just enough to want to play again and again and beat your best score.

Also, playing other games is essential, especially with your development team. The best solos in music come from a fusion of the passion and skill of the soloist with a responsive and iterative band. They listen to what the soloist is doing, and then play with and off of it. In turn, the soloist responds with his own intuitive iterations or departures. When a second soloist joins the fray, his performance is only augmented by what he has just heard if he can build upon the previous experience. As game developers, we should not be afraid to play other companies' games and learn from what they did, as well as playing our games and learning from our own mistakes. Seeing what has come before leads to new thoughts on where to go.

TM: How do you begin to test or prototype gameplay ideas or gameplay mechanics?

BR: The single best thing you can do is to find some way to get anything that represents the core idea of how the game will play onto the screen. This doesn't mean you need to have the best graphics engine in existence created first—even the simplest of shapes that allow the core concept to be tried is a good start. Depending on the genre of the game, there may be ways to use existing products and tools to whip up a quick, initial proof of concept. Team Fortress, for example, was created using a preexisting game and a set of tools to see if the idea that was scratched out on a notepad would be fun to play. Beyond sound design concepts and philosophy, you simply will never know if something is really fun to play until you can actually play it, so getting to that stage as early as possible—even with a rudimentary implementation—is essential.

TM: How do design decisions made in the past help to shape the decisions you make in the present?

BR: Historians say that those who do not learn from the past are doomed to repeat it. This is certainly true in the realm of game design and development. From game mechanics to implementation of technology to scheduling to test procedures to creation of art resources, each and every aspect of designing a new game should be compared to what was previously done on other projects. If it took four months to build a basic, playable prototype on each of the last three projects, there is no reason to assume that this time it will take two months. If players responded well to including an in-game auto-mapping system in your last role-playing game, they will probably want one in your next one, as well. Also, if you tried something and it failed, that is the more important lesson to learn. If trying to build levels before the storyline for the single-player campaign was completed cost your last project time and money to go back and either change levels or re-record dialogue, make sure you remember that when you get to the same decision point the next time around.

Doing a post-mortem on every project that both points out the good and bad decisions made in all aspects of the game's design and production is a great tool for future design work. Also, staying in close touch with the day-to-day gaming community and seeing what it is they like and dislike about your game is an immense help when making design decisions. While you may have been enamored with a particular gameplay mechanic, if none of your players like it (or even use it), then you should rethink its use. This is not to say you will automatically change what you did for the future, but you must be aware of the issues and give them real thought. We can learn a lot not just from analyzing, but from continually playing our own and others' games to see how the decisions made when those games were created can be best referenced when moving forward.

TM: How do you handle multiple design preferences and multiple design personalities on a design team?

BR: Being a producer or lead designer in this industry is like juggling cats. You will have numerous talented and highly independent people all giving input into the direction of the game, and it is your job to sort through them, pulling out the best ideas for the game. This is a key distinction from pulling out the best ideas in a general sense; it is important that in all design decisions it is the game, and not the individual personalities of team members or a desire to be hyper-innovative or the need to be on the cutting edge of technology, that drives the process. Whether you are diplomatic or hard-nosed in your interactions with your team members (and both will be called for), as long as they can see that you have only the best interests of the game in mind and at heart, they will work with you. This also means that you need to be able to lead by example. If you have a design idea that ends up not being as good for the game as a concept proposed by another member of the team, you need to be able to put your idea aside and go with theirs.

TM: Any suggestions for handling the communication loop between a design team's requests for features and functionality in tools, and the programming team tasked with building those tools?

BR: If you can get the programmers and designers to agree that the tools are an essential part of making a great game, you have won half the battle. Again, the focus needs to be on the game and not the programmers' "personal" interests or the designers' "petty" needs. The designers have a responsibility to give thought to what they are trying to accomplish with the requested tool as opposed to just saying, "We need feature X." The programmers have a responsibility to work with the designers to create a toolset that makes the creation of the game as quick and easy as possible. The huge benefit is that if there is a strong toolset that a designer can use to get all of his ideas onto the screen, the end of the project becomes much easier for the programmers because they won't be spending all of their time writing special-case code to do what the well-written tool will handle.

As an example, the design and implementation of the World Editor for Warcraft III was key to the successful realization of the role-playing-game aspects found in the game's single-player campaign. The level designers worked hand in hand with the programmers to create a tool that was not only powerful, but was also easy enough for them to use day in and day out. Although it is not uncommon to see tools created without much thought given to the end user, the growth of the World Editor was a cooperative venture between the people making it and the people using it. This was essential not just because we intended to ship it as a part of the game, but also because we knew that we wanted to free up our game programmers as much as possible from having to do special-case programming for the campaign.

By putting a heavy focus on designing a robust tool that the level designers could use to modify their work and then immediately review it in the game, we not only streamlined our development process, but we also gave ourselves many more chances to iterate on those designs while reducing our required quality-assurance testing time. It is said that a craftsman is only as good as his tools, so giving your craftsmen the best tools possible will help them create the best product they can.

TM: What advice would you offer to new designers? How do you prepare?

BR: Make a game that you want to play. It is frustrating to talk to a designer on a sports title that doesn't like sports, or to a developer on a real-time strategy game that only plays first-person shooters. Although you cannot always choose the projects on which you work, do everything you can to at least be involved in an area that sparks your interests and passions. Also, no matter what type of game you are designing, keep your eye on the following goals:

Easy to Play

This is the stage of getting your player into the game. The game must be simple to learn and have a very accessible interface. As the player progresses through the game, he or she is introduced to more sophisticated game mechanics while being given more tasks to do and places to explore. By the end of the game, the player is playing at a much higher level than when he or she started, but the development was made easy through a gentle learning curve.

Difficult to Master

This is the real meat of the game. After players know how to manipulate the interface, move around the world, and so forth, what is going to keep them coming back for more? Advanced strategies, an array of multiplayer options, and either random or player-created maps are all factors to making a game playable and replayable for months and years as opposed to days or weeks.

F-U-N

Above all else, the game has to be fun. While this is perhaps a very esoteric statement, it is surprising to see how this most basic of building blocks is overlooked by designers. Advanced enemy AI, cutting-edge graphics engines, or complete digital environmental surround sound can enhance a game that is, at its core, fun to play. These things do not, however, make the game fun to play in and of themselves. This is also the main contribution of the designer; making sure that the course is set for a compelling and fun experience is the designer's top job.

TM: How do you see the design role evolving with the scope and complexity of games always on the rise?

BR: We need to balance the increasing technology, size, scope, and complexity of games with keeping them accessible. It is easy to get caught up in all of the bells and lights and whistles and lose sight of the fact that when someone sits down to play the game for the very first time, they may have absolutely no idea how anything you have designed works. You need to ease people into the game, even if by the end you are going to have them typing tons of text, whipping the mouse around, frantically clicking on dozens of objects, and balancing a range of resources.

Also, we need to stay focused on the key elements of what is entertaining and captivating about our game design, and then embellish those areas as opposed to simply creating more and different ideas. Our job as developers is to define a play experience and then stay true to that vision. If we do a good job of that, the game will remain fun throughout for players who are excited and entertained by the type of experience that our game provides.

Finally, we need to create and maintain tools that not only help us build the game, but also track the progress and evolution of the design and development. If you have a massive role-playing game with hundreds of spells, thousands of quests, and tens of thousands of different items, for example, you need to not only be able to design and generate all of that content, but you need to be able to iterate on the balance, distribution, and use of all of those elements. The bigger a game gets, the more there is to follow and probably fix, so we need to make excellent tools to facilitate doing so in a timely and organized fashion. In more mundane terms, if you have 10 people in your community, you can remember all of their names and phone numbers. If you have 50–100, you need a pen and a notepad. If you have 1,000,000, you need a phone book, directory assistance, and a way to organize operators to facilitate your calls.

TM: What aspects excite you about the near future of gaming?

BR: Both what we can do as game designers and acceptance of the game industry as a mainstream form of entertainment are constantly on the rise, and there are no indicators that these are trends that are going to slow anytime in the near future. As this generation grows up, they are likely to consider PC and console games as much a part of their culture as past generations viewed art, literature, music, television, and movies. This means that there will be an increasing interest in games. There will continue to be a need for talented, dedicated developers who have a passion for making great games, and more and more people will be exposed to the great fun to be had. The systems we create and play those games on will continue to get more powerful, and the player's experience will just keep getting better and better. The best part is, in five years, we will probably be creating things that right now we could only dream about.

TM: For most game projects, how far away from the original game concept does the game travel by completion?

BR: The two opposing, but supportive, forces in game design are maintaining your persistence of vision while being able to let go of ideas. Once you have set the vision of your project—meaning the main goals, feel, gameplay mechanics, and so forth—you need to always keep them in mind as you design out the game. Although there will be innumerable changes, both grand and small, to your initial design, you must keep the concept of the game in the forefront of your discussions.

During the creative process of designing a game, you will come up with thousands of great ideas and also a lot of not-so-great ideas. Sometimes you come up with an idea that is destined to be a truly amazing and groundbreaking concept. Occasionally, these ideas simply don't work out. Regardless of the reason, you realize that these ideas need to be changed or even set aside. This can be a simple matter when you finally try out the idea in the game and immediately realize that it is just not fun. Other times, this can be an extremely difficult decision because you can see how it might work and are willing to try and find ways to keep the idea alive.

In either case, dumping an idea that you have conceived, fostered, and perhaps even implemented is a painful but necessary process. Not everything works out as planned, and it is a difficult thing to admit when that gameplay mechanic you thought would revolutionize the industry turns out to be an adventure into tedium. When you are faced with the need to pull the plug on something in the game—no matter what the cause—you have to do so as quickly and painlessly as possible. Do not be afraid to scrap ideas, because many times you will replace them with something far better or simply find that there does not need to be anything there at all.

Keeping your eye on the overall vision for the project will allow you to make major changes to even key elements of the game with the knowledge that you will end up with a cohesive and fun game design. This is where these two forces meet and actually work together, as long as you recognize they are there and are willing to accept them both as tools to use.

TM: The "design" role means different things to different developers. Should designers focus on the technical, the artistic, or something else entirely?

BR: First and foremost, find out what it is that drives your creative juices, and then focus on becoming the best you can in that area. Look at what else interests you and see how these elements of your life can intermingle with your job as a designer. If you love sports and are also interested in AI, start working on creating the best football coach that has ever competed on the digital gridiron. If you love westerns and horror, start working on a game that has a zombie gunslinger as the hero or villain. If you have an idea for a game that you just haven't seen yet, make it out of cardboard and pieces from other games, or build a level that shows the idea with an editor for another computer game. As a designer you should focus on the area where your passion and expertise can best help the game.

MEGA TIPS

1. Keep your approach, skill set, and mindset diversified. The game industry is a tough and turbulent business.

2. The best developers appreciate opportunities to "bring back" the results of their individual and collective explorations for the benefit of gaming.

3. Focus on the meaning of your skills growth as an individual *and* as a game developer, not *only* as a game developer.

4. You can start now by studying and exploring areas you believe are relevant to building new game ideas, or improving your game-related skills by extending them.

5. Make sure you focus on the foundations of game design: industrial design, writing and presentation, scripting, modeling, staging, dynamics, lighting, and, perhaps most importantly, learning how to truly *be* a team member.

6. Get out of the box. Don't be afraid to try to take gaming to new venues.

7. Focus on the fun. As a designer, don't fall victim to techno-distraction. A game is either fun enough to create a natural replay value or it isn't. You have to get this aspect right at the most basic level of your game design.

8. Don't ignore opportunities to expand the domain of gaming. You will be helping yourself and possibly creating opportunity for others.

9. Keep gaming.

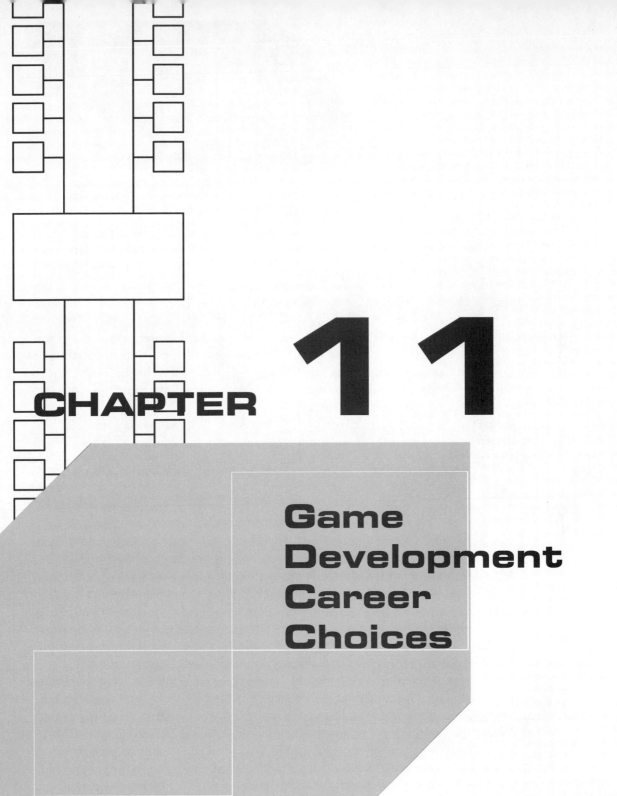

CHAPTER

11

Game Development Career Choices

AT some point in your skills growth, you have to make a choice about a career direction in games. It would be extremely difficult to be an artist/ programmer/audio engineer in today's game industry, since each of these disciplines alone requires so much focused knowledge depth. It's useful to remember that in a very real sense for many game development teams, each team member is a game designer, or at least a significant game design contributor. The specific role of "game designer" is a relatively new position and many game makers struggle to be clear about exactly which set of skills make up a potent game designer. Many programmers, artists, and producers have strong abilities in game design and will collaborate intensely with those taking on the game design role. Other developers prefer not to get into the muddy design details much at all. They are perfectly content to focus on their own area specialties and interests.

In this chapter, we're going to take a look at several of the major game development career tracks and talk about some of the factors you might want to consider in making game career choices.

PROGRAMMING

It's not easy to be a game programmer. Then again, it's not easy to be anything in game development. I've always said that if you're a programmer at heart you'll know it. What does this mean? It means that you can't really make yourself a programmer. You kind of take to it or you don't. I know that code editors and debuggers have gotten much better over time, but when I learned programming, it didn't feel like programming. It felt like I spent the majority of my time searching for misplaced semicolons in order to get something to compile correctly. If I could finally get something to compile without waving a rubber chicken over the computer, I was done for the day.

I started experimenting with games by writing text games in Basic and recording them to audiotape on a cassette recorder for the TRS-80 Model 1. If I mucked up the record volume, the game wouldn't save. I wrote little games with a friend, and we broke into the Basic code for arcade shooters and tweaked the code to get new results.

My professional game programming aspirations ended in a college programming class in the early days of computer graphics. I was building a dart board game using Pascal. I could barely get the darts to land on the board at all, and the guy sitting next to me had flashing animations indicating where darts had hit the dartboard, and he had colored darts. Damn. I knew it was time to wander back to the philosophy department, having just experienced the end of my programming career. Why Descartes seems to make sense but plunking colored darts on a screen doesn't I cannot even imagine.

Actually, you can "make" yourself a programmer and force yourself into programming; I've known a few who have tried. Unfortunately, you probably won't have the passion required to push yourself further every day. As a game developer in any capacity, it's important to understand programming (if only conceptually). Even if you never become a professional game programmer, it's well worth your time to take some programming classes. You need to understand at a very basic level what it's like to face a programming challenge, even if your challenge is writing a program to calculate your weight on Mars. Or, heaven help you, building a dart game.

In my own experience, game programmers need two core elements. They need a deep understanding of how to tackle 3-D programming challenges (in code, math, and physics), and how to inject life via code into the disparate elements that come together into a game. They also need to have played a ton of games to know what they're after content-wise. I've seen engineers with little gaming exposure try to build games. It's not a pretty sight. They sometimes have fantastic engineering instincts, but no sense for how to bend code into game fun.

Gathering knowledge of many games is the easy part. It's the fun part in building up your game understanding. The tough part seems to be gaining enough understanding of the pure foundational mathematics and physics to get the intended effect out at the other end of your code.

Many people have argued with me over the following point: I claim that these days you simply have to finish a B.S. in computer science or mathematics (or get the equivalent level of understanding on your own) to handle game programming. It simply has become too complex. Having worked with many teams under huge amounts of development pressure, I've seen the difference first hand. I've seen developers with a solid background get a complete 3-D engine off the ground from scratch in two months. I've seen developers without a solid background struggle for months to try to move something across the screen.

Game Programming as a Career Choice

Game programming is probably the best career choice in the game industry. Many game studio founders are ex-programmers, and some of them even still like to code. Some have left programming behind and have chosen to focus on the business side of running a game development studio. The game programmer as an individual has traditionally been the focus of the industry. In the past, they often delivered the entire game experience. Let's face it, without great programming, you won't have a solid game despite the best art, design, or audio.

If you are a natural programmer and enjoy programming, you can't go wrong in becoming a game programmer. It's a great job. Understand, however, that as a game programmer, you help control the code base for a game project. Any changes that need to be made in code will pass by you or your team. Game programmers work very long hours, and the work is intellectually challenging to say the least. You will constantly be problem solving, experimenting, and working to maximize efficiencies. It's tough work, and you simply have to love it or you won't last long. Good game programmers are paid well, but they earn it in spades. They are paid less in many cases than their peers in other industries. I've known programmers who have started their game programming careers earning $25K, and in five years are earning well over $100K. Like all game industry salaries, these figures are highly variable on a number of conditions.

The best way to get work is to have solid code examples of a game or game-oriented material. Maybe you wrote a great game tool with friends, or you wrote a pretty fun game in college. Many people have gotten into jobs this way. Don't worry if you can't walk in with a code base for a game engine to rival *Doom III*. If you can, let's talk.

Another nice aspect to game programming as a career is the fact that you can eventually run in a number of directions. You can focus on many areas that might meet your interests: graphics or rendering, audio, tools, compression, path finding or AI, or software development management.

And since game programming is one of the hardest types of programming in existence, it's easy to jump to a different sector if you don't like the hours. The demand for programmers may wax and wane, but the demand for programmers who can write *fast* code is more recession-proof.

There is always solid demand for good game programmers. You can't say the same thing for many other development roles.

ART

Games require the creation of many types of art assets (as discussed in Chapter 1), including, but not limited to: character models, character textures, environmental modeling, environmental textures, prop models, prop textures, character and prop animations, special effects, complete introductory movies, segues, and end movies, and, of course, plenty of interface and power-up details.

I've cleaned up the language, but I once had a boss tell me: "Find me a programmer. I can go out on the corner to spit in any direction and I'll probably hit an artist." An overexaggeration to be sure, but there *are* many aspiring game developers who would like to be game artists. Game companies are regularly flooded with demo tapes. How anyone thinks that they can get a game art job by sending in a screen grab of a sphere with a chrome texture on it, I will never know.

I've had woodcut printers send in a resume and a post card showing no "art" material at all. Game developers are not looking for art exhibitors; they are looking for people with art skills they can utilize to create game assets that help to sell games. That's it. This doesn't mean that you can't be an artist. In fact, you should be an artist, but you're going to have to know how to navigate the commercial world of the game industry versus the world of your art.

Primarily, as a game artist, game developers want your modeling, texturing, and animation skills. Good artists with a solid understanding of how to prepare game-ready low-poly artwork are in regular demand. However, learning how to deliver this kind of material reliably takes time.

As a game artist you will be asked to provide many kinds of in-game art assets, so you need to be able to demonstrate some versatility. Think about all of your favorite games and the kinds of games you've seen made. What do they have in common? Well, they probably feature either fantasy- or cartoon-style heroes and enemies. They probably offer a wide variety of vehicles. They are probably set in an environment.

The same boss also told me, "Every game setting can be traced back to outer space, a desert, a jungle, a castle, or a city." My point is that you probably already know what kind of art requirements games demand. Focus on drawing, modeling, texturing, or animating these exact elements. If you want to have a long and deep career and enable yourself to make career transitions, you should start with a solid foundation. Go get a B.A. or B.F.A. in art or design. Draw plenty of humans, vehicles, and animals. You will never stop learning, so it's really best to establish a strong starting point.

Game Artist as a Career Choice

Game developers always need good artists. There are now starting to be more people interested in and ready for positions than there are positions available. It's a very competitive field. If you eat, breathe, and sleep building game-oriented art assets, you'll probably do just fine.

If you find work with a game developer, being a game artist can be a fantastic job. If you love to draw or model and animate, it is rewarding to get paid for doing something that you love. That feeling will soon pass, and like any other game developer role, you will have to love what you do in order to make the sacrifices necessary to do it.

Game artists are primarily responsible for creating art assets. Modern games have tons and tons of art assets. Entire software packages are dedicated to managing the workflow for all of these assets. These assets regularly must be changed, redone, or deleted altogether. Sometimes a small art team is responsible for creating hundreds or thousands of art assets: every little icon, cursor, or screen element, every single power-up, projectile type, and projectile effect.

It can be very hard work to create all of these elements and still meet your deadlines. Game artists regularly work very long hours. Being a game developer can take its toll on personal relationships. Artists tend to get paid less than programmers. Some artists start working for a developer for free. Some start with a salary around $25K and can earn up to $75K. Some may earn even more. There are many factors involved in the pay allocated for an artist. Are they creating assets and managing a team? Are they helping train others? These kinds of "soft" factors enter into perceived value.

It can be a volatile world with frequent layoffs. Outside of entertainment companies, which can be seriously affected by a bad economy, where will you find work? You might find a few opportunities, but it could be very difficult. This is why I dedicated an entire chapter to keeping your skills and your mindset diversified.

Being a game artist can be a very rewarding and fulfilling endeavor, if you balance your passion with an understanding of how to dig in for the long haul.

DESIGN

As games escalate in scope, someone has to watch out for design flow issues and game play issues, and provide design-productive content. The game design role for most game developers is an interesting beast. Generally, game designers are not hired straight away into the game industry. More typically, you move into the design track by having worked in another area of game development first. In some capacity, you will probably have to demonstrate your design abilities before anyone will pay you for the position.

A level designer builds game levels. The best way into level design is to showcase the levels that you've learned how to build on your own. Many developers regularly or occasionally troll the sites dedicated to creating levels for their titles, looking for the best of the best from the level-design talent pool available. I won't kid you; it isn't easy to get noticed. Demonstrating that your levels have become popular in the mod community is one good way to get noticed. The pathway into level design is pretty straightforward—just build great levels!

Getting a job as a game designer, on the other hand, involves showing your previous design work. This can take the form of completed games, design documents, design materials, and so forth. There is some specialization in this area, since developers like to use designers who have a real passion and love for the kind of game they are preparing to build. If you are a die-hard sports designer, you may have little interest in designing a hardcore RPG, and vice versa.

If you can't find a direct route into game design, it's probably best to start in another area of game development and then try to work your way over to design if a position becomes available.

Game Designer as a Career Choice

If you have long-distance persistence and determination, and viable skills to accompany your pursuit, there are opportunities in game design. It is my hope that as the game industry expands, even more opportunities will be created very soon. Once you've worked on a couple of game titles, it becomes easier to show some of your work. However, getting a great design job is never really easy. The competition is always fierce. Let's face it, for many game lovers, what could be better?

Think about the pure numbers involved, too. On any given development team these days, you might have 25 developers. However, most of these development positions are reserved for programmers and artists. This means that game productions typically have many more programmers and artists working on a title than they do designers. So if you are competing for the few design slots available, the competition is going to be heavy, and it may drive your salary down. Simply put, others may be willing to do the same job for much less money than you.

Working as a game designer can be a beautiful avocation for those who are up to the challenge. What challenge? It's always a challenge to build content at the crossroads of innovation in art and technology. This endeavor is rarely simple or easy.

The salary range for game designers, like many other development positions, varies greatly. Entry-level designers might make $25–30K, while much more experienced designers can earn around $60K. If you are very well versed in 3-D tools, packages, and scripting, you are obviously adding value and flexibility to your role. "Superstar" designers can obviously earn much more than this range would suggest, but very few developers fit that classification.

PRODUCTION

Game developers and publishers have producers on staff. In other forms of nongame-related software development, these folks are called project managers, or software product managers. The game industry uses the more entertainment-oriented term of "producer." Producers work to manage all aspects of a game production by tasking, tracking, coordinating, budgeting, and facilitating. They are planners and project coordinators. They also usually have a large background and exposure to games (for obvious reasons).

Traditionally, producers come up out of the QA department. They begin as assistant producers, move on to associate producers, and then on to full producers. An assistant producer is usually mentored by an associate producer, while the associate producer is mentored by a producer.

If you like highly specialized, detail-oriented work that will throw you curve balls when you least expect them, then you might like to work in game production. You will often be responsible to upper management for meeting milestones, keeping game projects on schedule and on budget, and keeping a solid relationship established with your publisher at all times. This is a job that combines detail and communications work with a solid understanding of the technical tasks involved in building games. Before there were official game design positions available, many producers doubled as game designers. Many programmers and artists doubled as designers, too. These days, some have decided to stay on the game design side, while others have left more design-oriented tasks behind and are working in a pure production capacity.

There is no way to learn how to be a good game producer, other than by getting a chance to work with a few good ones along the way. There is no real "bar" or measuring post for the production role, so some suspicious characters sometimes make their way into production roles.

Your day to day duties would include team planning, milestone tracking, game build evaluation, design coordination, art approval, and training support, and then you'll also work on all the other details that no one else has time to deal with. This can include marketing, PR interfacing, special events, food runs, event planning, counseling, and making breakfast the morning after a milestone is successfully completed.

Production as a Career Choice

Developers tend to grow their own producers up through a company. This is not to say that companies don't hire producers from outside their current ranks—they do. Yet, since producers ultimately get a glimpse of the business game plan for a development studio or publisher, a trust factor needs to be in place. It can be hard for a development studio to find someone from the outside they're comfortable with. On the flip side, only promoting from within, and never or rarely hiring externally, can lead to a somewhat stagnant talent pool as developers only know how "they" have always done it, and cannot necessarily benefit from the learning that comes with seeing everyone else make mistakes first.

Production positions also suffer from the numbers games. Even in a relatively large, independent development studio, there are rarely more than just a couple of producers. There might only be two or three full-time producer positions available among many more positions available to programmers and artists. This tends to lower your individual odds of getting a position as a producer.

The production role can be very satisfying, especially after overcoming several production challenges along the way and finally shipping a solid game that will entertain many players. The pay range for producers varies by experience from $28K to around $90K. Again, pay ranges must always be considered with great latitude. Some developers prefer that their producers be ensconced almost purely in matters of business and studio growth, while others prefer producers to have a more technical inclination. Most successful producers seem to have some combination of both. They combine a solid understanding of game construction technology and a reasonable amount of business sense and experience.

AUDIO

Audio is a critical part of carrying emotion throughout a game. If you don't believe me, just try playing your favorite game with the sound off. It isn't nearly the same experience. Games these days have heavy audio requirements and support expanded audio formats like Dolby Surround sound. Games require large amounts of music to be composed along with numerous special effects or Foley audio. Several game developers are also musicians, and these folks see an ideal combination of their own interests by providing audio for games.

Learning how to prepare audio for games and working within the technical limitations and memory constraints are a few of the big challenges. Many of the audio engineers and music composers perform in music areas outside of games.

Audio Composer and Engineer as a Career Choice

The audio department at most developers is very compact. Several developers choose to contract their audio requirements out to audio pros that know how to prepare sound for various game platforms. If they work in-house with a developer, the audio department is typically very small. This means that only a few individuals per company are employed full-time creating audio in the audio department. It also means that competition for these few positions is very heavy.

For those who love to create music and sound effects and grew up in love with games, it can be an ideal job. Keep in mind that you are often assembling many versions of each sound requested for audition. You are also composing different versions of a music theme or movement for audition and assembly into the game.

Full-time audio engineers in game development make around $30K to $60K or more. You can sometimes earn more as an independent contractor taking on work for games and other venues concurrently. Overall, providing audio for games can be rewarding and challenging as long as you can work under the challenging budgets, timelines, and technical constraints that games place on audio content.

QUALITY ASSURANCE

Many developers see the QA department as a launching pad for their career. It certainly can be. You would be surprised by how many of today's industry pundits have passed through a QA department at one time or another. I think the QA department will end up being to games what the mailroom is to other entertainment companies.

QA allows any developers to see how a game becomes truly final, and how various kinds of decisions help to shape a game title. You can find out if you enjoy some of the process of game making while working in a QA department. Some developers become testers, but really want to be artists, programmers, designers, or audio engineers. This is fine. In fact, you sometimes stand a better chance of moving where you would like to go by starting in QA than by taking any job in one of the career tracks. These tend to nail you down.

So again, if you can't get in by any other means, go up through the test department. I did, and so do many others.

Some choose to stay in QA, and that's just fine too. If you become a QA manager and help to run an entire test department, you can rest assured that as long as games are being made, you're going to have work to do in testing them.

QA as a Career Choice

Many developers only want to spend a couple of years in the QA department and move on, while others choose to make a career of it. Both full-time and part-time work are available in QA, whereas virtually every other role is full-time only. QA testers can be paid hourly at $8–13 per hour part-time with no benefits. As a new developer, this is a great way to test the waters. Full-time QA personnel can be put on salary with benefits in the $25K range or more dependent on the scope of their duties and experience. With a full salary and benefits, the full-time testers are often the minority and are senior testers, as QA departments regularly rely on plenty of part-time help. They can ramp up help when their testing needs peak, and then let the part-time folks go after a big title finishes up. QA managers can earn $50K and upwards, but their role expands to include many responsibilities to support the entire testing effort.

OPENING AN INDEPENDENT GAME STUDIO

For many new and old developers alike, opening your own development studio has long been a dream. The ability to band together a group of dedicated and talented friends to build games together seems like a great idea—even for those with considerable industry experience. A great idea it may be (and this alone can change based on many extenuating factors), but the pathway to success as an independent game studio is covered with many perils. The days of opening an independent studio to work on cutting-edge titles seems to be fading into history. Even those developers with long track records on many prior consoles are finding it challenging to build a strong bridge into the future.

Publishers will only sign up titles with developers who have deep commercial track records. Based on the right connections to industry insiders and representatives, a really solid showing of your own proprietary game technology, and a top-notch team with solid title experience, you might get a low-paid shot at a low-priority title, but even this is becoming harder to secure.

Walking into a publisher as a startup developer with limited experience and saying, "Hey there, we'd like to make a game for ya!" will not get you very far. In fact, the walking-in part probably won't even happen. It's harsh for us game lovers, but publishers want to deal in a world of knowns. At the starting line, they already face too many unknowns for their liking. In short, they only want to risk development money on the knowns. Now, even a known can become an unknown very quickly in game development, but it will take the legacy of the known to get you close to a game development deal. They want to "know" and "believe" that you can produce a hit game for them. How will they come to know or believe this? Probably, it will be because you've produced a hit game for someone else. Someone has to give you a chance at some point, or no one would ever get to make that first hit game that allowed them to get a shot at making another one, right? Well, sort of.

If you think about it, the independent game studios that have been making waves recently are really just spin-offs from large publishers. This means that a team came together under a publisher's roof, learned how to work well together, delivered a solid-selling game or two, and then decided to go independent so that they could build games for more than just a single publisher (the publisher whose roof they first formed under).

Another common pathway to building up an independent development house is to gather together a group of developers who might have worked on games before as employees of several developers or developer/publishers and have recently banded together as a new development group. Often they must exercise their relationships with former publisher employers in order to gain work. This can work too.

What this should be telling all of us is that if you want to start an independent development studio, you're probably going to have to make your way into the industry first and gain some considerable experience before even trying. You can choose to go direct, get some seed money and some venture capital (good luck explaining the revenue model), but in today's climate, this would be an extraordinarily difficult way to launch a development house.

Does this mean that your dream of developing games as an independent developer is shattered right here and now? Not even hardly. There are plenty of ways to go about moving toward your goals. You can participate in the Independent Games

Festival at the yearly GDC. You can pursue shareware. Hey, it sure worked for id Software. Other delivery systems straight to your potential players will no doubt be available in the near future. You shouldn't feel ultimately frustrated by the risk tolerance and concerns of large-scale contemporary game publishers.

Let's be clear about the difference between game developers and game publishers. Game developers build game content and employ programmers, artists, designers, producers, and audio staff. Game publishers, in comparison, are responsible for packaging, manufacturing, marketing, promoting, and supporting game sales. Game developers are given development contracts to build games by game publishers.

Joining a Game Developer

The best way to get valuable development experience is to join a game developer. Most programmers, artists, designers, audio engineers, producers, and QA staff build their careers one step at a time by joining a game developer and learning the ropes of game development, and the nuances of the game industry, long before trying to launch out into the wilderness of independence.

It really is necessary to understand how a whole game development cycle works and how publishers collaborate with developers to build game titles in an everyday game work environment. By establishing yourself as a developer this way, you will learn answers to many of the critical questions you might have about developing games.

Industry Economics

If you were to look at the short history of the game industry, you would probably see that there have been several years where plenty of game jobs were available, and a few years where very few game jobs were available at all. The game industry, like any other industry, reacts to economic shifts in the total economy.

While it's true that games are somewhat recession proof, there are times when the industry definitely backs off on hiring. It's always best to try to anticipate some of the momentum behind the rises and falls so that you can be prepared. Again, this is part of keeping a diversified mindset.

GAME DEVELOPMENT STUDIO BREAKDOWN

The following sections break down the standard set of professional roles and give you a brief description of exactly who does what. Remember that an independent game developer builds game content, while a game publisher packages, markets, supports, and sells the game title.

There are hybrid developer/publishers, too, where the game publisher actually owns the developer engaged in building its own game titles. Probably the most common arrangement, however, is where a publisher contracts out the development of its game title to a developer.

Let's take a look at the role breakdowns for a developer/publisher hybrid. Figure 11-1 describes one common way a developer/publisher-hybrid company might be organized. There is considerable flexibility in these roles from company to company.

Executive Department

The *president/founder* might come from a pure business background or might be an ex-game programmer. There is plenty of variation in this executive capacity. As the chief executive, this person has ultimate responsibility to the owners/shareholders of the company for the fiscal performance and direction of the company.

The *VP of product development* is responsible for guiding all aspects of game product development. These individuals often work alongside a marketing team in pursuing and acquiring attractive licenses to build games around. They also negotiate development agreements with developers, and are entirely responsible for the successful delivery of profitable game titles. Generally, they tend to come from production and business backgrounds.

The *VP of creative* is the creative lead on all projects. These individuals usually have a track record of having helped guide various kinds of projects to successful creative conclusions, meaning that the creative material they have directed has been received well in the marketplace. Not every organizational structure has a VP of creative, and many companies operate with a *director of game design* working in or near this role.

The *VP of technology* or CTO is responsible for considering and directing all technology issues for a company. These individuals normally have deep experience in developing, crafting, and maintaining several kinds of sustainable technologies. They also have management and team-building experience. They assist in making company-wide directives that influence technology orientation for the company. Should we develop for this platform or that one? What kinds of internal technologies should we grow? These are among the questions they must help answer. They might lead the development effort of in-house game engines, proprietary technologies, and so forth. Any kind of company-based hard technology decision is usually deliberated by the CTO.

The *VP of marketing* is focused on bringing the finished game product to the players. They work in a number of ways, and collaborate with many other organizations to try to make sure that game titles receive attention, publicity, and adequate advertising support to help sell game titles. It should be obvious that if you have too many titles shipped without significant sales, you won't be making games much longer.

FIGURE 11-1

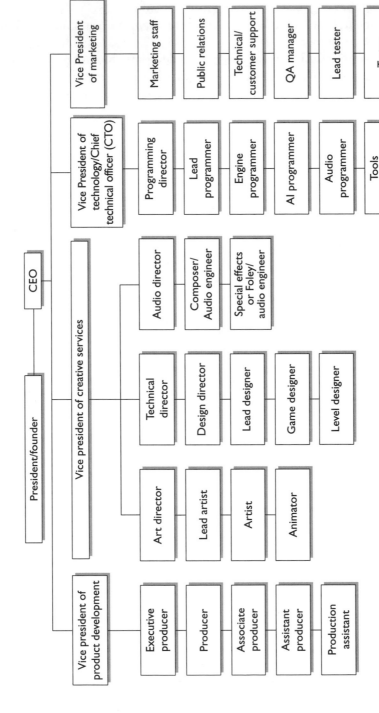

Organization of Developer/Publisher Hybrid

Product Development Department

An *executive producer* is often the lead producer in a company and is responsible for the efforts of other producers and their teams. They act in liaison with the VP of product development in helping to weigh the value of certain licenses and assist in making decisions about placing contracts with external developers. They can also be involved in helping to oversee all onsite game production efforts.

A *producer* helps manage all aspects of hands-on development for a game team, and is responsible for making sure that a game project or multiple projects are on time and on budget. They try to make sure that all the developers on their team have the necessary tools and resources to complete their development goals, resulting in the creation of a successful game title. Team building, tasking, tracking, budgeting, and maintaining game product vision and clarity are significant parts of their role.

An *associate producer* often works in collaboration with a producer on one or more game projects. Some associate producers even have full responsibility for smaller projects, like a game done for portables rather than a huge console title. Companies like to grow associate producers into producers by gradually increasing the scope of their project responsibilities. Good producers help to mentor associate producers by passing on whatever hard-earned wisdom they've accumulated by making (or watching others make) mistakes.

An *assistant producer* is commonly a new producer recently promoted from the QA department. These developers are just starting to learn about the frontline game development process. They usually work in collaboration with both associate producers and producers, assisting with a wide array of assigned project details.

Production assistants are unpaid or hourly interns with an interest in learning more about the game development process. They assist with peripheral project details like gathering reference material for artists or being project runners ("Go get this or that …").

Creative Department

All developers are creative, but art, design, and audio tend to fall under this province or category. As in all the other categories mentioned, there are senior, junior, and a few entry-level positions, although most developers need you to hit the work assigned to you with minimal support. There is very little time to ease an individual's skill shortcomings into a crushing deadline. If you are still growing your skills, that's okay; you simply end up working in the background until the skills you've developed can push you out to the forefront. This is a commercial reality.

An *art director* works in concert with a VP or creative director to make sure that a game title is living up to a high set of visual standards and that the material being produced will be pleasing to IPRH licensors. Larger companies tend to have a couple of art directors working on multiple titles simultaneously. Art directors normally take responsibility for identifying the strengths of the artists they work with, and helping to maintain some kind of training program for their artists to help keep their skills competitive.

As we've discussed many times before, artists have a wide area of contribution to building game assets. Some are dedicated only to modeling, texturing, conceptual drawings, or animation. Other artists do a little bit of everything (or a whole lot of everything!). A *lead artist* is commonly a senior artist who has both direct art responsibilities on a game (building models and textures, for instance) and managerial responsibilities in helping less-experienced artists make meaningful, game-ready art assets. In the best cases, lead artists are a point of reference and a valuable resource for other artists on the team.

An *artist* builds low-polygon models, textures, interface elements, storyboards, cinematics, and so forth.

An *animator* focuses on defining motion for objects and characters. An animator can treat any game element that requires sophisticated motion of any type. Some animators are model builders and texture artists too, but increasingly, as digital animation capabilities get more and more sophisticated, animators are focusing on animation alone. Actually, in many of the art roles discussed, specialization is increasing.

A *technical director* works to set up models for animation by animators. This includes rigging up characters with inverse kinematics (IK) and forward kinematics (FK) control handles for use in animation. Also, depending on the animation techniques required, a technical director might set up slider-based animation systems that give animators control over vertex groups.

The *design director* is the senior game designer on staff. Many companies operate without any specific design director, but this role is starting to become more common as larger teams of designers are assembled for game productions.

A *lead designer* is the design detail manager chiefly concerned with building in the best possible game play for players. All design-related issues, obstacles, problems, challenges, and work-arounds are shared between a design lead and their fellow team members.

A *game designer* works to flesh out or define any and all game design and game play details associated with a given game title. How will every single element present in a game work and relate to one another in excruciating and precise detail? Are the results of that detail fun to play? If not, several passes of adjustment and reworking may be required.

A *level designer* wraps up various game assets into levels, commonly using a specific tool created just for level assembly. Level designers have input into overall game structure, but are primarily focused on level-to-level play details and construction.

An *audio director* is responsible for all audio content created to support game titles. They help to manage teams of audio engineers, audio effects specialists, and composers. As part of their managerial component, they often assist producers and teams in setting up recording sessions, casting game voices, and so forth, among other duties.

A *composer/audio engineer* writes game soundtrack music to accompany game play. They write music for introductory movies, segues, and end movies. A composer produces any original customized music for in-game use that is required. Many companies contract independent composers to write music for their game titles.

The *audio special effects or Foley engineer* is tasked with creating sound effects for games. All of those fantastic punch, crunch, kick, and mortar shelling sounds are the work of these talented folks.

Programming or Technical Department

A *programming director,* usually a senior software engineer, can be in charge of several facets of code support for game development. They may lead up game engine development efforts, conduct limited research, suggest or make improvements to code sharing and cross-platform issues, or help keep coding guidelines and code resources current across a company.

A *lead programmer* is usually the senior programmer on a team. This individual leads the team-based coding effort on all project fronts. Most project-based code details lead back to the lead programmer in some important fashion. They also help to assess, mentor, and train new programmers.

An *engine programmer* focuses on game engine development, revision, and improvement. They may not be working on any particular game content, but rather on the code base that makes other game content development possible. Keep in mind that many programmers not classified as engine programmers per se (lead, team, programming directors, and so forth) often contribute to a company's game engine programming efforts in some way. As a programmer, you may be working on many other kinds of programming (audio, interface, tools) while also contributing to engine code development.

An *AI programmer* (or artificial intelligence programmer) focuses on AI-related programming topics like path finding, intelligent actor or agent systems, and building in, for example, sophisticated types of sports or boss behaviors as examples.

An *audio programmer* works on code to support the audio requirements for a game. They may be writing intelligent audio spooling systems to stream music sections as background music, rewriting the way resident audio uses memory, or developing custom code to handle specialized audio output formats.

One of my favorites, the *tools programmer,* works to build tools that support complex game creation requirements of all kinds. These tools might support audio tagging, level construction, actor property systems, or support for hosting custom events in an MMOG title.

Marketing Department

The *marketing staff* is comprised of several folks with specialty contacts in every area related to bringing a game to market. They are focused on doing everything possible to help build and inform the playing audience about every single game title released.

The *public relations* personnel help to build a bridge in a number of ways between players as customers and a game company. They host special events, try to support some player requests, and keep developers informed about public sentiment and reaction to certain issues.

The *technical/customer support staff* works to support the player base as a game title is released and then long afterwards. They run the help lines or hint hotlines, web sites, technical support FAQs, and so forth. They answer questions and assist players with resolving installation, patching, or compatibility issues. Without their work, a vital part of delivering a fun play experience to the customer would be lost. If players can't get support or help with a game title, they'll remember the experience the next time they see your logo on a box.

A *QA manager* directs all testing services and resources to help insure to the best degree possible that a bug-free game experience is delivered to the players.

A *lead tester* is a point of contact on a test team for any particular title. They filter much of the feedback from their test team, so that developers can get a clear picture of any outstanding bugs.

A *tester* works to find game bugs and "break" the game so that bugs can be reported to and fixed by a game development team.

Breakdown Conclusions

I hope you've found the role breakdown for a developer/publisher hybrid useful. It's best to keep in mind that many of these roles mean different things in different places. Much of the role specifics are determined by the size of a company, access to resources, and many other factors. Many of these roles are common throughout the industry, so they are worth mentioning here. As you pursue your own goals, you will at least have an idea about what kinds of positions are available in gaming.

CASE STUDY COMMENTS ON THE TESTING DOORWAY

It's important to remember that QA is the doorway to game development for most of us. Your first week in a test department will probably be a shock, and that's just fine. It shocks everybody. You won't believe that you're getting paid anything at all to play new games, and you won't believe the head-, neck-, and eyestrain. Be sure to take breaks.

You'll probably meet all kinds of interesting folks in the test department with you. I've met people with business degrees, people with law degrees, child actors, wrestling fanatics, chefs, a neuroscientist, a professional gambler, and a guy on trial for manslaughter. Everyone shares a certain love for games (you'd be insane to do this without loving them!), and most are looking for a way into a game development studio in a full-time capacity. You will probably even meet some "professional" or prize competition-oriented players. Some of these players have won game publisher-hosted competitions and are among the best players in their category. Don't worry if you're nowhere near as good. Test departments need a wide range of player abilities from total pro to near novice. It can be a badge of honor in the test department if you manage to beat a game champion at something (or at anything for that matter).

You will get to play a wide range of games. You may love some of them immediately and you'll probably hate others. It's easy to get tired of anything when you are playing it all day long. You will start to learn what is really a bug, and what isn't. Hopefully, you'll get good at writing up solid and descriptive bug reports. Even at this point, you want to be growing your communication skills.

From there you have to keep your eyes and ears open day and night. Soak up everything you can like a big sponge wearing contact lenses. Ask plenty of questions, but not too many. You want to gather information and express your interest without driving people insane. You'll undoubtedly make some great friends. If you enjoy the QA process, you might have already found your niche. If you want to move into development, start watching for opportunities. It can be difficult and it probably won't happen overnight. Like any other career, building games for a living asks for many kinds of sacrifice. Learn what you can and enjoy yourself. Remember that developers are not looking for people on the quick take; they are looking for people who genuinely enjoy building games.

INTERVIEW WITH YOU!

We've heard from many talented game developers in previous chapters (a big "Thank you!" to them again) about the process of building games, but this is a career chapter. It is your chapter. It's probably time to ask yourself some questions about gaming, and where you might like to go in the game industry. With that in mind, I've assembled a few questions to ask yourself as you pursue your own goals in gaming:

> *What kind of foundation do I need to achieve my goals in gaming?*

> *Which aspect of game development grabs my attention the most?*

> *Can I see myself doing something other than working on games?*

> *Can I be flexible about the opportunities that may come my way?*

> *Do I have a diversified approach in mind?*

> *What can I do now to start earning some relevant experience?*

> *How can I follow up with many of the topics encouraged here as essential to game design?*

> *Am I willing to go where the work is?*

> *Will my passion for games carry me through tough times?*

> *What can I do to become the best I can be in my area or discipline?*

I hope that you can use all of the information presented here to help you on your way toward building exciting new gaming content. Thank you for taking this journey with me. May all of your dreams in gaming be realized!

MEGA TIPS

1. QA is often the doorway.

2. Start now to build a foundation for your game development interests. Don't forget that your interests in gaming may change over time. You can always make adjustments to the work you've set on your foundation.

3. Ask yourself the hard questions about the intensity of your commitment level to games.

4. Take advantage of the material presented here as a springboard, and plot your course.

5. Understand the various development roles and let your intuition and interest guide you to available opportunities.

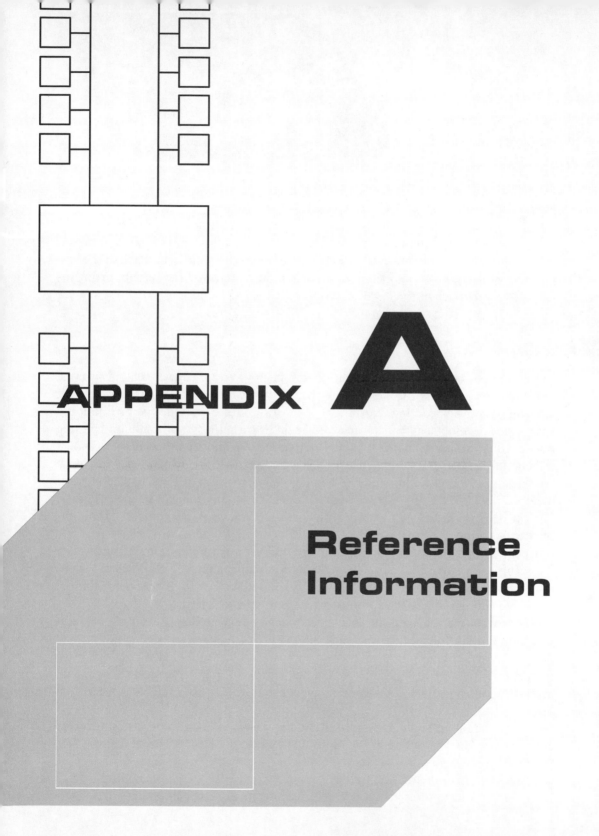

APPENDIX **A**

Reference Information

THIS appendix includes useful reference information in several categories to help you research the game industry. It is by no means an exhaustive listing of the many possibilities you can explore in the game industry. New opportunities become available every day in this dynamic field. Each of the listings mentioned here is intended to try to help point you toward some supporting information for much of the material covered.

EDUCATION

Many schools, colleges, and universities have begun to offer courses related to game development. In many cases, these are relatively new course offerings that are just starting to get their footing. Nothing will substitute for experience gained building games on a development team (even if you begin by gathering your friends and putting one together!), but you should explore every educational possibility available to you.

I encourage you to try to balance your game education by getting some experience with a game developer if possible. Remember that coming up through the QA department is still one of the best ways to begin. For part-time game education opportunities, you can always check with the extension department at your local university campus or search online.

Keep in mind that the common education track toward game programming is a B.S. degree in computer science or mathematics focusing on 3-D graphics programming, while the common track toward art and design is a B.A. or B.F.A. in traditional art and/or design (illustration, industrial design, and so forth).

My advice is to finish a solid B.A. or B.S. degree in a subject of your choosing. It will help build a foundation for everything you do in game development, and will demonstrate that you can start a project, face several forms of challenges, and, most importantly, complete a project! There are successful game designers with backgrounds in marine biology, anthropology, aeronautical engineering, and theatre set design, too.

Several online-oriented game education classes and opportunities are starting to appear also. Here are a few of the options for game-design-specific education:

❭ **DigiPen Institute of Technology (www.digipen.edu)** One of the first institutions to offer actual degree programs in game development.

> **ed2go (www.ed2go.com)**   I teach online game industry courses to students here regularly and have several courses oriented specifically towards game design presently in development.

> **Full Sail (www.fullsail.com)**   Full Sail offers trade-oriented coursework in game development.

> **Art Institutes International (www.aii.edu)**   Most of the Art Institute campuses located across the U.S. now offer game development courses.

It's important to point out that game design as a topic of investigation and exploration is also becoming part of conventional curricula (undergraduate and graduate level) at many prestigious universities including Massachusetts Institute of Technology (MIT), Rochester Institute of Technology (RIT), Carnegie-Mellon University, and Georgia Institute of Technology (Georgia Tech), among others.

EVENTS

The electronic gaming industry has several major industry events per year, the biggest of which are listed here:

> **Electronic Entertainment Exposition, or E3 (www.e3expo.com)**   The leading U.S.-based annual industry trade show.

> **The Game Developers Conference (www.gdconf.com)**   The Independent Games Festival held each year at the GDC is a great way to showcase your independent game work and have it seen by developers and publishers from around the globe.

> **SIGGRAPH (www.siggraph.org)**   The largest annual gathering of computer graphics and graphics technology companies. A great way to learn more about cutting-edge graphics technologies.

> **Electronic Consumer Trade Show (www.ects.com)**   Europe's premier interactive industry trade show.

> **MILIA (www.milia.com)**   An international game content event held in Cannes, France.

INDUSTRY MAGAZINE

Game Developer magazine (www.gdmag.com) is a must read. I suggest reading the "Post-mortems" offered in every issue very carefully. There are plenty of great design-related articles too. An annual "salary survey" provides industry salary range information.

INDUSTRY-RELATED SITES

Numerous industry-related sites are popping up all over the place. I visit only a few of them regularly. Here are my recommendations:

❱ Gamasutra (www.gamasutra.com)

❱ Blues News (www.bluesnews.com)

❱ Game Daily (www.gamedaily.com)

ORGANIZATIONS

One great way to meet other game developers, and those interested in learning more about all aspects of game development, is to show up at a meeting of your local IGDA chapter. Established chapters all over the world are listed on its web site. If you don't have a local chapter, but plenty of local interest, you can always start your own chapter!

❱ International Game Developers Association (www.igda.org)

❱ Academy of Interactive Arts & Sciences (www.interactive.org)

❱ Interactive Digital Software Association (www.idsa.com)

BREAKING IN!

If you aren't hired "out of school" based on your portfolio of work or a striking game demo/sample, then launching your career from the QA department is the way to go. You can always order back issues of *Game Developer* magazine, which contains many articles and stories about getting into the industry.

GameDev.net has several online articles with various suggestions offered on breaking into games: www.gamedev.net/reference/list.asp?categoryid=68.

AGENTS AND RECRUITERS

If you're just getting started in the industry, you must get some work experience before you approach agents and recruiters. If you already have industry experience, Studio Search (www.studio-search.com) is a great agency. Many other agencies are listed on the www.gamasutra.com site under Companies/Business/Legal.

JOB SITES

You can use the main job boards to search for game-related jobs even at the entry level. I have occasionally seen job listings for testers and QA support roles, which are both great ways to get started.

 ❭ Game jobs (www.gamejobs.com)

 ❭ Monster (www.monster.com)

 ❭ Gamasutra (www.gamasutra.com)

DESIGN DOCUMENT REFERENCE

Keep in mind that every developer has their own style and formatting preferences when it comes to preparing game design documents. However, the GameDev.net site (www.gamedev.net) is a good place to start looking. On this site, under "Articles and Resources," you will find several game design document templates. These will give you an idea about both layout and content for writing and formatting your own game design documents.

TV PROGRAMMING

Now available in many areas on cable, G4 TV (www.g4tv.com) is a 24-hour-a-day game channel that features nonstop game-related programming.

COPPA GUIDELINES

For anyone interested in learning more about how to make online game content COPPA (Children's Online Privacy Protection Act)-compliant, visit www.ftc.gov/bcp/conline/pubs/buspubs/coppa.htm.

SELF-PUBLISHING

For those interested in trying to self-publish an already complete/market competitive commercial title, there are a few companies like Tri-Synergy (www.trisynergy.com) offering publishing support services listed on www.gamasutra.com under Companies/Business/Legal.

OUTSOURCED TESTING SERVICES

For anyone in need of outsourced or "out-of-house" testing services, check out National Technical Systems (www.xxcal.com).

GAME INDUSTRY MARKET RESEARCH AND REPORTS

It's always good to stay informed about industry trends and sales patterns in the gaming business. Several companies offer reports:

> DFC Intelligence (www.dgcint.com)

> NPD Group (www.npdfunworld.com)

RECOMMENDED SITES

I recommend each of the following sites as points of reference and inspiration for anyone interested in studying the kind of concept reference material that helps inform and influence the early game design process.

> **Bay Raitt (http://cube.phlatt.net/home/spiraloid/)** Master modeler Bay Raitt (be sure to check out Bay's work in the *Lord of the Rings* movies) has some great advice on character construction, modeling, and applying sculpture techniques.

> **Doug Chiang (www.dougchiang.com)** Design director on the *Star Wars* prequels, be sure to see Doug's beautiful work on *Robota*.

> **Syd Mead (www.sydmead.com)** Legendary designer on *Blade Runner*, *Aliens*, and *TRON*, Syd's work is always exciting and inspirational.

> **Craig Mullins (www.goodbrush.com)** The jaw-dropping conceptual artwork of Craig Mullins.

❱ **Gnomon (www.gnomon3d.com)**   A great educational option for building up those Maya skills!

❱ **Eni Oken (www.oken3d.com)**   A great site for those interested in exploring texture creation.

ECOMMENDED READING

Most game developers keep a wide array of reference material on many topics handy on the bookshelf. I've included a listing of several titles that I think you might find useful in continuing your investigation of the game industry and game design fundamentals.

❱ *A Brush With Disney: An artist's journey told through the words and works of Herbert Dickens Ryman*. Edited by Gordon and Mumford. Camphor Tree Publishers.

❱ *The Art of Maya* (2003). Alias Wavefront Education.

❱ Ching, Francis (1997). *Design Drawing*. John Wiley & Sons.

❱ Hanks & Belliston (1992). *Rapid Viz*. Crisp Publications, Inc.

❱ Hogarth, Burne (1996). *Dynamic Figure Drawing*. Watson-Guptill Publications.

❱ Mencher, Marc (2002). *Get in the Game! Careers in the Game Industry*. New Riders Publishing.

❱ *Pieter Saenredam: The Utrecht Work*. Edited by Liesbeth M. Helmus (2002). Getty Publishing.

❱ Roberts, J.M. *The Illustrated History of the World – 10 volumes*. Oxford University Press.

❱ Thomas, Frank et al (1995). *The Illusion of Life: Disney Animation*. Hyperion.

❱ Thompson, Frank (2002). *Tim Burton's Nightmare Before Christmas*. Hyperion.

❱ *Visions of Light: The Art of Cinematography*. DVD. Image Entertainment.

I also recommend any visual concept books with production and reference drawings, like those featuring *Star Wars*, *Lord of the Rings*, and *Planet of the Apes*.

RECOMMENDED TOPICS FOR FURTHER RESEARCH AND REFERENCE

The following list includes many subjects for further investigation relevant to game design. Each of these areas of exploration, and others besides, can have a direct positive influence on several aspects concerning game design. Game designers must often do considerable amounts of research into various topics while helping to plan new game productions. Here are a few topics to get you started:

❯ Lighting (theatrical, film, TV)

❯ Writing (descriptive, dramatic, technical, comic)

❯ World history

❯ Military history (Osprey's military history books offer excellent reference material: www.ospreypublishing.com)

❯ Sports and sports history

❯ Basic acting

❯ Vehicle drawing and construction (preferably with exploded views)

❯ Building architecture (interiors and exteriors)

❯ Landscape architecture

❯ Set construction techniques (theatrical and film)

❯ Modular building

❯ Action movie "hotspots" and character motions (you can build your own library)

❯ Anthropology

❯ Painting and illustration

❯ Museum collection books (The British Museum, www.thebritishmuseum.ac.uk/, and many major museums publish these)

❯ World myths, fables, and legends (for example, Joseph Campbell's *Power of Myth* series)

❯ Art and artifact books (particularly those with great photo reference material)

❯ Costume design

❯ Interface design

❯ Life drawing, sketching, visual communication

❯ Anything fantasy or sci-fi oriented, classic or contemporary

❯ Storyboarding

❯ Comics

❯ Industrial design

❯ Product design

❯ Character design and construction

❯ Special effects for movies (www.cinefex.com)

❯ Creature sculpting

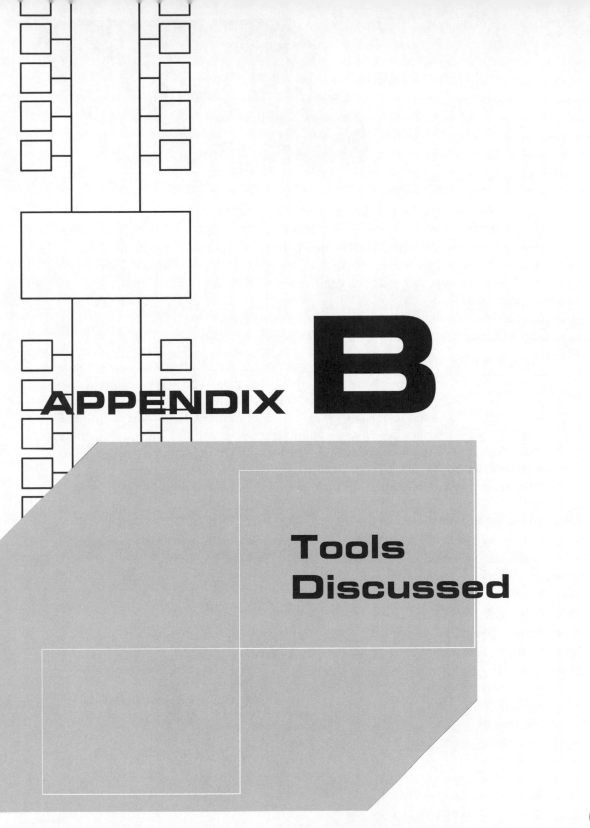

APPENDIX B

Tools Discussed

MANY types of software tools were discussed throughout the various topics of consideration, and I've assembled some reference material on these tools for you here. It's always best to remember that aside from some legacy tools in game development (like 3ds max or Maya), there is plenty of shift and room for growth in game tool development.

3-D MODELING PACKAGES

Each 3-D modeling package has its supporters and detractors. Many artists and designers are extremely passionate about their package of choice, where familiarity is often key. Each package has its own strengths and weaknesses (or perceived strengths and weaknesses). Rather than try to point out each, it's best to simply find the tool that works best for you in accomplishing your production requirements and goals. Don't be afraid to share knowledge with your peers. Training budgets for independent developers are very small or nonexistent. Developers are always learning more and trying to take their skills deeper into various packages.

Name	Web Address	Comments
Maya	www.aliaswavefront.com	Maya is my own preferred 3-D package of choice. Maya Personal Learning Edition is free on the site.
3ds max/gmax	www.discreet.com	Get a free version of gmax! A very powerful package used by many developers.
LightWave 3D	www.newtek.com	Another package of choice!
SOFTIMAGE|3D	www.softimage.com	Another package with many supporters.
Wings 3D	www.wings3d.com	A great way to start learning about 3-D construction.
Rhino3D	www.rhino3d.com	A nice application for design projects.
DOGA	www.doga.co.jp	A "starter" application for those with no previous 3-D exposure. This free program can help get you oriented toward building objects in 3-D.
MilkShape 3D	www.swissquake.ch/chumbalum-soft/	Another free application for your exploration.

ART TOOLS

A wide range of art tools is used to support game art asset creation. The following table lists a few of the very popular ones.

Name	Web Address	Comments
Adobe Photoshop	www.adobe.com	A favorite multipurpose application and the standby texture creation package.
Adobe Illustrator	www.adobe.com	Many artists prefer to draw within this package.
Painter 7	www.corel.com	Used for doing texture detailing and also in a number of other ways.
Wacom graphic tablets	www.wacom.com	A must-have for traditional artists working in digital.
ACDSee image viewer	www.acdsystems.com	A great image viewing and image management program.
Flash	www.macromedia.com	Great vector art tools allow for fantastic visuals with small file sizes. Not just for the Web, this package is starting to be used for many game interface requirements.
Bryce 5	www.corel.com	Nice choice for quick topographic construction.
Polytrans	www.okino.com	Converts model assets between formats/packages.

LEVEL EDITING

Many popular game titles in several genres ship with complete level editors included. These editors allow players to build their own levels and missions. Learning how to use these editors well and participating in the mod community is a great way to get noticed (and get hired) when you start building sophisticated maps. I suggest that you know one FPS/environmental editor well, know one RTS tool well, and, of course, have solid ability in a popular commercial 3-D package. With all of these editors in use, you can see why jumping from package to package powerfully can be tricky.

Name	Web Address	Comments
Unreal 2/UnrealEd 3.0	www.epicgames.com	The UnrealEd 3.0 level editor is included with the retail purchase of Unreal Tournament 2003 and Unreal 2.
Radiant	www.qeradiant.com	The radiant tools can be used to create levels for many popular games based on the Quake engine technology, like Jedi Knight II or Half-Life.
Serious Editor for Serious Sam	www.croteam.com	A fun game and a nice engine choice with a free editor included.

Name	Web Address	Comments
The DEdit tool is part of the Jupiter System behind No One Lives Forever 2 and Tron 2.0	www.touchdownentertainment.com	DEdit is the level editing tool specifically constructed for use with the Jupiter System engine technology. If you work with this engine, DEdit will be your level tool.
The Warcraft 3 editor comes included with the game	www.blizzard.com	Using editors that ship with popular game titles is a great way to get a feel for level construction. Use the Warcraft 3 editor to start exploring map construction. You can use many of the workflow suggestions offered in previous chapters.
Neverwinter Nights includes the Aurora Neverwinter Toolset, allowing players to create custom content	www.bioware.com	A solid choice for learning about event scripting for games. However, your scripts will be game specific. Don't forget to experiment with a multi-purpose scripting language like JavaScript or Python!

These listings are only a sampling of games that allow for player editing. There are many other game titles not listed here that ship with their own tools for custom content creation. These tools tend to vary greatly in stability and quality. It's not necessary or time sensitive to learn all of these tools. Focus on using a few of them well based on your own particular gaming interests.

IDDLEWARE

Middleware forms a technology layer between your development tools and game hardware, allowing developers to focus more on content creation than on the supporting technology construction.

Name	Web Address	Comments
Renderware	www.renderware.com	A portfolio of tools and technology solutions to support game development efforts and cut down external dependencies.

RODUCTION TOOLS

The following applications are general purpose production tools that are frequently used to support the game development effort in a variety of ways.

Name	Web Address	Comments
Microsoft FrontPage	www.microsoft.com/frontpage/	My HTML editor of choice for building intranet-based design documents. Any other editor you are familiar with will obviously work just fine too!
Microsoft Project	www.microsoft.com/office/project/default.asp/	Common project tasking and tracking application used to help manage and predict many facets of the development of a game project. The enterprise version now allows for network based project collaboration and file-sharing among other management teams and developers.
Microsoft PowerPoint	www.microsoft.com/office/powerpoint/default.asp/	Great application for quickly assembling design presentations.
Microsoft Visio	www.microsoft.com/office/visio/default.asp	Fantastic diagram and flowchart application. Very useful for helping to define game-flow logic and interface logic.
NXN Alienbrain	www.nxn-software.com	Asset management software perfectly suited for tracking large volumes of asset creation and editing workflow.

SOUND EDITING TOOLS

Many sound designers and audio engineers prefer to use Pro-Tools systems on the Macintosh for heavy audio work. For audio as it relates to the game design role, Sound Forge is extremely useful. SoundMAX is an interesting effort to broaden the audio horizon in gaming. For my tastes, it's taken way too long to even get this far with audio in games! If I had my way with development, audio would share equal billing with visuals in helping to define the game experience.

Name	Web Address	Comments
Sound Forge	www.sonicfoundry.com	Great audio editing tools! Easy to use and extremely powerful (if only all tools worked this way...).
SoundMAX	www.audioforgames.com	Helping expand the audio limits for games.

-D CONSTRUCTION FOR THE WEB

The following listings offer 3-D web based content exploration opportunities for those developers interested in exploring web possibilities.

Name	Web Address	Comments
WildTangent	www.wildtangent.com	Great for building web-based 3-D applications. Includes the free WTStudio tool, which can be a great place to start learning 3-D environmental editing.
Anark	www.anark.com	Another interactive media and web-based 3-D solution that interfaces with several popular 3-D packages.

SCRIPTING LANGUAGES

As you know now, you regularly end up using whichever scripting language has been chosen for the project, so it's best to be able to move around between scripting languages a bit. A passing familiarity is helpful. You will become quite knowledgeable in one of these languages when you use it for 15 months straight on a project.

Name	Web Address	Comments
Microsoft Visual Basic	http://msdn.microsoft.com/vbasic/	A common choice for behavior scripting.
JavaScript	www.ngweb.biz/software/djsedit.shtml	Another common choice for scripting.
Python	www.python.org	Open source language that is growing in popularity as a scripting language choice.

GAME DYNAMICS LIBRARIES

These software-based libraries can be folded into the construction of unique game engines in order to provide dynamics solutions of several kinds.

Name	Web Address	Comments
Havok 2	www.havok.com	Game physics/dynamics solution.
Karma	www.mathengine.com	Another great game dynamics solution.

MOTION TRACKING

The following are examples of a motion tracking studio and a motion tracking hardware provider.

Name	Web Address	Comments
House of Moves	www.moves.com	A frequently used motion capture facility located in Santa Monica, CA.
Polhemus	www.polhemus.com	Motion-tracking hardware solutions.

PROGRAMMING LANGUAGE FOR CONSOLE/PC

It's a world of C++ development for console and PC game titles.

Name	Web Address	Comments
C++	www.research.att.com/~bs/C++.html	The object-oriented programming language of choice for console and PC development.

MMOG BOX SOLUTIONS

With several parties attempting to create successful MMOG content, a couple adventurous companies are beginning to offer technologies to support this kind of game construction.

Name	Web Address	Comments
LithTech Discovery	www.lithtech.com or www.touchdownentertainment.com	An MMOG solution from the creators of the Jupiter system used in console and PC game development.
Tera Zona	www.zona.net	Providers of an MMOG development solution for game builders.

WIRELESS DEVELOPMENT

Wireless game and entertainment applications are still in their infancy. Two of the leading current development orientations are listed for you here.

Name	Web Address	Comments
J2ME	www.borland.com/jbuilder/	The JBuilder environment is a popular choice for J2ME development.
BREW	www.qualcomm.com/brew/	You can download the BREW SDK here and start exploring BREW development.

INTRODUCING CHILDREN TO GAME DESIGN

For those of you interested in helping to mentor future game designers from a young age, here's a great way to expose kids to game design thinking.

Name	Web Address	Comments
Klik 'N' Play	www.clickteam.com/English/klikplay.php	A very cool game construction system for kids.

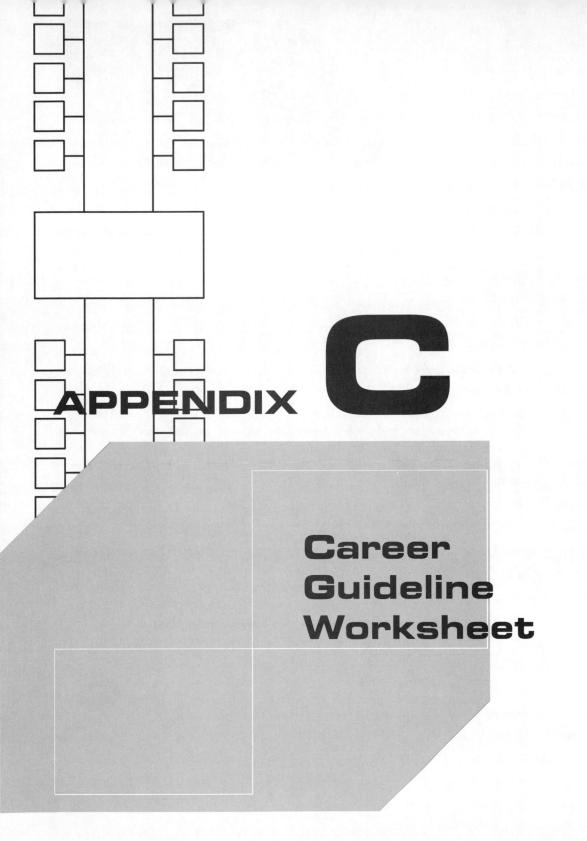

APPENDIX C

Career Guideline Worksheet

TO assist you to further define your goals in game development, I've put together a simple career worksheet with some suggestions by category. These are not intended to be rules, they are simply guidelines, and results will vary. I hope you find this material valuable. Hopefully, this can serve as a starting point for you to help determine where you would like to go within the game industry.

IF YOU WANT TO EXPLORE PRODUCTION

❭ Most producers get their start as game testers in QA. They are rarely (if ever) hired into a production role without some solid QA experience.

❭ A few game companies out there like producer candidates to have MBAs, because there is an obvious business component to the job, but this is by no means a requirement and there is no general agreement among developers or publishers looking to hire producers. Most game producers do not have MBAs or need them.

❭ I recommend getting a solid liberal arts degree. This is a common pattern among game producers I've met.

❭ Find other developers with a similar level of experience and start making games with your new friends! Everyone involved will benefit from the experience. In my game development classes, students take on development team roles (programming, art, design, audio, production) to start learning not only about the different roles but, more importantly, about how to deliver as a team. Learn how to manage simple game projects, solve problems, make design trade-offs, and multitask.

❭ As a producer, it helps to have a comprehensive knowledge about industry trends, patterns, and motivations. You must constantly do industry research. Work your way out of QA and into a production capacity.

IF YOU WANT TO EXPLORE GAME ART CONSTRUCTION

❱ Focus on building your traditional skills (drawing, painting, and sculpting).

❱ Finish a B.A. or B.F.A degree in art or design.

❱ Start early on to apply the traditional skills that you're developing to the digital world. Start to experiment inside your favorite software package using traditional techniques you've learned on the outside.

❱ Begin to focus on your favorite areas. If you prefer animation, pursue it aggressively. If you enjoy modeling, learn everything you can about it. If texture painting excites you, try to become an incredible texture artist. All development roles are increasingly heavily specialized.

❱ Remember that if you can't get an art job in game development directly, you can start in QA and continue to showcase your skills and desires to the developers around you. QA is always a doorway.

❱ Keep your mind and skills diversified. Don't ignore those storyboarding classes because you are convinced that you'll be an animator. Keep an open mind and take it all in. You'll be surprised to discover exactly what becomes useful later on. You can always work on the side to build your portfolio for nongaming companies, even while you explore every game opportunity available to you.

IF YOU WANT TO EXPLORE GAME PROGRAMMING

❱ Begin by starting to teach yourself programming. Keep in mind that console and PC development is done in C++, which is a great language to learn to cover the bases. To help you get started, many great reference books are listed at www.gamedev.net. Write your own games using your own art (or better yet, get your friends to help). Card games, puzzlers, arcade shooters, or a very simple RPG are great choices.

❱ It's a 3-D world. Doing interesting things in 3-D requires vicious math and programming skills. Independently, try to develop a solid understanding of 3-D graphics programming.

❱ Get a B.S. in mathematics or computer science.

❱ One of the best ways to get a programming job is to have solid code samples you can provide from game work that you've done in some capacity.

IF YOU WANT TO EXPLORE QUALITY ASSURANCE

❯ Play tons and tons of games! What an assignment. Game fanatics encouraged.

❯ Depending on your geographic location, do some research to find out if there is a game publisher in your area. You can find listings at www.gamasutra.com. Be respectful in approaching game publishers—they're really busy! Inquire about any testing needs that they might have or expect to have soon. Go to www.monster.com and search on "game tester."

❯ Get a degree in anything you choose. If you decide you want to work in QA management, a degree will definitely help you inside the bigger companies (and bigger companies are becoming the norm).

IF YOU WANT TO EXPLORE GAME AUDIO

❯ Become an excellent musician and audio effects builder. You can get many free sound design loops and editing software on the Web. Start tweaking gunshots, body punches, dinosaur shrieks, and big squishy splats. Try to make the most amazing sounds possible with the smallest file sizes possible. Check out www.fatman.com for more information on the crazy life of a game sound guru.

❯ An education isn't required, but it won't hurt either—at least you'll build a network of friends and fellow musicians you can call on later to help each other get work! So finish that B.A. Study computer music (according to Pythagoras, music is good for the soul). Many schools now offer computer music and music technology courses.

❯ In my opinion, some of the best PC audio tools can be found at www .sonicfoundry.com. Learning these tools is a great place to start.

❯ Pay attention to your competition! Listen for the best game audio of all kinds in every game that you play (interface, ambience, cinematic, effects, and so forth). Try to re-create the feel and sound of your favorites. Better yet, find someone locally who needs game audio work and offer to help out.

IF YOU WANT TO EXPLORE BUSINESS RELATIONS OR MARKETING

➤ Play plenty of games! You need to be able to relate directly to your audience—game players. There is no better way to help assure that you know where to find your audience, and that you can think like your audience when considering a game title purchase.

➤ Familiarize yourself with all aspects of the game playing community, including player preferences for genres, frequently visited sites, and all the relevant industry magazines.

➤ Having some direct knowledge of game development is very useful. Spend some time around a QA department, and around development teams. Learn as much as you can about the challenges faced by developers in delivering game titles.

➤ Get a degree in anything that you want.

➤ Some public relations and marketing departments within game publishers have internships. These are a great gateway into a company. Find a publisher near you and inquire about internship positions.

APPENDIX D

Quick Topic Summary for Designers

I'VE gathered together a few of the important concepts we've discussed in a synopsis for this appendix. Each of the following categories can be an important part of the designer's role on a team. Designers must remain flexible and open to challenge. The idea of deep, area-specific knowledge and role specialization stands in direct opposition to the "do more with less" situation that most developers operate under. While it's entirely understandable that game studios seek to find developers with wide experience, this desire must be balanced with finding developers who have particular area-specific skills oriented in the right ways to be of benefit to any particular game project.

The design role continues to evolve as its boundaries come into clearer focus. This material is offered in summary, and should be understood and used within the growing fabric of what defines a designer's contribution to game making.

REFERENCE MATERIAL

It's always helpful to have abundant reference material! I can't emphasize this enough. It's really an essential production requirement. Don't be afraid to build a general library that you move with you from project to project, and definitely build a library for each of your specific projects. The quick research phase in gathering adequate reference material to establish a visual style and for pure inspiration should not be overlooked. Failing to do this at the beginning of a project can set the tone for success or failure for an entire team.

I'm going to focus on interiors for the moment, since they are so readily used in games. Figures D-1, D-2, and D-3 show Pieter Saenredam's treatment of St. Bavokerk's Chapel. Saenredam (1597-1665) spent most of his life drawing cathedral interiors and exteriors, and is known for his mastery of perspective. Architectural drawings, paintings, and photographs are enormously useful as reference material. It's always best to be on the lookout for any material that you can add to your game reference library. One thing is certain: you're going to need plenty of interior and exterior reference material.

Some of my favorite drawings are by Giovanni Battista Piranesi, an archaeologist, architect, and engraver (1720–1778). I've had the good fortune to see some of these drawings in person. Piranesi has had a lasting influence on theatrical design and set design. He can just as easily influence game visuals. I want to share these drawings with you to underscore the importance of reference material to set visual style and to inspire.

FIGURE D-1

St. Bavokerk's Chapel, Haarlem, by Pieter Saenredam
(site drawing, 1634)

FIGURE D-2

St. Bavokerk's Chapel, Haarlem, by Pieter Saenredam
(construction drawing, 1634)

FIGURE D-3

St. Bavokerk's Chapel, Haarlem, by Pieter Saenredam
(painting, 1635)

Figure D-4 shows how easily a drawing might inspire prop design and prop detailing. Notice the chains and cantilevers near the upper left. A drawing like this might also influence staging (the relationships between props), overall scene setup, or prop placement specifics in a level section. You could easily refer to this image as reference in your level specifications for your design document.

Figure D-5 might partially influence how you build and lay out bridge systems in your level, including the construction of staircases like the kind seen encircling the columns. Notice how the center of the composition focuses on two suspended-bridge pieces. This might even inspire some light puzzle solving. It might inspire one to make some interesting bridge and transit placements, or it might just influence simple lighting prop ideas like the overhanging lantern posted on the column.

Figure D-6 demonstrates interesting alcove, tunnel, and bridge system reference material.

Figure D-7 is another one of my favorites. There is plenty of obvious influence here with the sweeping arches, implied dramatic lighting, menacing wall-sculpture reliefs, and jutting bridge systems.

FIGURE D-4

Piranesi's *Carceri d'Invenzione*, plate from Second Edition

FIGURE D-5

Piranesi's *Carceri d'Invenzione, plate VII*, Second Edition

FIGURE D-6

Piranesi's *Carceri d'Invenzione, plate XIV*, Second Edition

FIGURE D-7

Piranesi's *Carceri d'Invenzione, plate XV*, Second Edition

FIGURE D-8

Piranesi's *Imaginary Prisons, Prison VI*, The Lion Bas-reliefs

Figure D-8 is an example of more excellent prop and prop detailing reference for interiors—most notably the lion guardians set as relief sculptures carved into the walls. The ability to start to build into game environments this kind of complex detailing is just now becoming somewhat feasible. Despite the perceived beauty in a scene like this, for the purposes of game building, there are always the ever-present performance trade-offs to consider. You need to get plenty of mileage out of most props. They must be chosen wisely.

Figure D-9 shows more potential prop, detailing, and staging influence: spiked wheels, massive iron grills, chains, and suspension devices.

FIGURE D-9

Piranesi's *Imaginary Prisons*, Title Page

DESIGN DOCUMENT WRITING

There are several templates available to you at www.gamedev.net. These templates are a useful starting point. A design document needs to present dynamic and useful information to your development team quickly. A solid design document will leave no piece of feature or functionality undefined. Features and functionality will change, but each basic aspect of your game should have a reasonable starting point denoted in your design document. Your team will not be happy wading through densely worded opuses about general design direction, a designer's personal thoughts on some matter extending into paragraphs and then entire pages, a litany on every other page about what went wrong with the last game you worked on, endless comparison to every other title on the market, or massive and intimate backstory detailing.

Most designers format their design documents somewhat differently according to the kind of game or game genre the document is created to support. The size of a design document varies, too, dependent on genre, platform, and so forth. I've written 400-page design documents and 20-page design documents. These days, it's not uncommon for a document to reach over 200 pages, and a design document for an MMOG could easily reach 500 pages. I would set up access to game design information for a third-person action title differently than I would set up a document for a racing game. However, one similarity among design document formatting that I tend to carry with me is the use of a left-hand sidebar with a list of topics that loads information on the subject selected into a main "frame" view. This seems to work nicely and allows developers to rapidly find specific design details by subject with very little effort on their part.

You need to give your development team design information quickly and effectively. Artists and animators need to know how characters should be constructed, should be textured, and are supposed to move. AI programmers need to know how characters are expected to behave by instance. Virtually everyone needs to know something about intended use for an item, and its feature specifics.

If you bury this content deep into a document that can be used as a weight set, it will be lost on your team. I format my design documents differently depending on the kind of game the design document will be created to serve. I try my best to get information to everybody in easily comprehensible bites of blatant information. Use tables. Use summaries. Use simple bullet lists. Don't make people dig.

As I mentioned, I write it all up in HTML using long sidebars that load information into an associated frame. You can simply look down the left-hand sidebar and get any information you want by topic selection quickly and easily. "What does that thing do again?" wonders an artist or programmer. Click. "Oh, yeah!"

QUICK MODELING

Depending on your team structure, you may be doing plenty of modeling as a designer, or next to none at all. At the very least, it's best to be able to make temporary models so that you can start to try things out before final models are completed by your artists. Having basic modeling skills is important, and they too will grow over time and exposure.

You will have a basic polygon budget for each major category of required assets established for you by your technical team. Start throwing in your temporary props, temporary environmental details, and temporary characters! Your characters might have roughly 1500 polygons available each for construction. If your game has 30 characters, you've just spent 45,000 polygons! Props might average 300–500 polygons. Arena or environmental budgets are much higher and are dependent on several other factors. Be sure to collaborate early with your technical team to make these numbers available to your team.

Don't wait for final art! Model it up, even if it's ugly, and get it in there! Get things into the game and moving around early rather than late. Start finding out as soon as possible as many details as you can about what is and isn't working. You will save time in your art production by using temporary models to discover a wide array of problems.

For new designers, there are several great books and videotapes available on 3-D modeling. Don't hesitate to get Maya Personal Learning Edition from www.aliaswavefront.com, gmax from www.discreet.com, or Wings 3D from www.wings3d.com and start building some low polygon characters and props.

LAYOUT AND STAGING

In your design document, you will have your topographic maps and level specifications as discussed in Chapters 1–3, right? From this information, you will do your basic layout and staging. You will create an appropriate environment, and you will start to stock it with good guys, bad guys, props, and items. Designers spend large amounts of time helping to manage the layout/staging building and refinement process.

You will have new art, code, and audio assets coming into the game from all directions at almost all times. Asset management (www.nxn-software.com) and file referencing will quickly become your best friends. NXN are leading providers of digital asset management software. You can learn more about asset tracking software by visiting this site. You will need the ability to find game assets quickly and you will want the capability to replace existing parts of the game build with new, other, or updated parts as quickly and efficiently as possible. There might be 35 lampposts in your level, but the new improved lamppost just came in from the art department. You won't want to search you entire level by hand or filename to find all 35 lampposts; you'll want to simply change the file reference pointer once.

Designers spend plenty of their time building and refining game scenes due to sometimes shifting layout and staging requirements and concerns. Build your abilities to compose scenes in 3-D.

If you're entirely new to this process, get a copy of DOGA (www.doga.co.jp) and start setting up scenes with the free parts included with this shareware package. You won't use DOGA in actual game construction, but it will help familiarize you with working in 3-D. DOGA helps you learn to build up scenes using premade pieces in a 3-D setting.

SCRIPTING

Don't forget that scripting ability now seems to be a basic requirement for most design positions; so consider digging into at least one scripting language like JavaScript, Python, or Visual Basic. The better you get at writing and editing simple scripts the better!

A designer can't be expected to write huge convoluted scripts, but he or she needs to know how to use an editor to change basic script values with some ease.

MAPPING OR LEVEL BUILDING

Whether you're working as a level designer building levels or maps, or working as a game designer on overall game detailing, you will be using a variety of software tools to build in functionality. The only way to get really familiar with building up game play using tools is to do it repeatedly—to go through the labors of build, test, refine, build, test, refine, ad nauseum. There are more tools available to players and developers than ever before. This is great for access, bad for mastery.

I don't know which tool you are using, want to use, or will be using. Yes, we want powerful game development tools, powerful editors with amazing flexibility, but ultimately part of the true power is in what you bring to the tool—your own gaming insights developed over countless thousands of hours of play.

As a general piece of advice, try to know one FPS editing tool, one RTS/RPG-oriented tool, along with one 3-D package. This helps you to cover your bases and create opportunities for yourself.

AUDIO

Depending on team configuration, your game team might be working with an audio director via your producer. As designers and producers, we want to make sure to maximize audio impact at every turn. It's simply unacceptable to ignore audio detailing. It's best to know how to edit basic sounds and create placeholder sounds and effects. Sometimes you might even come up with something useable! Take advantage of the excellent tools available from Sonic Foundry (www.sonicfoundry.com).

Plan for audio early on. Push it closer to center stage in your design concerns. It's easy to get lost in nothing but the visuals, but that is a mistake! Audio will do wonders in helping you transfer mood and emotion.

TESTING

You'll be testing right along with QA. You'll try to make fixes before they become official bugs. You may not like the feedback coming from QA. Listen carefully—frustration is usually shared. If players are having a bad experience with your game, you'll need to do some real-time problem solving to try to address the situation. It will create more work. This is the cost of refinement; the alternative is failing to get your game where it needs to be in order to succeed. Make sure that testing continues among your peers as well.

SUPPORT SOFTWARE

Don't forget to try out new software to help support the design and production process. The stand-bys for me are Word, FrontPage, Visio, Project, and PowerPoint. With industry trends moving toward middleware (www.renderware.com), there may soon be some forms of standardization in actual production software and tools. To date, this has not happened.

Visio is a less popular application, but a great tool for setting up interface features and functionality, mapping screen flows for the game shell, and performing other charting tasks.

TEAM FOCUS

Always cross-check the game heartbeat with your plans and support your team's efforts in the face of problems. Be a problem solver, and strive to help those around you to be better. Make sure you apply the same rules to yourself. Stay hungry for learning. Address sagging morale issues early on and don't ignore team concerns!

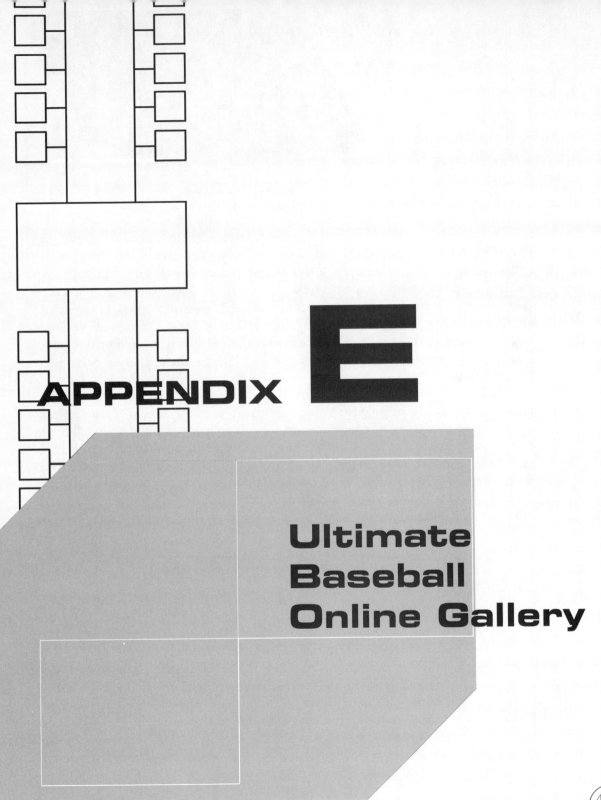

APPENDIX **E**

Ultimate Baseball Online Gallery

AS a point of reference and as a quick discussion about in-game art assets, I have assembled several screenshots from *Ultimate Baseball Online* (*UBO*), introduced in Chapter 8. I provide a few comments for each of the screenshots, which I hope you'll find useful. As I mentioned earlier, this game project called for much innovation in both technology and design—a factor I found very exciting from the beginning as a design and production consultant for the makers of *UBO*. An attempt to develop, produce, and market the very first MMOG sports title ever is rife with many risks and considerable challenges. I applaud each of the developers who have contributed to *UBO* for their dedicated efforts in building this game. I'd like to thank Andy Wang and everyone at Netamin for their generous permission to use various images from the game.

Baseball as an MMOG choice presented several unique design challenges. How do you entertain players waiting for action on the field or in the dugout? One potential solution is to have a roving spectator camera with a "quick jump" feature allowing players some freedom to essentially jump views during the game in order to participate and spectate the game in parallel. If you happen to be watching the game from the pitcher's view, the catcher's view, or the blimp overhead and you see the ball hit in your direction, a hot key snaps the camera back to your on-field position. There are other solutions currently in the works to entertain players when on-field action is low for your character or position.

UBO GAME INTERFACE

For every game, no matter which genre, it's extremely important to get the interface details right. This is why I always encourage designers to start with a thorough interface diagram put together in a flowchart application like MS-Visio.

Every game interface must be easy to understand and navigate, and must operate various game details with power and efficiency. This is a balance that is always hard to achieve. Most interface details evolve substantially with player and developer feedback as a game goes deeper into development. At the very minimum, you must always begin with a well-crafted interface diagram. Be sure to map your overall screen logic, your screen-to-screen transitions, and your single-screen logic details very carefully to avoid massive amounts of reworking.

Player Creation Screen

Figure E-1 is a very early version of the basic player creation screen, allowing the player to configure the most basic player details, but not nearly all game details just yet. This player creation screen is not yet complete. Keep in mind that each of your interface designs should allow for maximum expansion and adjustment as development progresses.

You will often revise your interface as you discover better and easier ways to control the flow of information between a player and the game. You always want to try to avoid running out of physical screen space for improvements.

FIGURE E-1

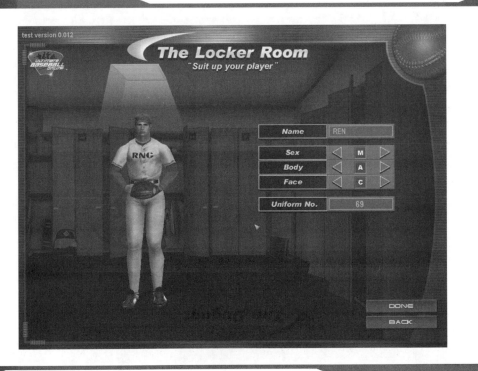

Locker room/player creation

Early Game Setup Screen

Figure E-2 is an example of a game management screen that allows players to join or create a game and to chat with other players in the game lobby while waiting for a game to begin. Ideally, you don't want to embed physical screen window sizes or backgrounds into the screen graphics. If you do, they become more difficult to change.

Instead, as best you can, you will want to allow these sizes to be tuned for optimum balance on the screen. As you might imagine, there are often one or two screen categories that simply require more display room by their very definition.

Game Details

The example shown in Figure E-3 demonstrates an early version of a game-detailing screen. Once a player has created a game, many game settings, like a player's choice of home stadium, game length, and/or several game conditions, can be adjusted

FIGURE E-2

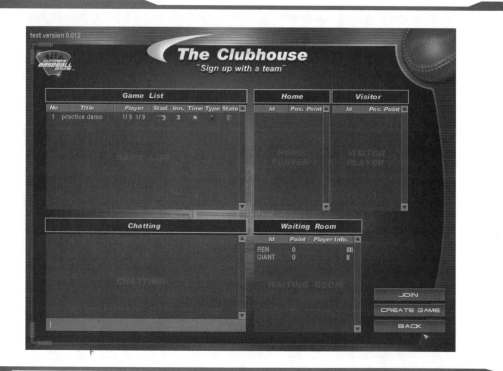

Clubhouse/game setup

FIGURE E-3

Manager's office/game details

according to player preference. Again, it's always best to keep these screens as flexible as possible in early development.

Position Selection and Batting Order

From each of the screens shown so far, you can see that there is a "screen logic" and a natural connection between these screens and the choices they offer a player. These should be illustrated clearly in your design document. Figure E-4 shows how players can set their field position and be entered into the batting order lineup.

FIGURE E-4

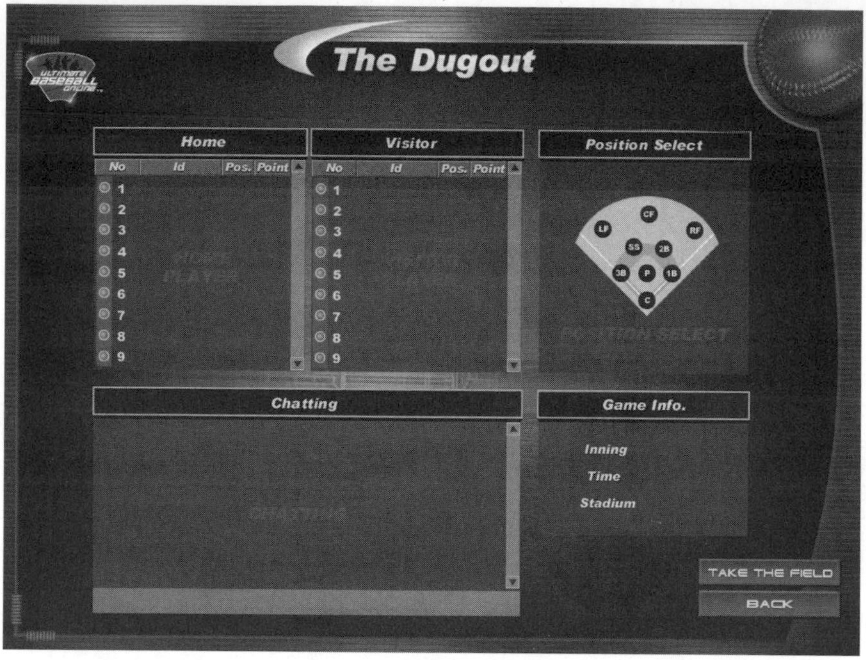

Dugout/position selection

BASIC CHARACTER CONSTRUCTION

There are four important character construction phases in character development: a concept drawing, a wireframe model, a flat-shaded model, and a fully textured model. Figure E-5 shows a character as a wireframe model, a flat-shaded model, and a fully textured model.

For each character, prop, item, and environmental detail, artists are given polygon budgets and texture size and resolution specifications for each game asset. Under these budgetary limitations, they are tasked with constructing the most compelling and visually attractive characters possible.

Figure E-6 demonstrates a dynamic pose of a fielding character in both a wireframe and fully textured view. Remember that motion capture information is applied to the model to create its animation within a 3-D package.

Specific motions can be captured as individualized custom motions or moves for the game, or motion can be taken from existing motion libraries. Motion capture libraries offer developers who might not want to incur the expense of custom motion

FIGURE E-5

Wireframe model, flat-shaded model, fully textured model

sessions to draw from a library of previously existing common motions (like walking and running). There is, of course, no guarantee that you'll be able to find each of the motions you require for your game in any standard library.

Many motion capture facilities offer libraries of stock motion for purchase. These tend to vary greatly in quality and usability.

FIGURE E-6

Dynamic fielder

The Motion Capture Process

Here are a few photos taken from the motion capture sessions for *UBO*.

Figure E-7 shows Major League Baseball All-Star Darrell Evans (center) directing Derek, a motion capture actor. The three digital cameras in view overhead bounce LED light off the reflective balls attached to the actor to record his motion details.

Collaboration with an All-Star like Darrell is an obvious advantage and offers game developers unprecedented real-world knowledge and insight into the game of baseball.

Figure E-8 shows Darrell Evans posing with the motion capture actors. Pictured from left to right are Derek, Darrell, and Tom. In this picture, you can clearly see the light-reflective balls attached to the actors' performance suits.

Finally, Figure E-9 shows the motion capture team conducting a motion capture session. Most game developers rely on experienced motion capture studios and capture teams for collaboration with motion details. From this control center setup, the capture team can monitor and process all of the motion data being generated by the actors on the capture stage.

FIGURE E-7

Motion capture direction

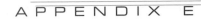

FIGURE E-8

Darrell with motion capture actors

FIGURE E-9

Motion capture team

BASEBALL STADIUMS

This section presents a few of the entirely original stadiums custom-built just for *UBO*. If you are constructing actual Major League Baseball (MLB) baseball stadiums under an MLB license, every attempt is regularly made to replicate the look of the actual ballpark, down to the smallest of details. In this case, there is true freedom to create a new and unique-looking ballpark for players.

Figure E-10 demonstrates an outdoor stadium as seen from the third-base line.

Figure E-11 represents another view of this stadium from a different camera position out in deep left field.

Figure E-12 shows another original outdoor stadium taken from *UBO* representing the look and feel of classic ballpark construction (notice the structure shading and the wear on the grass!).

Figure E-13 represents an example of an indoor or domed/covered stadium. For each of these stadiums, whether indoor or outdoor, it's always a challenge to get all of the construction details just right for players (the lighting, the look and feel, the audio, the wear and tear details). Without each element working together, the illusion for the player is broken. Developers try their best to avoid this scenario at all costs.

FIGURE E-10

Outdoor stadium

FIGURE E-11

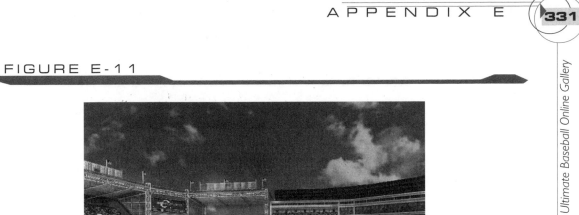

Outdoor stadium (left field view)

FIGURE E-12

Classic ballpark-style outdoor stadium

FIGURE E-13

Indoor stadium

GAME ACTION

With many of the elements discussed here in place within the game, it all comes down to just one thing—the game action! In many cases, the most design development time is spent trying to get the play details just right.

Figure E-14 shows the early stages of developing the game action, from the pitcher's view. Of course, *UBO* is unique in that every single field position is controlled by a unique player connected together in this suspended baseball world.

Figure E-15 shows a spectator's view of the batting action (a swing and a miss!). Who doesn't believe that the future for MMOG sports is bright indeed!

FIGURE E-14

UBO pitcher's view

FIGURE E-15

UBO spectator's view

Index

o

p

INTERNATIONAL CONTACT INFORMATION

AUSTRALIA
McGraw-Hill Book Company Australia Pty. Ltd.
TEL +61-2-9900-1800
FAX +61-2-9878-8881
http://www.mcgraw-hill.com.au
books-it_sydney@mcgraw-hill.com

CANADA
McGraw-Hill Ryerson Ltd.
TEL +905-430-5000
FAX +905-430-5020
http://www.mcgraw-hill.ca

**GREECE, MIDDLE EAST, & AFRICA
(Excluding South Africa)**
McGraw-Hill Hellas
TEL +30-210-6560-990
TEL +30-210-6560-993
TEL +30-210-6560-994
FAX +30-210-6545-525

MEXICO (Also serving Latin America)
McGraw-Hill Interamericana Editores S.A. de C.V.
TEL +525-117-1583
FAX +525-117-1589
http://www.mcgraw-hill.com.mx
fernando_castellanos@mcgraw-hill.com

SINGAPORE (Serving Asia)
McGraw-Hill Book Company
TEL +65-6863-1580
FAX +65-6862-3354
http://www.mcgraw-hill.com.sg
mghasia@mcgraw-hill.com

SOUTH AFRICA
McGraw-Hill South Africa
TEL +27-11-622-7512
FAX +27-11-622-9045
robyn_swanepoel@mcgraw-hill.com

SPAIN
McGraw-Hill/Interamericana de España, S.A.U.
TEL +34-91-180-3000
FAX +34-91-372-8513
http://www.mcgraw-hill.es
professional@mcgraw-hill.es

**UNITED KINGDOM, NORTHERN,
EASTERN, & CENTRAL EUROPE**
McGraw-Hill Education Europe
TEL +44-1-628-502500
FAX +44-1-628-770224
http://www.mcgraw-hill.co.uk
computing_europe@mcgraw-hill.com

ALL OTHER INQUIRIES Contact:
McGraw-Hill/Osborne
TEL +1-510-420-7700
FAX +1-510-420-7703
http://www.osborne.com
omg_international@mcgraw-hill.com